About

"In this superb biography of the life and teachings of the Emir Abd el-Kader one finds brilliantly manifested the deepest ideals of the Islamic faith. It is for this reason that he continues to be regarded in our times as the Muslim hero *par excellence*—a hero in whom the most noble chivalry was combined with the metaphysical insights of a true sage, and the spiritual graces of a realized saint."

—**Reza Shah-Kazemi**, Institute of Ismaili Studies, author of *My Mercy Encompasses All*

"This biography of the great Algerian leader—admired in his lifetime not only by his contemporaries such as President Lincoln, but also by his foes—will help us to rediscover in our own times the true spirit of Islam and to gain a better appreciation of the meaning of the misunderstood term *jihad*, whose qualities of nobility and magnanimity in the face of strife, were exemplified by the Emir's life."

—**M. Ali Lakhani**, editor of *Sacred Web*, and author of *The Timeless Relevance of Traditional Wisdom*

"This book is an excellent overview of the Emir's life, spirituality, and times. In an era of widespread misunderstanding about Islam, this biography provides a refreshing portrait of a classic 'defender of the faith' who was as fiercely dedicated to Muslim chivalry as he was to opposing colonial occupation, and who took full responsibility for the protection of the innocent and vulnerable, no matter their religion or birthplace."

—**Roger Gaetani**, editor of *A Spirit of Tolerance: The Inspiring Life of Tierno Bokar* and co-editor of *Sufism: Love and Wisdom*

"This wonderful and much-needed translation conveys the beauty and majesty of the original. It is an accessible and at times exhilarating account of a seemingly legendary individual. The translator's excellent introduction situates the life of the Emir in the political crosscurrents of his time and spiritual undercurrents of Islam, demonstrating how the former never compromised the latter. Through this work, one gains a true vision of the chivalry and sanctity that defines Islam when practiced in all its depth and breadth."

—**Joseph Lumbard**, Brandeis University, editor of *Islam, Fundamentalism, and the Betrayal of Tradition*

About the Emir Abd el-Kader

"There are few names in the list of modern notabilities which are better known than that of the 'Arab Napoleon,' the warrior who, in defense of his native soil, successfully defied, during several campaigns, the whole power of France, and kept her armies in a state of almost unremitting warfare for more than fifteen years. . . . [The Emir Abd el-Kader] was one of the few great men of the century."
   —*The New York Times*

"The most redoubtable adversary that France encountered on African soil, the man who for sixteen years of heroic battles fought for his faith and for the independence of his country, Abd el-Kader is, unquestionably, the most important personage that has arisen in the last century among the Muslim populations."
   —*Le Figaro*, French national newspaper

"Abd el-Kader disquieted Paris and challenged all the might of France in the reign of Louis Phillipe. The history of the French conquest of Algeria is in substance the record of the conflict which Abd el-Kader waged almost single-handed against the foremost military nation of Europe."
   —*The London Times*

"Today the Christian world unites to honor in the dethroned Prince of Islam [Emir Abd el-Kader], the most unselfish of knightly warriors, risking limb and life to rescue his ancient foes, his conquerors and the conquerors of his race and his religion, from outrage and from death."
   —*The New York Times*, October 20, 1860, reporting on the Emir's rescue of over 10,000 Christians in Damascus, Syria

"Such is the history of the man for whom our town is named. A scholar, a philosopher, a lover of liberty; a champion of his religion, a born leader of men, a great soldier, a capable administrator, a persuasive orator, a chivalrous opponent; the selection was well made, and with those pioneers of seventy years ago, we do honor the Shaykh."
   —**Elkader High School**, Elkader, Iowa, class of 1915

World Wisdom
The Library of Perennial Philosophy

The Library of Perennial Philosophy is dedicated to the exposition of the timeless Truth underlying the diverse religions. This Truth, often referred to as the *Sophia Perennis*—or Perennial Wisdom—finds its expression in the revealed Scriptures as well as the writings of the great sages and the artistic creations of the traditional worlds.

Emir Abd el-Kader: Hero and Saint of Islam appears as one of our selections in the Perennial Philosophy series.

The Perennial Philosophy Series

In the beginning of the twentieth century, a school of thought arose which has focused on the enunciation and explanation of the Perennial Philosophy. Deeply rooted in the sense of the sacred, the writings of its leading exponents establish an indispensable foundation for understanding the timeless Truth and spiritual practices which live in the heart of all religions. Some of these titles are companion volumes to the Treasures of the World's Religions series, which allows a comparison of the writings of the great sages of the past with the perennialist authors of our time.

Abd el-Kader in Paris,
photo by Mayer and Pierson, 1855

Emir Abd el-Kader
Hero and Saint of Islam

Ahmed Bouyerdene

Foreword by
Éric Geoffroy

Translated and Introduced by
Gustavo Polit

World Wisdom

Emir Abd el-Kader:
Hero and Saint of Islam
© 2012 World Wisdom, Inc.

Translated by Gustavo Polit.

Cover:
Abd el-Kader, photo by Etienne Carjat, 1865.
Al-hamduli'Llahi wahdahu ("Praise be to God alone").
Personal wax seal of Abd el-Kader.
Map of Algeria, by Jean Baptiste-Louis Charle, 1852.

Library of Congress Cataloging-in-Publication Data

Bouyerdene, Ahmed.
 Emir Abd el-Kader : hero and saint of Islam / Ahmed Bouyerdene ;
foreword by Éric Geoffroy ; translated and Introduced by Gustavo Polit.
   p. cm. -- (The perennial philosophy series)
 Includes bibliographical references and index.
 ISBN 978-1-936597-17-8 (pbk. : alk. paper) 1. 'Abd al-Qadir ibn Muhyi
al-Din, Amir of Mascara, 1807?-1883. 2. Algeria--History--1830-1962.
3. Statesmen--Algeria--Biography. 4. Soldiers--Algeria--Biography. 5.
Muslim saints--Algeria--Biography. I. Geoffroy, Eric. II. Polit, Gustavo.
III. Title.
 DT294.7.A3B694 2012
 965'.03092--dc23
 [B]

                                                          2012032679

Printed on acid-free paper in the United States of America

For information address World Wisdom, Inc.
P.O. Box 2682, Bloomington, Indiana 47402-2682
www.worldwisdom.com

To the Shaykh.

To my wife Jamila and to Arif,
who was born when this was being written.

CONTENTS

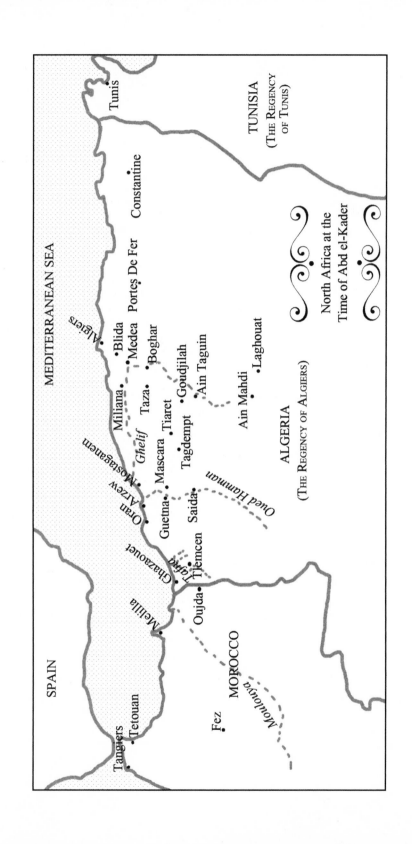

ILLUSTRATIONS

FOREWORD

"Every human being will find his way smoothed in order that he may realize the destiny for which he has been created." Doubtless, the Emir Abd el-Kader often meditated on this saying of the Prophet during the course of his life: in 1832, when, although *a priori* dedicated to a life of study and contemplation, he was invested, despite himself, with the command of the resistance against the occupying French; in 1847, when, having laid down arms, he hoped to trade cavalry gear for the rough wool of the Sufi; when, from 1847 to 1852, during his captivity in France, where he had clearly understood that if the French power had materially colonized his land, he was going to "colonize the hearts" of the French, and bear witness in that country to Islam and to Sufism; in 1855, when after having sworn to the French that he would never return to Algeria, he settled in Damascus, following exactly the way traced by his master centuries before, the Andalusian Ibn 'Arabi; in 1860 when, after having saved thousands of Damascene Christians from being massacred, he was congratulated on all sides for having done what to him seemed simply to be his duty . . . as a Muslim; in 1863, in Mecca, when having quite unexpectedly become the disciple of an unknown Sufi shaykh, he is told: "I have been waiting twenty years for you"; a little later, when this shaykh led him to the "initiatic death" by putting him into spiritual retreat in the cave of Hira, precisely where Muhammad became the Prophet of Islam; finally, in 1883, although his physical death had been mistakenly announced earlier by rumors worldwide, he left his fleshly envelope.

It is said that the death of a saint is always an apotheosis. But is the saint aware of being a saint, that is, of being a "friend of God" (*wali Allah*)? The question has been debated in Sufi circles from earliest times. "I have not made events," the Emir said, "it is they that have made me." For Ibn 'Arabi as for him, the life of the world and of individuals is an uninterrupted succession of theophanies, of divine manifestations which are never repeated. Abd el-Kader was revealed to himself through these "second causes" which gnostics know how to identify. More than others, he had experienced the various meanders of life: study and contemplation, knighthood and war, politics and leading of men, exile and captivity, humanitarian engagement and involvement in modernity and, since time is cyclic, a luminous return to his first vocation: spirituality, that is to say, the intimate conviction that the acceptance of paradoxes enables one to be reabsorbed in Oneness. His intention to lead a life of the Spirit was already taking place when in 1848 he announced to Bishop Dupuch: "All my life I should have been—and at least, I wish to return to being so before I die—a man of study and prayer; it seems to me, and I say this from the bottom of my heart, that henceforth I am as though dead to all the rest."[1]

A complex being was this Emir: the multiple facets of his personality were fixed upon by some, reified by others, for rarely did people want to see him for what he was: namely an "heir of the Prophet Muhammad," having realized Unity within himself and, consequently, working for the advent of unity between men, between Islam and the West. "The entire creation is the family of God," he liked to repeat in imitation of the Prophet: every form of life is sacred. His humanitarian ethic (the decree which he enacted during the war concerning respect for French prisoners; the rescue of the Christians of Damascus. . .) follows the example of the prophetic model; and one can understand that his clear enemy, General Bugeaud, had seen in him "a kind of prophet."

According to this model and the principle of wholeness (*shumuliyya*) that governs Islam, each level of reality has its "due" (*haqq*). "Universal being" (*al-insan al-kamil*) has no individual attributes; as Abu Yazid al-Bistami put it: horizontality is as spiritual as verticality. The Emir was *insan kamil* in the measure that he accepted, like the Prophet, to be at one and the same time *masculine* (the man of war and of action) and *feminine* (made fruitful by inspiration and mystical ecstasy). His very love of women, and the consideration which he gave them, sprang from the Muhammadan vision of woman, the most profound support in Manifestation and way of access to Union.

The Muhammadan heritage also explains the Abrahamic, and above all, the Christlike, aspects of the Emir's personality, which impressed all those who came into contact with him. This book furnishes many testimonies of it. Indeed, it is by the inclusive and synthesizing function of the Prophet Muhammad, that the Muslim saints become heirs to the prophets prior to historical Islam. Heredity is also spiritual. Is this surprising?

Let us continue with genetics: for some Europeans, Abd el-Kader was too handsome, too good, too charismatic, to be a Muslim, an

1 Mgr. Dupuch, *Abd el-Kader au château d'Amboise* (Paris: Ibis Press, 2002), pp. 21-22.

Arab, in short, a "native." He must have had exogenous forbears (Italian, Spanish, Maltese, have been proposed). Similarly, generations of orientalists have attempted to find—in vain—the foreign origins of Sufism: how could Islam, the religion of the hereditary enemy, and then of colonized peoples, contain such inward riches? The scholar of Sufism, Louis Massignon, in particular, put an end to this ideology.

A model is of no use if it is not actualized. Such indeed was the function of the Emir Abd el-Kader: to introduce the doctrine of Ibn 'Arabi into modernity, to prepare Sufism for its providential role for the West and, beyond that, to vivify the teaching of the Prophet in its most ample universalism. The Emir was aware of the counterfeits to which Muslims had already subjected their religion, but he looked far ahead. To be sure, he did not fall prey to the pseudo-religion of "Progress," but he had been following European technoscience and had warned its promoters of the near closing of "Heaven" upon them. He considered the geographic drawing together of peoples (symbolized by the excavation of the Suez Canal) and the economic globalization which would follow as a necessary passage towards the globalization of the Spirit, and this in a properly eschatological perspective. I must cite him here: "Religion is one. And this is by the agreement of the prophets," he wrote in 1855. "For they have not differed save regarding certain matters of detail. . . . If the Muslims and the Christians had wished to heed me, I would have put an end to their quarrels: they would have become brothers, outwardly and inwardly. But they ignored my words: the Wisdom of God decreed that they would not be reunited in a common faith. Only when the Messiah [Jesus] comes, will he make their differences cease."[2] Henceforth, the Emir invalidates the theory of the "clash of civilizations," while having a foreboding of its advent. As an Abrahamic heir he warns us that humanity cannot be united, and therefore saved, except through spirituality, and a supra-confessional brotherhood.

As a "son of the Moment," a Sufi such as Abd el-Kader could not but be receptive to the fluctuation of theophanies which, according to him, were in the process of changing the configuration of the world; he could not but be resigned to Western modernity, for he saw in it

---

2 *Lettre aux Français, notes brèves destinées a ceux qui comprennent pour attirer l'attention sur les problèmes essentiels*, translation by René Khawam (Paris: Phebus, 2007).

the expression of the divine will. What tidings did its message bear? I note that, particularly for contemporary young Muslims, especially the descendents of immigrants and who often feel caught in the jaws of a social, cultural, and even religious vise, the Emir Abd el-Kader incarnates the sovereign freedom of the Spirit, which awakens and frees from the mentality of resentment. Broadly speaking, he announces that spirituality cannot be rehabilitated unless it is lived in action itself, and that it cannot be dissociated from the different modalities of human life. Had he lived during our time, he would have worked to address the major contemporary challenges, related to ecology, the rights of man, bioethics, the relationship between the North and the South. . .

*   *   *

Ahmed Bouyerdene, through the totally unpublished information he brings, through the intimate knowledge he has acquired of the Emir Abd el-Kader, and the particular sensitivity he has developed for his subject, was able to go beyond the images that have been forged here and there. To each his Emir: with a concern for balance and temperance which never stifles his enthusiasm, he tries to open the reader to the complexity of this great man. And could one deny the evidence? It would be vain to try to hide the fact that for the author it is the spiritual dimension, Muhammadan in this case, that allows one to apprehend him who was "a prince among saints and a saint among princes."

Éric Geoffroy
University of Strasbourg

INTRODUCTION

In this beautiful and moving work, the reader will be lifted into the life and soul of a man whose deeds and whose order of personal grandeur transcend the ordinary and pertain almost to the stuff of legend, as of glorious tales of times long past. At the same time, however, this is no happy fairy tale, but rather the sometimes harrowing recounting of a life lived in a context of maximum danger, fierce battles, grievous trials and suffering; times of deepest despair, bitter disappointments and humiliation, betrayals, and deaths of his nearest and dearest loved ones and comrades, but also of great faith and forbearance, and ultimate spiritual victory and glory.

It is not easy to summarize the life and personality of a man of the scope and complexity of the Emir. The author has accomplished a difficult and admirable work, giving us a balanced view of this great man who was at once an outstanding and chivalrous warrior and strategist, a leader of men, a hero, a man of profound learning, and a mystic and saint of the highest order. All these facets of the Emir come before the reader's view, but at the same time, the author never loses sight of the essential: it is the virtues and the inner life of the spirit, which in this soul have precedence over all else and stamp the outward life to such an extent that even his enemies became his admirers because they perceived his extraordinary quality. Above all, the Emir is this fascinating combination of hero and mystic, this extraordinary combination of immense courage, magnanimity, and holiness that recalls the Prophets. Indeed, if one had to summarize the Emir, it would have to be by saying he truly incarnated the essence and fullness of his Tradition of Islam, and therefore also necessarily represented a kind of reverberation of the Prophet of Islam, much as St. Francis represented a reverberation of Christ.

The life of the Emir Abd el-Kader spanned almost the entire nineteenth century—the century that saw the beginning of the modern period of world history, in which can be seen the beginnings of what would in time spread out to encompass the entire globe. That century would see the tremendous expansion of the European powers into Africa and into the East, an expansion in large measure made possible by the technological developments of the so-called Second Industrial

Revolution which also took place in that century. During this time, Europe underwent the sweeping changes that began to modernize it. The mass production of iron and the use of the steam engine had already been achieved, and these were followed by the manufacture of steel, which in turn revolutionized almost everything: steel machinery, new modes of transportation, and a host of other industrial developments transformed the European world, and these along with new and much more powerful weapons of war were crucial factors in the expansion of colonial power. In this race to colonize, Great Britain and France were the two great rivals. Great Britain was the first to industrialize, for it had the necessary supplies of coal and iron which France lacked. France, unlike England, also suffered from the political instability that was the legacy of the French revolution, and it only achieved stability with the Third Republic, following the very short-lived Second Republic headed by the Prince-President Louis Napoleon, under whom, however, Paris was transformed into a modern city, and thanks to whom Abd el-Kader was released from captivity and returned to the Muslim world.

The France which the Emir Abd el-Kader had to confront was therefore part and parcel of the new modern world, which was then in the full vigor and confidence of its youth, ready to engage in the race with the other European powers to colonize the rest of the globe. At that moment, then, there were two worlds in existence: the ancient pre-industrial worlds and the dynamic, rapidly evolving and industrializing Europe, including its prolongations, above all in North America and Oceania. In the traditional East, the modernizing West encountered civilizations which in many respects were far more refined than its own, but which at the same time were also undergoing a very gradual process of decay and decadence, which in the Muslim world may be said to date from 1258, with the sacking and total destruction by the Mongols of the city of Baghdad, the seat of the Abbasid caliphate.

The sharp contrast between Europe and the Muslim world at the time of the Emir was therefore not merely a difference of technological or material development, because the character of modern civilization implies above all a mentality different in kind from that of the traditional East. In the East the West encountered worlds which on the whole had been formed by religious traditions which shaped everything in the society, and this was something foreign to the West, for it had not shared that kind of mental formation, that outlook on life, since the end of the Middle Ages, when it was part of the larger world of Christendom, its culture and institutions formed by Christianity. The modern mentality had been forming gradually in the Christian world ever since the end of the Middle Ages and, as is well known, it received a sudden impetus at the time of the Renaissance, and finally crystallized decisively during the period of the so-called Enlightenment, at which point the modern mind came into view unmistakably. The philosophical and other cultural developments during that period laid the necessary foundations for the rise of the industrial modern world. These developments, which represented something entirely novel in human history, were therefore unknown to the Emir, who at first interpreted the French invasion in terms of a religious conquest, attacking in order to gain Christian territory. The response of the Muslims was in terms of the defense of *Dar al-Islam*, of the homeland of Islam, and so they legitimately and logically declared holy war. In due course, however, and very quickly at that, the Emir realized he was facing not men formed by a religious tradition as he had been, but men who had been formed by something quite different, which they called "civilization," for which religion had ceased to be the determining factor.

The European drive to colonize was motivated partly by a need to control territory for military purposes and for the control of resources, partly by the desire for national glory, and also by a kind of "proselytizing zeal," which the French termed *la mission civilisatrice*, "the civilizing mission." This was akin to Kipling's famous phrase, the "white man's burden." Underlying the notion of a "civilizing mission" was the supposition of Western superiority, the conviction that modern civilization was the only one really worthy of the name, and it is this sentiment which in turn rationalized the drive to eliminate all obstacles to the expansion of the colonizers, often by the most ruthless and barbarous means, and which moreover sought to impose the colonizer's culture on that of the conquered peoples. This assumption of cultural superiority resulted from the philosophical ideas of the Enlightenment and the French Revolution, according to which the past was in large measure backward and superstitious, whereas man was now proceeding according to reason and experimental science, the discoveries of which had begun to open a cornucopia of material benefits and material power stemming from the technological applications of this science. These changes were so revolutionary, so breathtaking, that they swept everything before them. It seemed that man had finally discovered the way to create an earthly paradise and that natural limits could be overcome: reason and science beckoned with a sort of siren's call towards a realm of infinite opportunity, truths hitherto unknown and ready to be discovered, mysteries to be unveiled, yielding secrets and powers to be harnessed for man's benefit.

No doubt, the key idea of the age was "progress"; it is this idea which characterizes modern civilization. This means that for modern man change is something essentially positive; it represents a future that is "open", in which everything is possible. Without change there can be no progress. To resist change is practically to resist progress. This attitude lies behind the thinly veiled contempt of modern man for the non-modern peoples, who often seem maddeningly and irrationally "fatalist," pathetically "resigned" to their lot, in a state of "stagnation," to which the response was a fierce determination to "improve" them, by force if necessary. The material and scientific superiority of the West was obvious and overwhelming, and this evidence was taken for absolute superiority. Seldom was it considered that this vaunted superiority might be quite fragmentary, relative, and provisional.

At the same time, however, by the nineteenth century, it could be said that, with some exceptions, the traditional worlds were in fact decadent in many respects, and some of their conventions even exhibited aspects which were more or less barbarous and represented various kinds of abuses. Hence, the West certainly had the right to note this as well as other factors of decadence, many of which the Emir himself castigated, in particular the progressive sclerosis of Islamic law, which rendered it unfit to adapt to changing conditions and even could drive the best people away from religion owing to its pharisaical quality which, however, made it attractive to fanatics. This dangerous and slowly worsening condition would form the basis for the truly deviant pathological developments that would see the light of day in the twentieth century. However, the decadence of the age in the East was not absolute. If the culture as a whole had ceased to flower, nonetheless the East continued to produce the sort of men which its several religions intended to produce: great scholars, sages, and saints; and it still offered a traditional framework, a cultural and spiritual environment which served to support the realization of "the one thing needful" for the people, which is the essence and chief purpose of their religions and therefore of their civilizations.

*   *   *

One of the current stumbling blocks to understanding Islam as a millennial religious and cultural tradition and civilization is the memory of the attacks in September of the year 2001. Since then, everything Islamic has been seen through a dark lens, a view scarcely conducive to a receptive attitude towards the religion. At the same time, the West has become embroiled in a continuous series of military engagements in territories of people of the Islamic faith. In addition, of course, the history of conflict between the Christian and Muslim worlds goes back almost to the very beginning of Islam.

To surmount all this, we need to gain some perspective. A millennial civilization cannot be judged by the aberrant actions of barbarous fanatics at a late moment of its history, and as if they had occurred in a vacuum rather than in an extremely complex and violent global context. But be that as it may, it is a fact that, in the eyes of its faithful, Islam is first and foremost a religion, a Revelation from God. This religion gave rise to one of the very great historical civilizations, and one which was crucial as well in the cultural development of the Christian world. To elaborate for a moment on just one famous and vital example, there is the figure of Avicenna, a Persian who was of the greatest importance in the formation of medieval theology, philosophy, science, and medicine. During the so-called "Golden Age" of Islamic history, translations of Greek and Indian texts were made, and the sciences of mathematics, astronomy, and medicine were developed. Algebra and trigonometry are also products of this time. Avicenna alone wrote a staggering number of treatises—nearly 500—in fields as diverse as medicine and Islamic mysticism, including an entire vast encyclopedia of science and philosophy. His *Canon of Medicine*, which developed the Greek medicine of Hippocrates and Galen, was used as a basic text in European universities as late as the seventeenth century. The Muslims conveyed not only the treasury of their own sciences and philosophy to the West, but also acted as the transmitter to the West of the entire Mediterranean culture. The importance of the contribution to the development of the West by the Muslim civilization cannot be overemphasized.

An important as well as beautiful element in the contribution of Islam to the West was its influence on the idea of chivalry, which is essential to this tradition, in part owing to its pre-Islamic antecedents, and, more fundamentally, owing to its spiritualization of combat, "holy war," *jihad*. This spiritualization is expressed in the famous incident in which the Prophet Muhammad, returning from a battle against the idolatrous polytheists, remarked that they were returning from the "lesser holy war" to the "greater holy war" against the passions of the soul which impede its spiritualization. In his book on Moorish Spain, Titus Burckhardt notes that for the European Christian observer it is not easy to understand that "the knightly attitude towards women is of Islamic origin. And yet, such is the case, for it has, so to speak, a double root: on the one hand, the famous [pre-Islamic] knights of the desert, who not only were brave fighters and good horsemen, but also poets and frequently great lovers; on the other hand, it is based on the value that Islam attributes in a general manner to the relationship between men and women: 'Marriage is half the religion,' said the Prophet."[1] Indeed, among the most engaging aspects of the Prophet's life are those episodes which reveal his indulgent and generous behavior towards women. One could say exactly the same of the Emir, as the reader will discover in the pages of this book.

Burckhardt recounts an example of the chivalric spirit of the Muslims, related by a Spanish chronicle of the twelfth century. This took place in Spain, in territory under the rule of the Moorish Almoravids, who were Berbers from the Sahara. The Moors attacked Toledo, but at the time only the Empress was in the city, while the castle was defended by a great number of knights, children, and crossbowmen on the towers and walls of the city. When the Empress observed the damage being done to the surrounding countryside by the invaders, she sent messengers to ask them if they were aware that they were attacking a woman, the wife of the Emperor, and that this was not honorable and that if they sought combat, they should go to Oreja where the Emperor awaited them with ready arms. As soon as the Saracens heard this, they raised their eyes and saw the Empress seated at the ramparts of the highest tower, surrounded by her court. Before this spectacle, the Saracens were filled with admiration and shame. They bowed to salute the Empress and returned to their lands, taking all their troops with them.

No doubt the most famous exemplar of chivalry in the Muslim world is Saladin. An example of Saladin's magnanimity was his peaceful occupation of Jerusalem, granting amnesty even to the Christian

---

1 Titus Burckhardt, *Moorish Culture in Spain* (Louisville, KY: Fons Vitae, 1999), p. 93.

army, in stark contrast to the savage slaughter perpetrated by the Crusaders when they originally conquered Jerusalem, for then, according to Saladin's biographer Stanley Lane-Poole, "the blood of wanton massacre defiled the honor of Christendom and stained the scene where once the gospel of love and mercy had been preached. 'Blessed are the merciful, for they shall obtain mercy' was a forgotten beatitude when the Christians made shambles of the Holy City."[2] The historian Jonathan Philips relates, "Saladin was viewed in the most glowing terms. Western writers on the Third Crusade lauded his generosity, his courteous treatment of women, his diplomatic skills and his military prowess. They were also aware of his peaceful conquest of Jerusalem in 1187 and the fact that he had chosen not to emulate the bloodbath of the First Crusade. In these aspects, his behavior matched the highest standards of chivalry. In fact, Saladin occupied a central place in the most popular medieval 'handbook' of chivalry—such was his fame that he had penetrated the very essence of Western knighthood!" He continues, "Richard marched on Jerusalem in June 1192. However, by now even Richard Lionheart was suffering. He had a fever and appealed to his enemy Saladin to send him fresh water and fresh fruit. Saladin did just this—sending frozen snow to the Crusaders to be used as water and fresh fruit."[3] There is also the well-known incident where, in the midst of battle, Richard Lionheart lost his horse, at which point Saladin halted the battle and sent King Richard two caparisoned horses. Although the two great knights never met, they held each other in highest regard. The historian Morris Bishop records that King Richard proposed that his sister, Joan of England, Queen of Sicily, marry Saladin's brother and that Jerusalem could be their wedding gift. This arrangement, however, could not be realized.[4] As for his merciful and chivalrous side in regards to women, the historian Baha ad-Din records that a Christian woman's baby had been stolen and had been sold. She went to Saladin and he with his own money bought the child for the woman. On another occasion, the Muslim forces attacked the defenses of Kerak with catapults. Within the walls, however, a royal

2 Stanley Lane-Poole, *Saladin and the Fall of the Kingdom of Jerusalem* (Beirut: Khayats Oriental Reprints, 1964), p. 233.

3 http://www.channel4.com/history/microsites/H/history/heads/footnotes/lionheart.html.

4 Morris Bishop, *The Middle Ages* (Boston: Houghton Mifflin Harcourt, 2001), p. 102.

marriage was taking place, and Saladin ordered the troops to avoid catapulting the young couple's quarters.[5]

Principled warfare, which is commanded by the Koran and is exemplified in the first place by the Prophet Muhammad, is the subject of the Islamic scholar Reza Shah-Kazemi's essay, "From the Spirituality of *Jihad* to the Ideology of Jihadism." In it he recounts the following interesting event:

> Some fifty years before Saladin's victory, a telling mass conversion of Christians to Islam took place, as a direct result of the exercise of the cardinal Muslim virtue of compassion. A Christian monk, Odo of Deuil, has bequeathed to history a valuable record of the event; being openly antagonistic to the Islamic faith, his account is all the more reliable. After being defeated by the Turks in Phyrgia in 543/1147, the remnants of Louis VII's army, together with a few thousand pilgrims, reached the port of Attalia. The sick, the wounded, and the pilgrims had to be left behind by Louis, who gave his Greek allies 500 marks to take care of these people until reinforcements arrived. The Greeks stole away with the money, abandoning the pilgrims and the wounded to the ravages of starvation and disease, and fully expecting those who survived to be finished off by the Turks. However, when the Turks arrived and saw the plight of the defenseless pilgrims, they took pity on them, fed and watered them, and tended to their needs. This act of compassion resulted in the wholesale conversion of the pilgrims to Islam. Odo comments: "Avoiding their co-religionists who had been so cruel to them, they went in safety among the infidels who had compassion upon them. . . . Oh kindness more cruel than all treachery! They gave them bread but robbed them of their faith, though it is certain that, contented with the services they [the Muslims] performed, they compelled no one among them to renounce his religion."[6]

---

5   Malcolm Cameron Lyons and D.E.P. Jackson, *Saladin: The Politics of Holy War* (Cambridge: Cambridge University Press, 1982), pp. 325-326.

6   Reza Shah-Kazemi, "From the Spirituality of *Jihad* to the Ideology of Jihadism," in *Islam, Fundamentalism, and the Betrayal of Tradition: Revised and Expanded*, edited by Joseph Lumbard (Bloomington, IN: World Wisdom, 2009), pp. 122.

He concludes:

The episodes recounted here as illustrations of authentic *jihad* should be seen not as representing some unattainably sublime ideal, but as expressive of the sacred norm in the Islamic tradition of warfare; this norm may not always have been applied in practice—one can always find deviations and transgressions— but it was continuously upheld in principle, and, more often than not, gave rise to the kind of chivalry, heroism, and nobility of which we have offered a few of the more striking and famous examples here. The sacred norm of chivalric warfare in Islam stood out clearly for all to see, buttressed by the values and institutions of traditional Muslim society. It can still be discerned today, for those who look hard enough, through the hazy clouds of passion and ideology.[7]

And in this book the reader will discover that the conduct of the Emir, throughout the years of his resistance to the French invasion, perfectly exemplified this principle of noble warfare.

Finally, in this book the reader will have the full story of the heroic rescue by the Emir and his men of over 10,000 Christians in Damascus. His biographer, Charles Churchill, summarized this great episode in the Emir's life, which earned him worldwide tribute and honors, as follows: "All the representatives of the Christian powers then residing in Damascus, without one single exception, had owed their lives to him. Strange and unparalleled destiny! An Arab had thrown his guardian aegis over the outraged majesty of Europe. A descendant of the Prophet had sheltered and protected the Spouse of Christ."[8] For the Emir, all men belonged to God's family. In this he followed the saying of the Prophet that "all creatures are like a family of God, and God loves the most those who are the most beneficent to His family."

* * *

The universalism of Islam may come as a surprise to the reader, but it results strictly and immediately from the Koran. A few verses will con-

---

7 Ibid., pp. 140-141.

8 Charles H. Churchill, *The Life of Abdel Kader* (London: Chapman and Hall, 1867), p. 318.

firm this, and will also recall Christ's words that "in my Father's house there are many mansions" (John 14:2).

> Say: We believe in God and that which is revealed unto us, and that which is revealed unto Abraham and Ishmael and Isaac and Jacob and the tribes, and that which was given unto Moses and Jesus and the prophets from their Lord. We make no distinction between any of them, and unto Him we have submitted (3:84).

> And they say: None entereth Paradise unless he be a Jew or a Christian. These are their vain desires. Say: Bring your proof if ye are truthful. Nay, but whosoever submitteth his purpose to God, and he is virtuous, his reward is with his Lord. No fear shall come upon them, neither shall they grieve (2:111-112).

> The Messenger believeth in that which hath been revealed unto him from his Lord, and [so do] the believers. Every one believeth in God and His angels and His scriptures and His Messengers—we make no distinction between any of His Messengers (2:285).

> Truly those who believe, and the Jews, and the Christians, and the Sabeans—whoever believeth in God and the Last Day and performeth virtuous deeds—surely their reward is with their Lord, and no fear shall come upon them, neither shall they grieve (2:62).

> For each We have appointed a Law and a Way. Had God willed, He could have made you one community. But that He might try you by that which He hath given you [He hath made you as you are]. So vie with one another in good works. Unto God ye will all return, and He will inform you of that wherein ye differed (5:48).

> For every community there is a messenger (10:47).

The universalism of Islam clearly does not have in view a false ecumenism that would dissolve the essential formal boundaries of a particular religion—"Had God willed, He could have made you one community" (5:48). On the contrary, it affirms that each religion has been revealed in accordance with the Divine Will to different sectors of humanity, at different times and places, and in varying circumstances, and his religion commands the Muslim to respect them—Christianity and Judaism in particular—as "People of the Book." The Emir himself forbade any of his men from trying to convert Christians, and this attitude of respect for a Divinely revealed religion was manifest even at the very beginning of Islam, an example being that of the Caliph 'Umar who, after the capture of Jerusalem, refused to pray in the basilica the Patriarch had placed at his disposal, so that the Muslims would not claim it later.

Thus, the reader will see that on the one hand the Emir was strict in his adherence to the prescriptions of his religion while at the same time completely accepting, out of principle and in conformity to Koranic injunction, of Christians and Christianity. Each religion is intended as a guide for men in this life, so that at the time of the inevitable death of the body they may save their immortal souls. Therefore, as coming from God, each religion is good, and each one is even the best in a certain unique respect, even as each color of refracted light is unique, for it is God who reveals Himself in a different manner in each one, and it is intended thus for those who were born into it according to Divine Providence, so that his own religion necessarily appears as the best to the believer—and this is in accordance with God's intention. As the Koran expresses it: "Unto God ye will all return, and He will inform you of that wherein ye differed" (5:48). Therefore, it was the Emir's rule to respect each man's religion, each man's sacred relationship to his Creator.

It is this universalism, which respects the formal differences of each religion, that the Emir hoped fervently would be the attitude of both Muslims and Christians. Instead, he saw that Islam was becoming sclerotic and enclosed in itself, becoming increasingly unable to adapt to an age in which exclusivism was no longer possible; for now each religious "world" was becoming fully aware of the others, and travel to and fro between them was becoming far easier and more generalized. The times required an attitude that accepted the right to exist of each religion or else risk constant tensions and eventual outbreaks of bloodshed. The Emir insisted that Islam in fact prescribed these important attitudes, but that they were not being heeded.

The reader will be struck not only by the Emir's religious universalism, but also by his unusual openness of mind in the face of a completely foreign culture, during the years of his captivity. This attitude has its deepest source in the conviction that the state of the world, as well as one's individual destiny, are due to Divine Providence. He doubtless would have fully assented to the famous Gospel verse, "And even the very hairs of your head are all numbered" (Matt. 10:30).

Given this view that God is the author of all things, and in accordance with the fact that change is inevitable in the world, it follows that the Emir would confront situations outside his usual experience with an attitude of intelligent openness and suppleness. At the same time, since he never lost contact with his spiritual center, and therefore with the principles of his Faith, he was able to maintain his personal integrity and balance. The Emir was insistent that the religious laws are there to favor man's spiritual as well as earthly equilibrium, and are not to be regarded in a superstitious and rigidly fanatical manner, for in his view, God is necessarily the first to be aware of changing conditions requiring fresh adaptations in accordance with immutable spiritual principles as well as with the invariable laws of nature. It is for man to adapt intelligently to inevitable change, hence without betraying his deepest nature and purpose, which is spiritual, and hence without sacrificing the essential obligations and prescriptions of his religion which are their indispensable support and means of fulfillment. Of course, this complexity of adaptation requires an intellectually active attitude that implies an unflagging and lucid discernment. The reader will see that the Emir admired the critical sense of the Europeans, which was being lost in the Muslim culture, but at the same time he warned Europeans that reason without the light furnished by a sacred tradition leads to impasses and a soulless sterility.

* * *

The attitude of the Emir towards the European development of the sciences and their technological applications reveals a desire to achieve a balanced view of contemporary reality in the light of his inner spiritual life and of the primacy he always gave to the Eternal and to sacred science. On the one hand, there was no denying the efficacy and power of modern science and technology, and therefore no denying the efficacy of the modern scientific method. The traditional approach by no means precluded the practical investigations of medicine and other natural sciences, but nonetheless there is a fundamental difference in attitude. For traditional man nature is the garment and manifestation of God, whereas modern science remains always within the sphere of what is observable and measurable. For the traditional sciences, the explanations of natural phenomena reside above all in their symbolism, their character as intelligible reflections of superior realities. This outlook presupposes that the way things actually appear to man is providential, even if it comprises a certain sensory illusion, as in the blueness of the sky. "What" something is, for traditional science, has to do with its essential qualities, which ultimately have their source in divine Reality. As for God, as it was declared at the Burning Bush, and as the Koran unmistakably declares as well, His "whatness" or essence is that He "is" absolutely, as distinct from existence or creation, which depends on the unconditional reality of God.

The Emir affirmed that the discoveries of science are precisely that, and for this reason it is foolish to deny their reality or to try to prevent men from making discoveries. What counts is to discern their degree of reality and importance, to situate them in accordance with a multi-dimensional and sacred, and not merely a "flat" and purely phenomenal and profane view of reality and scale of values, which can only lead to a serious loss of equilibrium in men and nature. In his view, technology is capable of lightening certain material burdens, but it is also capable of doing immense harm, which amounts to saying that the intelligence that gives rise to technological progress can deviate and become abusive and dangerous. As the author of this biography points out, a given technology is "no more than a tool," and requires wisdom for its use, and therefore prudence, self-control and, in some cases, the wisdom to renounce certain possible advantages because these comprise equally possible catastrophes. We who live in the age of the atom bomb can certainly appreciate this point of view.

The Emir, in the goodness of his heart and generous spirit, held out the fondest hopes that accomplishments such as the Suez Canal, which established a kind of bridge between the Christian and Muslim worlds, and whose conclusion was celebrated by an ecumenical ceremony attended by representatives of both religions, would help bring about a spirit of brotherhood in men of different faiths and cultures. He tried his best to inspire the men involved in the project with a sense of its spiritual meaning, and therefore with a vision of its most positive possibilities. No doubt subsequent developments in the next century would have saddened him immensely, even while being fully aware that all things unfold according to a Divine plan, and that through this firm awareness and trust, men can find peace and hope in their hearts amidst the world's inevitable changes.

*   *   *

Finally, we would inform the reader that the original work in French is presented in the form of an academic thesis with a considerable number of footnotes. With the author's permission, a number of the notes have been incorporated into the main text of the book, so as to enhance the book's readability for the general reader, yet without losing the references. This entailed a great deal of detailed labor and discerning selection, and we are very grateful to Mrs. Catherine Schuon for having volunteered her talents for the work required, as well as for reviewing the entire translation and making many valuable suggestions.

Gustavo Polit

CHAPTER 1

The Last Breath

La ilaha illa 'Llah
"There is no god but God. . ."

"Damascus, May 26, 1883.

"To His Excellency Jules Grévy, President of the Republic.

"With sorrow, I have the honor of conveying the great misfortune that has struck us regarding my father's person . . . who died this Saturday evening at midnight" (*Le Figaro*, May 28, 1883). It is in these laconic terms that Muhammad Sa'id announced the death of the Emir Abd el-Kader to the French President Jules Grévy.

During the first days of the spring of 1883, his state of health had dangerously worsened. "An illness of the heart," *Le Figaro* specified, "which, for several years, had slowly used up his strength and held his entourage in incessant fear of an approaching end" (*Le Figaro*, May 28, 1883). His entire life had prepared him to "give up his soul." Far from dreading this moment, it was with a feeling of fulfillment that he prepared to welcome it, "rejoicing," he wrote to one of his sons, "in going to meet the Almighty."[1] The Sufi Abd el-Kader had made of his existence a place of discovery of the inexpressible. A spiritual way which had led him to die to the world a little more each day, until the physical death which placed him at the threshold of what he designated as the "greatest deliverance and the highest bliss."[2] He dedicated the breaths that separated him from this decisive moment to the mention of the supreme Name *Allah*. . . . The last breath took place at midnight, Friday, May 25, 1883, at Doummar, in the outskirts west of Damascus.

---

1 Cited in Marie d'Aire (née Boissonnet), *Abd-el-Kader. Quelques documents nouveaux, lus et approuvés par l'officier en mission auprès l'émir* (Amiens: Impr. de Yvert et Tellier, 1900), p. 247.

2 *Mawqif* 320. *Kitab al-Mawaqif* (pl. of *mawqif*), or *The Book of Halts*, is the spiritual compendium of Abd el-Kader. We refer to the translations of Michel Chodkiewicz (Abd el-Kader, *Écrits spirituels* [Paris: Seuil, 1982]) and of A. Khurshîd (Lyon: Alif édition, 1996). The references are given as follows without further specification: *Mawqif* followed by a number.

At the first light of day, the inert body of the son of Sidi Muhyi ad-Din and Lalla Zuhra was placed in a bus going towards the old city. There, where formerly the deceased regularly met with his "brethren in God," the remains were left in the care of the religious dignitaries who undertook the funeral washing. Among them was one of his closest companions, the Shaykh[3] 'Abd ar-Rahman 'Illaysh, "his equal in sanctity,"[4] his son pointed out. Outside, the crowd had not ceased to grow as the news of his death spread. After receiving military honors in the presence of the city authorities and representatives of the consulate, the casket was conveyed in a funeral procession to the Grand Umayyad Mosque where an initial ceremony was celebrated. The convoy, followed by a compact throng of 60,000 persons, then headed north towards Salahieh, at the foot of Mount Qasiyun, the mountain of the Forty Saints.[5] He was buried in the mausoleum of the famous Sufi of Andalusia of the 13th century, Shaykh Ibn 'Arabi. The burial was done on orders of the Ottoman sultan, at the request of the governor of Damascus, Izzet Pasha. He thus shared the final resting place of him whom he considered to be one of his spiritual masters, and of whom he was the most eminent disciple of the 19th century—a divine favor, to which was added the one which the Andalusian considered to be the greatest: to be buried by men extinguished from themselves, of whom God is "the ear, the eye, and the tongue."[6]

Many men of letters paid a last tribute to the "Knight of the Faith," expressing mixed joy and sorrow in their soaring lyrics: "if for us thy departing tastes of Hell, Paradise is honored at thy coming,"[7] a poet wrote. And another, more somber one: "I see the universe darkened; the days without sun, the nights without moon. . . . Whilst the birds

---

3 The principal Arab terms are defined in a glossary at the end of the book.

4 Al-Hachemi, cited in Marie d'Aire, *Abd-el-Kader*, p. 247.

5 Mount Qasiyun contains some forty natural grottos called the "Sanctuary of the Forty Saints." The spiritual tradition of Islam mentions the existence of an "Assembly of Saints," *Diwan as-salihin*, who govern the universe. In the present case, the "Forty Saints" refer to a category of saints termed the 'Abdal or "substitutes."

6 *Futuhat*, I, p. 530 cited by Claude Addas in *Ibn 'Arabi ou la Quête du soufre rouge* (Paris: Gallimard, 1989), p. 337.

7 Nizar Abada, *al-Amir Abd al-Qadir al-Jazairi, al-'alimu al-Mujahidu* (Beirut: Dar al-Fikr al Mu'assir, 1414h [1994]), pp. 34-38.

were in continual song, suddenly they fell silent."[8] There also is an inspired poem that was retained as an epitaph. Composed by Abd al-Majid al-Khani, a fellow disciple in the Sufic Way of Shaykh Ibn 'Arabi, it pays homage to the spiritual heir of the Prophet: "Saint and son of the Prophet, thou assuredly art. Thou hast received from the supreme Companion the grace of contemplation in the most sublime Stations of nearness."[9] The most significant tribute, however, came from the crowd that had swarmed into the surrounding narrow streets, representing the cultural and religious mosaic of the ancient Umayyad capital, reconciled for the duration of the ceremony around the memory of a man whose most fervent prayer had been precisely to unite the human family around a common principle.

In France, beginning Monday the 27th of May, most of the national dailies dedicated an article to the death of the Emir Abd el-Kader. Ranging from the most simple dispatch to the most glowing tributes, all acknowledged the historical significance of the event. *Le Figaro* (May 28, 1883), with the pen of the well-informed Henri d'Ideville, recalled the stature of the deceased: "The most redoubtable adversary that France encountered on African soil, the man who for sixteen years of heroic battles fought for his faith and for the independence of his country, Abd el-Kader is, unquestionably, the most important personage that has arisen in the last century among the Muslim populations." And he ended his article with the famous quote of Marshal Soult, the former president of the Council: "At present in the world there are only three men who can legitimately be called great, and all three pertain to [Islam]:[10] they are Abd el-Kader, Muhammad Ali, and Shamil."[11] *Le Temps* (May 28, 1883), which dedicated its front page to the event, emphasized the exceptional character of the personage: "His career was divided into two periods: the first was a true heroic epic; the second

8 Ibid.

9 Ibid.

10 "Islamism" in the original. In the nineteenth century, this term meant Islam, and not political Islam as it has come to mean in our day. In order to avoid any misinterpretation, and as an exception, we have substituted "Islam" for "Islamism."

11 Mehemed-Ali, or according to another spelling Muhammad Ali, was the viceroy of Egypt until his death in 1849. He introduced important reforms in his country. Imam Shamil (1797-1871) was the hero of the independence of the Caucasus against the Russian troops. He met the Emir Abd el-Kader in Egypt in 1869.

was a renunciation of all the tumult of the past. Judged from the stand-point of history, and aside from all the prejudices of our civilization, Abd el-Kader will appear as one of the most extraordinary men of our times." Some famous newspapers published engraved portraits of the Emir on the front page of their issues; for example, the *Journal illustré* (June 10, 1883) and also *La République illustrée* (June 9, 1883). The English and American newspapers were part of this editorial movement. On May 27, the *New York Times* published the dispatch of the son of the deceased in its obituary, in order to complete it several weeks later with a signed article by Ferdinand de Lesseps. The day after his demise, the *Chicago Daily Tribune* (May 27, 1883) summed-up the general feeling prevailing then with the headline, "Death of Abd el-Kader, who once filled the world with his name."

Le Temps (May 28, 1883) recalled a curious fact that had occurred three years earlier. Between the years 1879 and 1880, the rumor of Abd el-Kader's death went around the world.[12] At the time, it gave rise to a succession of laudatory articles that were brought to the notice of the "deceased," who had "recovered from the attacks that had put his life in danger, and who read them with deep emotion, and then collecting himself for a few moments said, 'I rejoice that in France it was believed that I was dead; for through your newspapers I have acquired the cer-titude that my memory will be respected by the French; and that is a great happiness for me.'" Abd el-Kader al-Hasani, however, had never sought gratitude or any notoriety, nor still less posthumous glory. He was acutely aware of the evanescence of things human and had never claimed any of the merits attributed to him—an abnegation that he formulated in these terms: "I have not made events: it is events that have made me what I have been."[13] Nevertheless, it was the historical events in which he took part and the responses he gave to their chal-lenges marking his life that have revealed him whom the chroniclers and historians have immortalized with the title of "Emir Abd el-Kad-er," and that have made him one of the great figures of his century.

---

12 *Le Petit Journal* of November 1879 and also *Le Monde illustré* of November 1879 announced on their front page the death of the Emir with a full page portrait. The *New York Times* of November 12, 1879, had the headline: "Death of Abd el-Kader, the Defender of Arab Nationality." It seems that a similar rumor was disseminated by the press at the beginning of 1874.

13 A.F.P. de Comte, *Mémoires d'un royalist* (Paris: Perrin, 1888), vol. 1, pp. 363-374.

Abd el-Kader bin Muhyi ad-Din was born seventy-five years earlier, in 1808,[14] in the West of the Ottoman Regency of Algiers, in a family of the religious nobility. In the religious and spiritual institution led by his father, seat of the Qadiriyya Sufic brotherhood of which he was also a representative, he acquired a classical knowledge that destined him to be dedicated to a religious career. The landing of French troops at the outskirts of Algiers in June of 1830 decided otherwise. In the fall of 1832, at the insistence of his father, he was placed at the head of the tribes of the province of Oran and acquired the title of Commander of the Faithful: that date marked his entry into history. Starting from almost nothing, without experience, within the space of a few years, the Emir Abd el-Kader developed a military organization and established the basis of a fledgling State. For more than fifteen years he held off the foremost army in the world and was able to impose two peace treaties allowing him to consolidate his administration. His refusal to compromise, his strength of soul in the face of setbacks, his magnanimity, aroused a current of sympathy in the very ranks of his adversaries. Already at that time, numerous testimonies emphasized

14 According to numerous sources, the birth date of Abd el-Kader bin Muhyi ad-Din al-Hasani lies between the years 1221 and 1223 of the hegira, which corresponds to the years 1806-1808 of the Julian calendar. The biographical essay that his son Muhammad Sa'id dedicates to him, *Tuhfat az-zair fi tarikh al-Jazair wal-Amir* (henceforth cited as *Tuhfat*; "Gift to the Pilgrim concerning the History of Algeria and the Emir" [Alexandria, 1903; Beirut, 1964]), indicates a precise date, 23 *rajab* 1222, which corresponds to the month of September, 1807. The same month and the same year are also indicated by another son of the Emir Abd el-Kader, al-Hashimi (Marie d'Aire, *Abd el-Qader*, p. 242). The family hagiography certainly draws from the same source as the English biography of the Emir: Charles Henry Churchill, in his biography *The Life of Abd-el-Qader, ex-Sultan of the Arabs of Algeria* (London: Chapman Hall, 1867), opts for the month of May 1807. Alexandre Bellemare, who in 1863 published his biography of the Emir, places his birth at the "beginning of the year 1223 of the hegira (1808)" (*Abd-el-Kader, sa vie politique et militaire* [Paris: Hachette, 1863], p. 10). The work of Léon Roches, *Trente-deux ans à travers l'Islam* (Paris: Firmin-Didot, 1884), mentions 15 *rajab* 1223, which corresponds to September 6, 1808. According to a biographical essay written under the supervision of Abd el-Kader during his captivity, it is the years 1221 and 1222 that are used, and thus repeat the data given by the sons and by Churchill. However, it is impossible to affirm anything on this question and to exclude one date over another. The only thing we are sure of is that everyone bases himself on an approximate oral tradition, hence subject to caution. Let us add finally that most of the later biographies published in France use the year 1808; such is the case, among others, of Paul Azan, or P. d'Estailleur-Chanteraine, to cite only the authors of the first half of the twentieth century.

the paradoxical character of the personage, at once warrior and saint: the Emir had chosen to nourish his political action by continual meditation. However, the scorched earth policy practiced by his emblematic adversary Marshal Bugeaud, reduced years of efforts to naught. Abandoned by a party of his own, harassed on all sides by French and Moroccan troops, Abd el-Kader agreed to give himself up, and in December of 1847 signed a treaty of surrender with the French Africa Army. Thereupon ended the first phase of his life. Victim of a perjurer, he was placed in captivity with a hundred of his companions. First held in Toulon, then in Pau, he spent four of his five years in captivity in Amboise, which in many respects was like a spiritual retreat, revealing a dimension that until then had been masked by the man of politics. It was also a period rich in dialogues at once cultural, intellectual, and religious. In October of 1852, the Emir was set free, and he definitively renounced political action.

The new stage of his life unfolded in the East. After a stay of two years in Bursa, Turkey, which he left in the spring of 1855, Abd el-Kader settled in Damascus, where he would end his days. He returned to France three times, notably in 1855 and 1867, on the occasion of the Universal Expositions which were then held in Paris. His intervention in favor of the Christians during the uprisings which took place against them in the Syrian capital in July of 1860, emphasized his humanist dimension and, more fundamentally, his conviction of a supra-confessional brotherhood. Yet, while tributes poured in from the whole world, the Emir continued his quest of the inexpressible through the study and teaching of the religious and spiritual traditions of Islam. In particular, he embarked on a subtle exegesis of the spiritual works of Shaykh Muhyi ad-Din Ibn 'Arabi, of which he became one of the first modern editors. During this time as well, the hidden face of the Sufi Abd el-Kader was fully revealed. In 1863, the encounter in Mecca with his spiritual master, Sidi Muhammad al-Fasi ash-Shadhili, gave a final decisive turn to his life. Under his direction, he entered into a spiritual retreat from which he emerged transfigured, full of an experience that illumined his view of the world, a view that was lucid and serene. Spiritual speculations did not, however, cut him off from the realities of his time, of which he became an enthusiastic and active witness. His support of the project to construct the Suez Canal, the inauguration of which he attended in November of 1869, attests to this. Proof of a resolutely modern thought, the support given to this project—the key event of its century—had also been a tangible manifestation of his faith in a reconciliation of the human family. In the 1870s, the man little by little withdrew into silence, ending "his years," wrote a witness, "as he had begun them, in a retreat lit by his writings, and in the practice of his worship."[15] Nonetheless, he was not to fade into oblivion. He who during his very life had become at once a legend and a major figure of history would leave a posterity which he did not suspect.

15 Lady Anne Blunt, *Voyage en Arabie, pèlerinage au Nedjed berceau de la race Arabe*, translated from the English by L. Derome (Paris: Librairie Hachette, 1882), pp. 27-28.

CHAPTER 2

His Roots

In the Messenger of God ye have a fair example.
Koran 33:31

Never ask about a man's origins; ask rather about his life, his
courage, his qualities, and you will know what he is.
If the water drawn from a river is wholesome, agreeable,
and sweet, it is because it comes from a source that is pure.
Abd el-Kader

A Prestigious Ancestry

Abd el-Kader ibn Muhyi ad-Din al-Hasani did not become what history has retained of him by his faculties alone—extraordinary faculties, which divine providence bestows only upon rare chosen ones. The natural, cultural, spiritual, and human environment of his youth, although removed from the major events of modern history and from the troubles of the century, was of an exceptional fecundity. It is impossible to understand the Emir's distinction without taking it into account.

Abd el-Kader came from a family of the religious aristocracy. His father, Sidi Muhyi ad-Din was the *muqaddam** (see Glossary), the representative, of an institution of religious instruction and spiritual teaching, a *zawiya** affiliated with the important Qadiriyya or Sufi brotherhood (*tariqa**). It was located in Oued al-Hammam, on the outskirts of Mascara, a large town to the west of what is still called the Regency of Algiers, which would become Algeria. Borrowing a Koranic metaphor, we could say that he was the fruit of a vigorous tree with deep roots planted by memorable ancestors.

Among the numerous articles dedicated to the Emir after his surrender in 1847, one of them had attributed a Spanish ancestry to him. "Nothing more was needed to provoke his pain and anger," wrote Alexandre Bellemare, ". . . indignant that someone had dared to darken the religious halo borne by his name as a descendent of the Prophet."[1]

---

1 Alexandre Bellemare, *Abd-el-Kader, sa vie politique et militaire*, p. 13.

After that, the Emir frequently had to recall the genealogical tree (*sha-jara*) of his family: "I am Abd el-Kader, son of Muhyi ad-Din, son of Mustafa, son of Muhammad, son of Mukhtar, son of Abd al-Qadir, son of Ahmad, son of Muhammad, son of Abd al-Qawi, son of Khalid, son of Yusuf, son of Ahmad, son of Sha'ban, son of Muhammad, son of Mas'ud, son of Taus, son of Ya'qub, son of Abd al-Qawi, son of Ahmad, son of Muhammad, son of Idris ibn Idris, son of Abd Allah, son of Hasan . . . son of Fatima, daughter of Muhammad the Prophet of God."[2] For an individual coming from a society governed by ties of blood and religion, the recital of the *shajara* is a form of social identification. Tocqueville rightly stresses this when he writes: "The Arabs are a strongly aristocratic society; the influence given by birth, wealth, holiness, is very great."[3] In the Maghreb of the beginning of the nineteenth century, prey to the divisions and power relations inherent in all tribal societies, descent from illustrious ancestors gave families a status that singled them out, and from which they drew a certain pride: some facts attested to by local chronicles, narratives recited by bards, names which had become mythical over time . . . sufficed to construct a family epic and a genealogy with which following generations identified. This nobility by blood was often associated with the religious nobility, which lent a family further legitimacy: the *shajara* then went back further into history and was added to the family of the Prophet.[4] These families were called *shurafa'* (sing. *sharif**) and its members became the heirs of the Prophet Muhammad and of his blessed influence, his *baraka.**

Abd el-Kader was one of these *shurafa'*. This title was authenticated by a written document whose existence was confirmed by Léon Roches, who belonged to the entourage of the Emir between the years 1837 and 1839:[5] "Abd el-Kader possesses, in the archives of his fam-

2 *Autobiographie, écrite en prison (France) en 1849*, translated from the Arabic by Hacène Benmansour (Paris: Dialogues, 1995), pp. 14-15.

3 Alexis de Tocqueville, *Sur l'Algérie*, presentation of S. Luste Boulbina (Paris: Flammarion, 2003), p. 16.

4 *Ahl al-Bayt* means literally "people of the house." It includes the descendants of the Prophet through his daughter Fatima and son-in-law Ali ibn Abi Talib as well as their two sons Hasan and Husayn. The genealogical trees of all the *shurafa'* lead back to one or the other of the two grandchildren of the Prophet, which is why they add to their patronym the term al-Hasani or al-Husayni.

5 Originally from Grenoble, Léon Roches was twenty-four years old when he joined

ily, a genealogical tree that establishes his descent from Fatima, the daughter of the Prophet married to ʿAli ibn Abi Talib. Consequently, he is a *sharif*."[6] This title authorized him to add to his name and to that of his father the patronym al-Hasani: "descendant of al-Hasan," the grandson of the Prophet Muhammad. According to family records, his family was from the Saquiat al-Hamra, a southern region in the kingdom of Morocco, from which, precisely, came most of the families of *shurafa'*.[7] This parentage made him a descendant of the Idrisids and thus of the founder of the kingdom of Morocco, Idris I, or Mulay Idris, also known by the name of al-Kamil (the Perfect); the great-grandchild of Hasan, son of Ali, son-in-law of the Prophet, he had exiled himself to escape the Abbasid dynasty and took refuge in the Maghreb where he founded the kingdom of Morocco.

Aside from religious prestige, the title of heir of the Prophet allowed Abd el-Kader, after his investiture with the title of Commander of the Faithful, to legitimize his political and military function and to overcome, to some degree, the clan divisions he faced. Later on, this "consanguinity" with Muhammad would take on a significance of another and deeper nature, making him spiritual heir.

"My forbears are famous in books and in history for their knowledge, their piety, and their respect for God,"[8] wrote Abd el-Kader. The family annals kept the remembrance of all their forbears, some of whom were exceptionally illustrious. Powerful men such as Abd al-Qawi, who ruled in Tiaret and in Tagdempt, and was assassinated by

his father, one of the first colonists, in Algeria. There he learned Arabic and became an expert interpreter and translator. He converted to Islam following a platonic love affair with a young Muslim girl. A rather complex, not to say ambiguous, person, Léon Roches nonetheless remains an essential source owing to his direct testimonies regarding Abd el-Kader. It appears that he was above all moved by a desire for adventure and escapism, but also by the desire to bring together "the native and European races." Although written late in life, the Memoirs of one who became the first French representative in Japan reveal a fragile personality and an excitable character. It seems that in the numerous upheavals of his life, he allowed himself to be led by events, without ever assuming the consequences, and then justifying them afterwards. Regarding the complexity of this person, see the study of Marcel Emerit, "La légende de Léon Roches," *La Revue africaine*, no. 91, 1947.

6 Léon Roches, *Trente-deux ans à travers l'Islam (1832-1864)*, vol. 1, p. 140.

7 Marie d'Aire, *Abd el-Kader*, p. 243.

8 *Autobiographie*, p. 15.

his vizier;[9] learned men such as Abd al-Qadir ibn Ahmad who lived during the seventeenth century and attained great renown throughout the province of Oran for his knowledge "of grammar, dialectic, and arithmetic. . . . In addition, he was versed in the branches of theology and in the divine precepts. . . . To see him and to hear his classes, people came from the furthest points East and West."[10] He left behind many religious works. A mausoleum is dedicated to him in Cacherou in a large cemetery, to which the diminutive of his name, Sidi Qada, has been given. He had many disciples throughout the province, who themselves were learned men of repute.

More than the source of a puerile pride, the future Emir had a relationship of admiration and consideration towards his ancestors. From a young age, he was steeped in the family hagiography which vaunted their piety and learning: eloquent tales in which reality is at odds with legend, and in which these real personages are often haloed with a supernatural charisma. Later on, these became so many models of heroism and virtues, models which the adolescent doubtless cherished the dream of equaling or even surpassing.

Abd el-Kader inherited another equally prestigious title, that of "marabout"* of the Qadiriyya *tariqa*.[11] For many generations, his family had belonged to this spiritual Way. Abd el-Kader, "servant of the All-Powerful," a common name throughout the Maghreb and particularly in the west of the Regency of Algiers, is also the name which appears most often in the genealogical tree of the family, for it is that of the founding saint of the Qadiriyya, Mulay Abd al-Qadir al-Jilani of Baghdad. The "bird of the heights" or the "gray falcon"—the most famous names of this ancestor—was deeply revered throughout the west of the Regency, where he is known as the "Sultan of the Saints,"[12] and

9 According to al-Hashimi, the son of Abd el-Kader (cited in Marie d'Aire, *Abd el-Kader*, p. 243).

10 V. Desjardins, "La commune de Dublineau," *Société de géographie et d'archéologie de la province d'Oran*, vol. 73, fascicule 228, p. 50.

11 In our time, the word "marabout" (*murabitun*) has not kept its exclusively spiritual meaning which it had originally. More generally, let us recall that the term "marabout," "khouan," "brotherhood," minor details aside, amount to Sufism. Let us also specify that, in colonial discourse, they had a strong political connotation.

12 Louis Marie Rinn, in his work, *Marabouts et Khouan, Étude sur l'Islam en Algérie* (Algiers: Adolphe Jourcan, 1884), p. 175, cites several other titles and surnames given to the celebrated saint: "the Qutb of the Aqtab [the pole of poles], R'out [succor], the

his adepts consider him "the greatest and most perfect of men after the Prophet."[13] The building of mausoleums here and there attests to this popular fervor, and they attract numerous visitors and pilgrims in search of a cure or in hopes of benefiting from his *baraka*. Thus his name is called upon in all circumstances: "It is he who is repeated ceaselessly by beggars asking for alms. . . . He is invoked when an accident has suddenly occurred. . . . The sick in their suffering, the women in the pangs of giving birth pray to him to intercede for them."[14] The representatives of the Qadiriyya *tariqa* living within the territory of the Regency had a great influence on the religious, spiritual, and social life. Such was the case of Muhyi ad-Din, the *muqaddam* of the Qadiriyya in the Oued al-Hammam, whose prestige was based both on his descent from the family of the Prophet and his descent from the founder of the *tariqa*, as Alexandre Bellemare emphasizes: "Muhyi ad-Din joined the dignity of Marabout to that of Sharif; it would be easy to understand the influence that was attached to his respected name in a province where the religious nobility has been and still is the only nobility."[15] The family tradition possessed, moreover, another version of its genealogy, which attached it directly to the Saint of Baghdad, a filiation claimed the Emir himself: "During our journey to Baghdad, we were assured by all the descendants of Sidi Abd al-Qadir al-Jilani that their origin and ours was the same; that without a doubt we were *sharifs* and that no one could contest our rights."[16]

As the heir of this double filiation, Abd el-Kader nourished a profound veneration for his ancestors to whom he felt tied not only by blood but also and above all by the spirit. To these revered names will be joined his own. Thus, he would become, by reference to the rich metaphor of the tree, the fruit of a sum of individual histories and the heir to a patrimony, symbolical and real, of which he in turn

Greatest Weapon (Qus al-Aʿzam), King of the land and the sea, the Support of Islam, etc."

13 A. Cochut, "Compte rendu du livre du capitaine de Neveu sur les Khouans, ordres religieux chez les musulmans d'Algérie," *La Revue des Deux Mondes du 15 mai 1846*, p. 592.

14 Édouard de Neveu, *Les Khouans, Ordres religieux chez les Musulmans d'Algérie* (Paris: Impr. de A. Guyot, 1846), pp. 23-24.

15 Alexandre Bellemare, *Abd-el-Kader*, p. 12.

16 Ibid., pp. 13-14.

would be the depository: for this reason, Abd el-Kader was conscious from an early age of the responsibility he had to assume to deserve this dignity. His illustrious ancestors, which blood relationship rendered closer, were, in a certain sense, the living teachers who accompanied him in the numerous stages that would mark his life. Such a dynamic of memory would have an emulatory affect on the future Emir.

The Guetna of Oued al-Hammam

It is likely that at the end of the eighteenth century Sidi Mustafa, Abd el-Kader's grandfather, established his encampment on the plain of Ghriss, in Cacherou, some twenty miles from Mascara. Having for many generations been affiliated to the tribe of Hashim,[17] he quite naturally established himself in their territory, where he founded a *zawiya*. The new religious institution, according to the family chronicle, had such success and prosperity that Sidi Mustafa would say that he was leaving his son "a caparisoned mule."[18] It was probably upon his father's death, at the very beginning of the nineteenth century, that Sidi Muhyi ad-Din replaced him and became the new *muqaddam*. For unknown reasons, he left the location chosen by his father and encamped a few kilometers away from it, on the left bank of a watercourse, the Oued al-Hammam. Occupied since Roman times, notably by a Christian community, this Oued, called at times by other names, lies upstream some twenty kilometers from the Guetna, a thermal spring having water with curative properties. Henceforth, his camp took on the name of Guetna.[19] It is here that in 1808 Lalla Zuhra bint

---

17 The tribe of Hashim, which is subdivided into several factions, became a *makhzen* tribe after the eighteenth century; in other words, it was put in the service of the Turkish administration of the province. It participated in this capacity in the collection of taxes for the bey's account and had to furnish armed contingents in case of a threat to the province. In return, it benefited from some advantages, such as the release from certain taxes and the concessions of land, in particular the left bank of the Oued al-Hammam. Regarding the Hashim, see E. Lespinasse, "Notice sur le Hachem de Mascara", *Revue Africaine*, 1877, p. 141.

18 *Autobiographie*, chap. 1.

19 "Al-Guitna, or al-Quitna, or al-Guiatna, is etymologically the place where one's tent is pitched. For the natives of the environs of Mascara, al-Guitna is the place where one comes to spend the winter, after having left the place where one spends the rest of the year" (Georges Yver, *Correspondance du capitaine Daumas, consul à Mascara (1837-1839)* [Algiers: Impr. de A Jourdan, 1912], pp. 302-330).

Duba, the second wife of Sidi Muhyi ad-Din, gave birth to Abd el-Kader.[20]

Abd el-Kader's cousin gives some interesting details concerning the founding of the new institution: "Sidi Muhyi ad-Din, having left the land of Cacherou, settled with his family in the Oued al-Hammam, at the foot of the mountain. There, he dug an irrigation canal and erected a mosque similar to that of the towns, as well as a home for himself. In the courtyard of the house there were camel hair tents and a flour mill."[21] At the beginning, the Guetna of Oued al-Hammam probably numbered only the families of Sidi Muhyi ad-Din and his servants. In time, it grew to around a hundred inhabitants, a figure that is explained by the growing influx of students accompanied by their families. Indeed, its notoriety went beyond the limits of the Regency of Algiers; according to the words of Abd el-Kader himself, students came from "Marrakech, Sousse, Chankrit, and Africa. It even had pupils from Alexandria." The *zawiya* would have received up to "500 or 600 persons. Studies were undertaken in the mosque, where there were some seven teaching circles,"[22] that is, classes, grouping the pupils according to their level. Thanks to alms, new constructions progressively completed the original building. For, aside from the salaries of the teachers, the *zawiya* also had to feed its guests: the students, young and old, but also the needy and travelers, which often placed the institution in a difficult situation, to the point that, at times, "nothing remained for the salaries."[23]

The *zawiyas* were the image of their *muqaddam*. The radiation of Oued al-Hammam owed much to the personality and prerogatives of Sidi Muhyi ad-Din. His reputation as a pious scholar, but also as a generous and just man spread rapidly throughout the province. The *muqaddam* was responsible for the material management of the insti-

20 According to Alexandre Bellemare, Abd el-Kader had only two elder brothers, whereas Charles Henry Churchill writes that he is the fourth son. Let us recall, moreover, that the Emir had a sister from the same mother, Khadija, who married Mustafa Ben-Thami, his lieutenant in Mascara, and who would follow him in captivity and then in exile.

21 "Histoire d'El-Hadj A'bd-el-K'ader par son cousin El-Hossin Ben 'Ali Ben Abi Taleb," translated by Adrien Delpech, *Revue africaine*, 1876.

22 *Autobiographie*, p. 34.

23 Ibid., p. 55.

tution, notably the tithes donated by the faithful and the production of the *habus* properties.[24] Not infrequently, he financed the needs of the school from his own funds, as Alexandre Bellemare recounts: "His relatively considerable fortune was less his own than that of the poor, for the sick or the traveler never made vain appeal to his generosity. Each year, the greater part of the produce from his crops were dedicated to alleviate the unfortunate, and it is estimated that no fewer than 500 *saas* [a measure of 160 liters] of wheat were distributed by him to the Arabs in need."[25] The popular chronicle recounts that his generosity was equaled only by his sense of justice. Thus it happened that the *zawiya* was transformed into a kind of "court of justice wherein all quarrels were aired, and into an inviolable sanctuary."[26] The proverbial probity of Muhyi ad-Din made him a mediator: "It was not unusual for Arabs to come from thirty and forty leagues distant to the Guetna of Muhyi ad-Din in order to submit their differences to him; and not only individuals would take him for a judge, but often tribes ready to take up arms would appeal to his arbitration and accept his decision as the expression of God's will."[27] The *zawiya* was not only a place of justice, but also a sanctuary (*al-hurm*), a sacred and inviolable space, on pain of incurring the disgrace of both heaven and men. The local chronicle illustrates this with an edifying case. A fraction of the tribe of the Smelas had left their lands in view of establishing themselves in the proximity of Sidi Muhyi ad-Din's *zawiya*, in order to flee from the abuses of their *quda* (sing. *qadi*).* This function of intercessor and protector heightened the reputation of the *muqaddam* to such an extent

---

24 The property endowments of *habus* were rights of "mainmorte," the revenues of which were intended for pious works. [Translator's note: These correspond to what is usually termed a *waqf* in Islam. It is an inalienable religious endowment—typically, real property—for religious or charitable purposes. "One typically Muslim institution that played an important part in shaping the city was the religious foundation, or *waqf* (pl. *awqaf*), equivalent to what is called *habu* in North Africa. The general principles of the *waqf* are well known: in fulfillment of religious obligations, property (in the form of money, land, or a building), is deeded in perpetuity to a religious or charitable foundation, in order that the proceeds from that property may benefit the foundation in question" (André Raymond, *Cairo*, trans. Willard Wood [Cambridge, MA: Harvard University Press, 2002], p. 234).]

25 Alexandre Bellemare, *Abd el-Kader*, p. 12.

26 V. Dejardins, "La commune de Dublineau," p. 53.

27 Alexandre Bellemare, *Abd el-Kader*, pp. 12-13.

that he played an important role among the tribes of Tlemcen after the landing of the French troops. Between 1830 and his death in 1833, he was an arbiter in the conflict between the Hadar and the Kouloughli of Tlemcen. During the same period, the bey and his family asked him for asylum. He also led several armed operations against the French garrison of Oran.

Abd el-Kader's father had all the qualities of a holy man. The following poem, by Shaykh as-Sanusi, a man of letters of the region, and extracted from the hagiography dedicated to Sidi Muhyi ad-Din, is particularly significant: "By God, thou art always walking on the way that leadeth to the truth. . . . Thou givest to thy guests the repast of hospitality and thou strivest to minister to their needs: thou support-est them all, dispelling all deception and misfortune. Thou passest thy nights in reciting the Koran from memory, in the darkness, and in the morning, like the morning star, thou promisest more light to come. At times thou teachest science, at times thou transmittest the *dhikr*,* thy soul ever in vigil."[28] There is no doubt that his father, admired by all, like his distant forbears, was an edifying model for Abd el-Kader. This patriarchal figure, who generously dispensed his learning and his goods in the service of the community of men, without distinction of tribe or origin, and who combined rigor and indulgence, probity and good will, was for him the personification of an ideal of justice and generosity.

From his father, from whom he inherited the sense of the virtues, Abd el-Kader also received the ability to read and write, a legacy of which he certainly was most proud and which opened to him the universe of the Koran and the *hadith** and the ancient texts. It is with his father that Abd el-Kader discovered the world of books and the taste for knowledge. And it is within the *zawiya* that his intellectual formation and spiritual initiation were set in motion.

The *Zawiya,* Place of Charity and Spiritual Initiation

At the heart of the plain of Ghriss, far from the commotion of the towns and the pressures of the government, Abd el-Kader's father had been able to preserve an atmosphere of peace in the midst of the *zawiya* of

---

28 In M. Bodin, "La Brève chronique du Bey Hassan," *Bulletin D'Oran*, 1924, cited in V. Desjardins, "La commune de Dublineau," p. 54n.

the Oued al-Hammam despite the troubles affecting the province.[29] In a region in which the population was entirely occupied with work in the fields and pastoral activities, the religious institution was a cultural and spiritual oasis.

In its first meaning, *zawiya* signifies "corner" or "recess," a mysterious etymology designating an intermediary space, situated between the sensible world and the suprasensible world. An acute awareness of the preeminence of the permanent over the ephemeral, of the spirit over matter, was transmitted and cultivated there. In this protected enclosure, the world here-below was viewed as a path towards the hereafter, a path for which all things are merely means to the only absolute necessity, the contemplation of the Face of God. The times of prayer were adapted to those who were dedicated to work, meditation did not exclude action, and religious learning did not forbid profane knowledge. The individual was considered in his complexity and in his contradictions, and it was necessary to take into account his spiritual as well as material needs.

On the strictly religious plane, the *zawiya* was the place of public worship, towards which the faithful converged for the collective Friday prayers and feast days. This purely religious function did not exclude a social anchoring: open to society, the *zawiya* offered help and assistance to the most needy and a shelter for the homeless. It also had a common origin with the ancient *ribat al-fath*, religious and military compounds that had spread over the south of the Regency of Algiers in order to confront the Spanish threat: a function that had placed the institution at the head of the *jihad** for the defense of *Dar al-Islam.** But the fundamental role of the *zawiya* was transmission in the broadest sense. The rules of courtesy (*al-adab**),[30] necessary for the perfecting

29 During the first quarter of the nineteenth century, the province of Oran experienced many disruptions: in addition to the sporadic rivalries between tribes and the latent tension which existed between these and the Turkish power of the *beylik,** there were the revolt of the Darqawi brotherhoods which had lasted until around 1815 and, some ten years later, that of the Tijani, in which one of the paternal uncles of Abd el-Kader had been involved. This situation had somewhat fueled the tensions between Bey Hasan of Oran and most of the brotherhoods, including the Qadiriyya *tariqa* of Oued al-Hammam directed by Sidi Muhyi ad-Din.

30 Jean-Louis Michon gives the following definition of *al-adab*: "Applied to the individual, it signifies politeness, innate and acquired or, better, the sense of propriety, the science, also infused and cultivated, which consists in treating each thing and each being, including God, according to its essential reality. Hence also its collective sense

of character, as well as the reading and writing that encourage speculation, were taught there. The Koran and collections of *hadith* were at one and the same time the supports and the end of this pedagogy. The families who entrusted their children to the *zawiya* knew that they would lack nothing: nourished on the Word of God and the Prophet, they were assured of receiving sufficient sustenance and of being properly dressed. Thus, it was in a traditional institution open to the world that the son of Muhyi ad-Din would take his first steps.

As a veritable microcosm, the *zawiya* of Guetna doubtless was the model of an ideal universe. There, as well as within the household, the child was steeped in a warm and dynamic atmosphere in which were mingled numerous foreigners who came for study or to lodge for a time in the tents that were appointed for guests. The conviviality of the meals taken together, the studies in classes ordered by age, the common prayer, the group games, developed in the students the meaning of sharing and communal living. The *zawiya*, opening onto the vast green plain of Ghriss, placed the child in immediate proximity to nature, an environment that was at times difficult, in which the rigors of the climate forced one to live precariously and in discomfort and to come up against one's own limitations—a school of life favorable to a full development.

Reciting in chorus the verses of the Koran written on wooden slates, the students simultaneously learned to read and to write and were steeped in the Word of God. According to Charles Henry Churchill, Abd el-Kader knew how to read and write at the age of five. In traditional Muslim society, a child remained in the care of women throughout the stage of play, until the age of six or seven years. It is only in his seventh year, which most often corresponded to the age of circumcision, that he was admitted into a circle of study. However, it is not impossible that Abd el-Kader benefitted from a precocious instruction. According to Churchill, Sidi Muhyi ad-Din was very close to his son, to whom "a secret and indefinable impulsion obliged him to dedicate an exceptional attention and care."[31] Alexandre Bellemare

of civility, of good manners (the "honesty" of the seventeenth century) and, in the arts, that of the fine arts and, more generally, of literature" (*Le Shaykh M. al-Hashimi et son commentaire de l'Échiquier des gnostiques* [Milan: Archè, 1998], p. 116).

31 Charles Henry Churchill, *The Life of Abd-el-Qader*, French trans. Michel Habart, *La Vie d'Abd el Kader* (Algiers: Sned, 1991), p. 47.

added: "Abd el-Kader was . . . the object of the predilections of his father. The old marabout delighted in cultivating the lively intelligence
he had recognized in the future Emir, and in teaching him, as well as
the art of writing, the first elements of grammar."[32] The precociousness
of this education was doubtless also facilitated by the boy's mother,
Lalla Zuhra, who, it seems, was one of the few women of the household
who knew how to read and write. Let us specify that aside from the
upkeep of the areas, the preparing of collective meals, and welcoming
guests, the women of the *zawiya*, in any brotherhood, were the keep-
ers of the traditions and the wisdoms which they transmitted to their
children from their earliest years.

Regarding the exact content of the studies undertaken by Abd el-
Kader, there is very little known other than what is said in the family
history, which is very laconic: "He learned *tafsir* [exegesis], *hadith*, jurisprudence, grammar, and religious principles, from his father."[33] The
future Emir probably benefitted from a traditional education com-
parable in content and method to that which his father had received.
After the strict memorization of the Koran, the collections of *hadith*,
and the chains of transmission, this immutable pedagogy led the most
gifted students to compose commentaries on the classical texts that
were considered difficult. Regarding this, the family history recounts
that Abd el-Kader admired his father who "clarified the difficulties in
the laws"[34] for his comrades. The pupils were in the right place to form
their thinking and develop their faculty of reasoning.

For the advanced students, the teaching, in breadth and depth,
went beyond the strictly religious field. Traditionally, any knowledge
that led the individual to awaken to the principle of the Oneness of
God, *tawhid*, was considered useful knowledge. To the specifically
doctrinal corpus were added the "positive" sciences,[35] which could
assist in deepening reflection and meditation on the Creation, such
as algebra, the natural sciences, historical chronicles, and Greek philosophy. The quality and level of the teaching offered varied from one
zawiya to another, and depended partly on the material means of each

---

32 Alexandre Bellemare, *Abd el-Kader*, p. 43.

33 *Autobiographie*, p. 55.

34 According to al-Hashimi, cited in Marie d'Aire, *Abd el-Kader*, p. 242.

35 The classical tradition of Islam distinguishes *al-'ulum al-'aqliyya* (philosophy, logic)
from the religious sciences, *'ulum naqliyya*.

one. The best endowed could afford to offer lodging for a relatively large number, a seminary with a high quality of education, and a good library—of decisive importance for teaching in general.

Books were rare, and therefore precious. The *zawiya* of Oued al-Hammam was considered to have a rather extensive library. There were, of course, volumes of the Holy Book in calligraphy written by forbears, which were jealously guarded as treasures, writing being all the more sacred in that it served as the support for the transmission of the Divine Word. There were also collections of *hadith*, in particular the most famous of them, the *Sahih al-Bukhari*, considered to be almost as sacred as the Koran. But the school also possessed, in all likelihood, treatises of classical exegesis, of grammar, historical chronicles, as well as classical Sufi texts used by the Qadiriyya brotherhood. This profane contribution, it might be said, considerably enlarged the intellectual horizon and developed the curiosity of the pupil Abd el-Kader, arousing in him a pronounced taste for books, which would not change with the passing of time. According to the family history, it seems that the future Emir was particularly gifted, for at the age of twelve Abd el-Kader became a student, and was thus in a position to comment on the Word of God and the Prophetic tradition. Two years later, he completed learning the entire Koran by heart, and received the title of *hafiz.** He could then in turn take charge of a class in the family mosque.

Because the Koran evokes the unenviable fate of those who "resemble a donkey carrying books" (62:5), transmission in the *zawiya* was not limited exclusively to the acquisition of the exoteric science and book learning. To be effective, this apprenticeship had to be accompanied by an awareness of one's manner of being and of nobleness of character. This is why, in the educational program dispensed at the *zawiya*, and more generally in the families of the religious aristocracy, there existed the practice of virtuous qualities, *as-salihat*. A common theme in the classical treatises recalled that the quality of the relationship to the Creator depended on the respect given to His creatures. Each individual was supposed to compete in generosity, good will, forgiveness, patience, courage, etc., so as to approach the ideal of humanity incarnated by the prophets and saints, who were so many models to be imitated. The Qadiriyya *tariqa* had placed generosity towards "all human creatures, without distinction of religion"[36] at the heart of this

36 Louis Rinn, *Marabouts et Khouan* (Algiers: Jourdan, 1884), p. 183.

21

apprenticeship. This virtue was associated with the figure of Jesus, for it was said that of all men, Sidi Abd al-Qadir al-Jilani was "he who by his virtue and his spirit of love, was closest to Sayyiduna 'Isa" (Our lord Jesus).[37] Because the Koran (68:4-6) attributes a "lofty character" to the Prophet Muhammad and because he himself said that he was sent "to perfect noble characters," he represents the model par excellence in this quest for virtuous comportment. In order to understand the preeminence of the figure of the Prophet in the pedagogy of the religious and spiritual institutions of Islam, one has to remember the notion of Mercy.[38] It proceeds from the two divine attributes, *ar-Rahman* and *ar-Rahim*, the Clement and the Merciful. It is through these Names that the Muslims are invited to steep their daily lives in the spirit of mercy, notably by preceding each of their actions with the consecrated formula, "In the Name of God, the Clement, the Merciful." It is only through this intentionality that all the virtues become possible. And the Koran institutes the Prophet, precisely, as the archetype of the Divine Mercy.[39] The faithful who thus follow in the steps of the Prophet "full of goodness and mercy" (Koran 9:128), to the point that their inwardness resonates with that of Muhammad, become his heir. This imitation must not become servile, however, but consented to and transformed by the love of the Prophet, which leads to the love of God, as the Koran informs: "Say (O Muhammad to men): Follow me, if thou lovest God; God will love thee and thy sins shall be forgiven. God is He who forgives, He is Merciful" (3:31). This seeking for the correct attitude, agreeable to God, was taught from the youngest age. But because it demands a total commitment and because it is comprised within the project of perfecting one's being, mature students and adults generally who desired to follow an initiatic path combined it with a spiritual practice.

37 Ibid., p. 175. [Translator's note: In Islam, it is part of spiritual courtesy to always precede the mention of a Prophet by the honorific "our lord" (Sayyiduna) and afterwards by the invocation of God's peace upon him.]

38 Mercy occupies a central place in the economy of sanctity in Islam, but also, in a more fundamental manner, in the animation of the living. By it, life is made possible and can be maintained; a centrality perfectly illustrated by a holy tradition authenticated by the Imams Bukhari and Muslim, which relate that on His throne God has inscribed: "My Mercy precedeth my Wrath."

39 According to the verse: "We have sent you only as a Mercy for the worlds" (Koran 21:107).

The Qadiriyya *tariqa* reconciled at one and the same time a popular practice and a more learned approach: a tolerance that was necessary, on account of the heterogeneity of the disciples. Contrary to certain *zawiyas* that had been affected with a kind of decadence for having conserved only a passive ritual lacking a true initiatic engagement, it is confirmed that Sidi Muhyi ad-Din, following his father, firmly established the transmission of the *wird*,* which linked the disciple to the initiatic chain.[40]

The spiritual education provided by the *muqaddam* took place essentially within the framework of spiritual reunions (*jam'*), in which all the disciples took part without any distinction of age. The "brethren in God," gathered to recite litanies that invoked the Names of God (*dhikr*). Placed at the center of the Sufi spiritual method, the *dhikr* could be practiced in solitude or in a group, in silence or aloud. It was symbolized by a rosary composed of ninety-nine beads, reflecting the number of the divine Attributes upheld by the tradition. Through this form of prayer, the disciple actualized his relationship with God and achieved a certain peace, according to the verse: "Are hearts not appeased by the remembrance of God (*dhikr Allah*)?" (Koran 13:28). The formulas of the *dhikr* could vary from one *tariqa* to another, and from one disciple to another, the formula most in use in the Qadiriyya being that of the affirmation of the Divine Unity, *la ilaha illa 'Llah*, the first pillar of Islam and the basis of all the doctrines attached to it. It is in reference to a holy tradition (*hadith qudsi*) that Abd el-Kader explains to the novices the power of this all-integrating *dhikr*: "*La ilaha illa 'Llah* is my fortress and he who penetrates into my fortress is preserved from My wrath." He doubtless had been constant in the sessions of *dhikr* presided over by his father. His pronounced taste for this form of prayer dates back to this time, and he would be ever faithful to it thereafter.

In addition to these sessions of litanies, and in accordance with the intention of the most advanced disciples, certain *zawiyas* offered the practice of spiritual retreats, *khalwat*,* undertaken in cells reserved for this purpose. Regarding this practice, a witness recalls a visit to the site of the Guetna and the ruins of what he made out to have been a cell for retreats: "A collapsed tunnel led to a *khalwa*, where one could imag-

---

40 This is confirmed by the written testimony of a member of the family: "If Sidi Mustafa . . . were dead, it is Sidi Muhyi ad-Din who would continue to give the *wird* to the Muslims ("Histoire d'El-Hadj A'bd-el-K'ader", p. 420).

ine that the future adversary of Bugeaud practiced meditation."[41] It was during the spiritual lesson, *al-mudhakara*, which closed the spiritual assemblies, that the *muqaddam* transmitted the initiatic doctrine. The fundamental principles in force in the *tariqa* were set forth, such as the action of grace in all circumstances, *al-hamd*, the need for renunciation, *az-zuhd*, patience, *as-sabr*, and so on for the other virtues. At the heart of all these principles was "reverential fear of God," *at-taqwa*, an inner attitude that creates in the disciple a state of intimacy with God, establishing an increasing inward vigilance in relation to passions and corrupt desires. For according to Sufi teaching, the enemy is not without but within oneself. By placing himself under the gaze of God the aspirant discovers in this superior will a support for mastering his inner enemy. "Fear" is thus not understood as a submission to the inquisitorial gaze of God, but rather an attitude of individual responsibility. Educating in introspection, this teaching on the gaze of God leads the disciple to one of the pillars of the faith, Excellence, *al-Ihsan*, which, according a famous *hadith*, consists in "Worshiping God as if thou seest Him, for if thou seest Him not, He certainly seeth thee." This inner disposition, which in all circumstances, fortunate or unfortunate, places the individual beneath the benevolent gaze of God, was at the heart of the education received by the son of Muhyi ad-Din. Alexandre Bellemare emphasizes this dimension that characterized the *muqaddam* of the *zawiya* of Oued al-Hammam, who, he writes, was "a man solely concerned with the fear of God; his children were raised by him with this sentiment."[42]

To these rituals and teachings of great moral rigor, which called upon the student to conform to a spirit of ascesis, were joined more festive practices which gave the *zawiya* a joyous air. Large gatherings were organized on the occasion of religious feasts: the *'Id al-Fitr*, which marked the end of the month of *Ramadan*, the *'Id al-Adha*, which takes place two months later and commemorates the sacrifice of Abraham, the *Mawlid an-Nabi*, the Prophet's birthday. To these holidays were added the commemorations proper to the brotherhood, the *wa'dha*, "votive festivals" which were the occasion for reunions between the brethren of one or several brotherhoods, and which were attended by the local populations. Such times, moreover, lent a savor and a depth

---

41 É. Dermenghem, "Les souvenirs de l'émir Abdel-kader dans la région de Mascara," *Bulletin des études arabes*, Algiers 1948, p. 216.

42 Alexandre Bellemare, *Abd el-Kader*, p. 11.

to the received exoteric teaching. These sessions, in which religious fervor was expressed at once forcefully and gently, shaped the imagination of the children, sensitizing them very early to the world of mystery and the inexpressible.

It is in this ambience, which mingled moral rigor and brotherly warmth, that Abd el-Kader would develop until his adolescence. After having received the bases of the religious and spiritual teaching, the adolescent left the plain of Ghriss for a time to complete his intellectual formation. He went to the city of Oran, the seat of the Turkish administration, in order to study "grammar, eloquence, and logic with the scholars."[43] Scarcely fifteen years old, he lived through a real expatriation, a wrenching, it might be said. In this large city, the first in the west of the Regency, he came into contact with a reality that radically severed him from his land of birth. Everything that he encountered was new to him: faces, dress, attitudes, etc. The students he mingled with were mostly from the prominent families of the province, sons of Turkish functionaries or of rich merchants, very different from the barefooted, the orphans, the old men without family who were welcomed to the paternal *zawiya*. And unlike the children of the tribal chiefs and these notables, the son of the *muqaddam* possessed nothing of his own. He had lived according to sheer necessity, and the principles of solidarity and sharing had governed his existence. As enriching as this may have been, this discovery wounded his sensibility, while the loose mentalities and behavior of the city dwellers clashed with the simple and strict education of a son of a *zawiya*. Alexandre Bellemare recounts that the imagination of the young man "was struck by the scandalous disorders furnished by the spectacle of the Turkish militia."[44] No doubt, Abd el-Kader would have been able to identify with the following commentary by a Sufi of that time: "The cities have exorbitant customs and great disorder reigns in them; they are not suitable for those who aspire to God!"[45]

It is likely, however, that this difficult episode tested the education he had received and allowed him to detach himself from the fam-

43 *Autobiographie*, p. 55.

44 Alexandre Bellemare, *Abd el-Kader*, p. 16.

45 Saying of Sidi Buzidi, the disciple of Sidi Mulay al-'Arabi ad-Darqawi and master of Sidi Ahmad ibn Ajiba, who relates it in his autobiography, *L'Autobiographie (Fahrasa) du Soufi Marocain Ahmad Ibn 'Agiba*, trans. J.L. Michon (Milan: Archè, 1982), p. 84.

ily Guetna, the place of his childhood. He acquired a maturity that prepared him for another major stage of his life. Upon entering his eighteenth year, it was indeed he whom Sidi Muhyi ad-Din chose as a companion on the pilgrimage to Mecca.

An Initiatic Voyage

Sidi Muhyi ad-Din, who had already acquired the title of *Hajj*,* that of a pilgrim to holy sites, decided in 1825[46] to renew the experience. His eldest son, Sidi Said, had to renounce accompanying him, probably in order to take charge of the general functioning of the *zawiya* of Oued al-Hammam during his father's absence. Designated as his helper, Abd el-Kader would be responsible for "the affairs of his father's entourage"[47] during the two years that the journey would last. Muhyi ad-Din knew that the theologian the young Abd el-Kader was destined to be, would complete his religious formation with this experience. At the beginning of the nineteenth century, the "great pilgrimage" or *hajj*,[48] was undertaken with little guarantee of return: the departure of the pilgrims probably had all the aspects of a definitive farewell. Hence, to joy mingled with pride, Abd el-Kader had probably felt a certain dread in responding to the call of God, and it is probably in this state of mind that some weeks prior to the fast of the month of Ramadan,

---

46 The date of the first pilgrimage of Abd el-Kader is indicated in the manuscript "Chevallier" in chapter 4. The manuscript, written in part under the dictation and supervision of the Emir during his detention in France, specifies 2 *sha'ban* 1230 (July 10, 1815). If the day and month of the hegira are plausible for the departure for the *hajj*, the year cannot be considered to be possible. The young Abd el-Kader was 8 years old in the year 1815, an age which contradicts other information given in the manuscript: for example, the fact that he had finished his education and that he had just married. We have preferred to retain the date of 2 *sha'ban* of the year 1240 (March 22, 1825), which is corroborated by Churchill's biography save for an error regarding the month (*La Vie d'Abd el Kader*, p. 53). This date is plausible if it is compared with the other events, in particular with the disturbances between the Tijaniyya brotherhood and Bey Hasan, which go back to the year 1826 and to which the "Chevallier" manuscript alludes, and at which time Abd el-Kader and his father were in Syria.

47 According to al-Hashimi, cited in Marie d'Aire, *Abd el-Kader*, p. 242.

48 There are two types of pilgrimage to Mecca: *al-hajj*, the "great pilgrimage," which takes place during a fixed period of the lunar year and which the faithful must observe at least once during his life, if he has the physical and material means to do so, and *al-umra*, the "lesser pilgrimage," which can be accomplished at any time of year.

the caravan set off eastwards. It successively crossed the Regency of Algiers, then the domain of the Turkish bey at Tunis, where the pilgrims embarked on a French merchant ship[49] in order to arrive at Alexandria during the time of the *'Id al-Fitr.*

For pilgrims from the Maghreb, Alexandria was the doorway to the Hijaz* and a spiritual halt for Sufis. In this city was located the mausoleum of Sidi Abu'l-Abbas al-Mursi, the successor of Sidi Abu'l Hasan ash-Shadhili, the founder of the Shadhiliyya, one of the most important Sufi *turuq* (pl. of *tariqa*). Abd el-Kader discovered there a religious ambience different from what he had known: the animated fervor of the Egyptian Sufis, the ambience of intense recollection within the mausoleums and in the *zawiyas* he visited with his father surely impressed him. Confronted with these "brethren" from the East, he who until then had had only his land of birth as his horizon, became fully aware of belonging to a great family. The remainder of the voyage would unfold to the rhythm of encounters with religious personages and pious visits. After Alexandria, the pilgrims continued their way through Tanta, the site of the mausoleum of Sidi Ahmad Badawi, the holy patron of Egypt, then through Cairo, where they made a short stop, time to visit the famous mosque of al-Azhar, and most likely the tombs of the great Sufi masters located in al-Qarafa, among which is that of Ibn 'Ata'illa, the author of the *Hikam*, and that of 'Umar ibn al-Farid, the "Sultan of the lovers."

Finally, they arrived at Mecca, the "navel of the world," *surrat al-'ard*, in time for the beginning of the rite, two months after their departure from the Guetna. An austere city, set in a semi-arid landscape, Mecca is the most important point of assembly of the Muslim world, *Dar al-Islam.* Faithful Muslims converge from all four cardinal points, responding to the call of God, crying: *Labbayka 'Llahumma labayk*, "Here I am O Lord, here I am. . .". Everything in the ritual of the *hajj* reminds man of the need to prepare his return to God and to regain his primordial state (*fitra**), when he was penetrated by the pure spirit. To each rite of the pilgrimage there corresponds a stage in this marked-out itinerary. The first condition for the pilgrim is to be clothed in two

---

49 It seems that the French captain Jouves ou Jovas, accompanied by his two children, left Abd al-Kader with good memories; he mentions them in the "Chevallier" manuscript (pp. 56-57). Léon Roches also alludes to them in his work (*Trente-deux ans à travers l'Islam*, vol. 1, p. 141).

sheets of white unhemmed cloth; it signifies the entry into the sacralized state, *al-ihram*. This garment symbolizes the shroud, for the return journey towards God is conditioned by the death of the ego, *an-nafs*. The ritual circumambulation, *at-tawaf*, around the Kaaba, takes the soul through a gradual purification from all its attachments until its total extinction, *al-fana'*. The young Abd el-Kader, like the tens of thousands of pilgrims, will scrupulously follow this marked-out rite. The sayings of the masters who encourage renunciation and to empty "the heart of illusion," come to his mind. Upon seeing the Kaaba, the empty "cube" that symbolizes the heart, precisely, he understands that the spiritual organ of man must be empty if it hopes to be "visited" by God. In this human tide, he perceives the fundamental unity of the Muslim community, *al-Umma*, and, beyond it, of all humanity. Everything there also recalls the figure of the patriarch Abraham, who according to tradition built the Kaaba with the help of his son. The rite between Safa and Marwa recalls the trial undergone by Hagar, seeking water for her son Ishmael, a trial which gave birth to the well of Zam Zam, from which the pilgrims drink. On the ninth day, all converge upon the plain of 'Arafat which metaphysically prefigures the Day of Resurrection. After a final circumambulation of the Kaaba, the pilgrims leave the state of sacralization. Then comes the time of preparation for the departure. The pilgrims are recommended to go the "Mountain of Light," Jabal an-Nur, to visit the cave of Hira. It is there, according to tradition, that Muhammad, while not yet a prophet, received the first revelation. The narrative of the pilgrimage specifies that after "forty-six days, we finished the rites of the Hajj and the Umra, and we went to Medina where we spent the day of 'Ashura'."[50]

The discovery of the city which welcomed the Prophet after his departure in exile, and in which his mausoleum is located, was no less moving. The Sufis draw from the love of the Prophet, the source of Mercy, the necessary strength to follow the way towards the Absolute. That is why the stage of Medina "the Radiant" is for them, more than for the other faithful, a stage as sacred as that of Mecca. After the tumult and tensions that the *muqaddam* and his son left behind, Medina, with its wholesome air and its mild temperature, was like the reward for the fatigues undergone. At the end of the first lunar month, they

---

50 Translator's note: 'Ashura' is the tenth day of *Muharram* in the Islamic calendar, on which day it was the custom of the Prophet to fast.

continued northwards. In Damascus, ennobled by the Prophet, who had declared "Go to Syria, it is the most pure of God's countries, and the chosen of His creatures live there," Abd el-Kader discovered still more forcefully all the richness of the Sufi tradition. The vastness of the cathedral mosque of the Umayyads impressed him. The pilgrims, who had the custom to include in their itinerary the mausoleums of the illustrious figures of Islam, certainly visited those of Salah ad-Din al-Ayyubi (the Saladin of medieval fame), liberator of Jerusalem, Shaykh Arslan, the eminent Sufi who had also led the *jihad* during the Crusades, and also that of Shaykh Ibn 'Arabi, surnamed *ash-Shaykh al-Akbar*, "the greatest master," whose spiritual works were well known in the Sufi circles of the Maghreb. At this time, Abd el-Kader already knew most of the great classical figures of Sufism* (*tasawwuf*). In one of his late writings he compares the numerous religious dignitaries he met in Damascus to the greatest spiritual Sufi masters in history, such as "Junayd, Shibli, al-Bistami, Ibn Ayadh, al-Ma'arri, Ibn Adham, and al-Ghazali."[51] Among these personalities there was the Shaykh Khalid al-Naqshbandi,[52] with whom Sidi Muhyi ad-Din and Abd el-Kader very likely made an initiatic attachment, thus affiliating themselves with the Naqshbandiyya *tariqa*.

However, Damascus for the pilgrims was merely a stage on the way to Iraq, the cradle of the Qadiriyya, where the caravan of the pilgrims sojourned for almost two months, the time necessary for the Qadiris from the Oued al-Hammam to restore themselves spiritually where the mausoleum of the founder reposes under a majestic tiled dome. Indian, Afghan, Egyptian, and Maghrebi pilgrims were welcomed by the Shaykh of the *tariqa*. The young Abd el-Kader participated with them in the spiritual sessions, punctuated by chantings, prayers, and teachings. It had been an intense journey during which, after Egypt, the Hijaz, and Syria, he had discovered all the spiritual and scholarly riches of Sufism. Part of their stay was dedicated to visiting the leading dignitaries of the mother *zawiya*, with whom Sidi Muhyi ad-Din and his son renewed their initiatic attachment. The cohesion between the local *zawiyas* and the mother-*zawiya* had always been guaranteed by emissaries coming from Iraq, who confirmed the function of the

---

51 *Autobiographie*, chap. 4.

52 Shaykh Naqshbandi died in 1827, shortly after the visit of Sidi Muhyi ad-Din and his son.

muqaddimun and transmitted the Shaykh's instructions. In each generation there had taken place spontaneously a renewing of the initiatic attachment to the living Shaykh of the Qadiriyya. In view of the distance and the dangers involved in a voyage to Iraq, the successive *muqaddimun* of the *zawiya* of Oued al-Hammam took advantage of their pilgrimage to the holy places of the Hijaz to also visit the ancient Abbasid capital.

After two months, the caravan took the return route they had taken from the Hijaz: a further stay in Damascus prior to heading towards the holy places where father and son undertook a second pilgrimage, after which they returned to Cairo where they regrouped with the caravans of the Maghreb. Several weeks later, the pilgrims from the Oued al-Hammam returned to the Regency of Algiers. The narrative that Abd el-Kader has left of the pilgrimage ends with a remark that announces a new epoch: "During the summer after our arrival, everyone spoke of the news concerning the Pasha and the French and of the Coup d'Eventail," namely the famous "Fly Whisk Incident" or the "Blow of the Fan," depending on the version, dealt by Dey* Husayn to the French consul Deval in 1827, and which served as the pretext for the conquest of Algeria. This was an event with considerable consequences for the future of both countries and for him whose close associates would henceforth use the title *Hajj* Abd el-Kader.

Upon the return from the voyage, the young *Hajj* had matured, his outward and inward horizons considerably expanded. The pilgrimage had allowed him to discover the extent and the complexity of *Dar al-Islam*: the diversity of faces, languages, cultures, customs. The contact with different religious brotherhoods, the exchanges with spiritual masters and theologians, probably sealed his vocation for religion and spiritual speculation, just as the sessions shared with the brethren in the Way, punctuated with chanting, prayers, and teachings, would have nourished his inwardness. But this initiatic voyage also allowed him to discover the human and social realities of *Dar al-Islam*. The observations he was able to make, the exchanges with the public officials and notables of the cities visited, contributed to his political maturation. From all this he would be able to draw in part his inspiration once elected as head of the tribes of the West.

CHAPTER 3

The Warrior-Saint

*The Prophet said: We have returned from the lesser holy war (jihad)
to the greater holy war. The Companions asked: What is the greater holy war?
The Prophet replied: The fight against the passions of the heart.*
Hadith

The Birth of a Figure of Sanctity

During the course of the summer of 1830, when Abd el-Kader learned
of the landing of the French troops in Algeria and the departure into
exile of Dey Husayn, the ruler of the country, he was far from sus-
pecting the consequences that these events would have on his destiny.
Settled in the paternal *zawiya*, he took up his vocation of teaching religious sciences and regarded his future serenely. At this time, he was
unknown outside the restricted circle of his family and of the Qadiriyya *tariqa*. His reputation was limited to the fact that he was the son of
Muhyi ad-Din, who enjoyed considerable renown throughout the west
of the Regency.

The French Africa Army extended its dominion over the entire
coast and, in January 1831, landed in Oran, where it established a garrison after having run off the Ottoman militia and Bey* Hasan. Feeling
the threat approach the Oued al-Hammam, Sidi Muhyi ad-Din called
for a *jihad*, and joined the first sporadic attacks that took place under
the walls of the city. It is there, in the spring of 1832,[1] that in the wake
of his father, the young Abd el-Kader underwent his baptism by fire.
Events unfolded rapidly thereafter, and a few months later, Abd el-
Kader ibn Muhyi ad-Din became the Emir Abd el-Kader.

The entry into history of Muhyi ad-Din's son is paradoxical in
two respects. The first has to do with the circumstances of his emer-
gence; destined to live in the shadow of his father, and in the silence

---

1 Charles Henry Churchill indicates the spring, as does Léon Roches, who specifies
March 1, 1832 as the date (see Léon Roches, *Trente-deux ans à travers l'islam*, vol. 1,
p. 211). Melchior-Joseph-Eugène Daumas gives other dates. He writes that the future
Emir distinguished himself "in the battles that took place under the walls of Oran, the
16th and 23rd of October and the 10th and 11th of November, 1832" (in Georges Yver,
Correspondance du capitaine Daumas, p. 305n).

of a provincial *zawiya*, yet it was a war of conquest which literally revealed him. The second paradox, resulting from the first, lay in the opposition between his new function and his first vocation as a "man of the rosary." Placed at the head of the *jihad*, Abd el-Kader added the sword to his rosary. From an eminently spiritual function he passed to the temporal function of Commander of the Faithful. This double paradox defined both the figure of legend that was crystallized during his lifetime and the one that entered into history. If the society of his birth, molded by a fruitful spirituality and the sense of the marvelous, nourished the hagiological dimension of the personage, the French or European witnesses had a more rational, but no less charismatic, interpretation. And it is just this balance between the imaginary and reality, hagiography and history, that will constitute the Emir's aura.

His entry into official history was fixed in the fall of 1832 with his election; as for the legend, the chronicle situates it during the time of the pilgrimage of father and son in the East between 1825 and 1827, and functions as a symbolic justification for the raising of the son of Sidi Muhyi ad-Din to the title of Commander of the Faithful. A letter taken from the correspondence of the French consul in Mascara relates the visit of the two pilgrims from Oued al-Hammam to the tomb of Sidi Abd al-Qadir al-Jilani, the patron saint of Baghdad: "They arrived there overcome by the heat and by fatigue. The moment they crossed the threshold, a venerable old man emerged from the tomb, offering them honey, dates, milk, encouraged them to rest, and disappeared. The next day, he returned and, not seeing the young Abd el-Kader, he asked where the Sultan was. Muhyi ad-Din, quite astonished, replied that they were poor God-fearing people, that there was no sultan among them, and that he had only his son, who had gone to take the horses to pasture. He tried, in vain, to defend himself by calling attention to the dangers they might face if the Turks became aware of all this. The old man completed his prediction saying that the reign of the Turks was going to end and that the young Abd el-Kader would one day rule the *Gharb* [the Arab West]." It seems that this story, of which there are several variations, was very widespread among the Muslim population. In this version, it is the founder of the Qadiriyya order in person who leaves his tomb in order to confirm the future Emir: the well-wishing attitude of the old man and the very symbolic offerings given to the pilgrims leave no ambiguity regarding the meaning of this vision: Abd el-Kader is destined to accede to important political functions. Another source has the old man exclaim: "What! The Sultan tends the camels! In that thou doest something astonishing!"[2] This family chronicle brings to mind an episode of the *Sira*, the traditional biography of the Prophet, featuring an old Nestorian monk who, after having seen the young Muhammad, who had remained behind to guard the mounts of the caravan, declared to the young man's uncle, Abu Talib, that an unparalleled destiny awaited his nephew. The two stories, that of the forthcoming Prophet and that of the future Commander of the Faithful, are very similar, which had certainly led the contemporary Muslims of the Emir to mingle them, to the point of merging them into one and the same tradition.

There is nothing astonishing in this, if one keeps in mind the centrality of the figure of the Prophet in the traditional Algerian society which, as regards the sphere of social organization, the place of religion and certain customs, reminds one, to some extent, of Arabia's at the time of Muhammad. The affinity thus established between the founder of the Qadiriyya order and the Prophet of Islam considerably enhanced the prestige of the new Emir and allowed him to further legitimize his new function. According to several French witnesses, this story, and other similar ones, circulated even prior to the onset of the conquest. Alexandre Bellemare, while trying to keep from mingling "the marvelous and the truth in the history of such an important figure," specifies that it "exercised a certain influence on the elevation of the son of Muhyi ad-din."[3] The French consul at Mascara was still more explicit: "It was during a voyage to Mecca that Muhyi ad-Din prepared the destiny of his son. Upon returning from this pilgrimage, he recounted several visions he had had at the holy site, all of which announced his son's future greatness. These predictions spread throughout the land, and even reached the Turks, who at that time ruled Oran. Nothing more was needed to alarm such a despotic government."[4] In attributing to Muhyi ad-Din an ambition for his son,[5] the French agent

---

2 Among the variations, that of Abd el-Kader's cousin, Sidi Husayn, which we cite here, was published in the *Revue africaine*: "Histoire d'El-Hadj A'bd-el-K'ader," p. 421.

3 Alexandre Bellemare, *Abd-el-Kader*, p. 22.

4 Georges Yver, *Correspondance du capitaine Daumas*, p. 303.

5 An interpretation shared by Léon Roches when he writes: "His father took great care to compile these predictions, and upon his return made haste to spread among the Arabs of the province" (*Trente-deux ans à travers l'islam*, vol. 1, p. 141).

was attempting to find a rational explanation and a political justification for the tales that were circulating regarding Abd el-Kader. Charles
Henry Churchill is more circumspect regarding their veracity and
seems to want to clear the Emir from such beliefs: "Each time Abd
el-Kader was asked if he himself had any faith in such superstitions,
he invariably replied, pointing an index finger towards heaven: 'My
trust is in God alone.'"[6] In the eyes of the European authors, if these supernatural tales played a certain role, they were nonetheless irrational,
hence subject to caution.

The debate over the authenticity of the reported facts is impossible to settle. What counts is what is revealed by their profusion and
success, namely the sensibility and point of view of Abd al-Kader's
contemporary Muslims, and how this "taste for marvels"[7] was able to
play such a determining part in the attribution of an aura of sanctity
to their Commander of the Faithful. The powerful symbolic charge
linked to the pilgrimage and to the holy places of Islam explains in
part the credit granted these tales, but the eschatological reading of the
political events which unfolded subsequently[8] must also be taken into

6 Charles H. Churchill, *La Vie d'Abd el Kader*, p. 55.

7 An expression of Léon Roches.

8 The reference is to a recurring affirmation in the writings of the colonial era. Regarding the Algerians, Depont and Coppolani, in particular, write: "They live in the
perpetual expectation of the arrival of a Redeemer. This idea of Mahdism dominates
the entire Muslim existence and the brotherhoods exploit it to the hilt. It is the expectation of the 'Master of the Hour'" (*Les Confréries religieuses musulanes* [Algiers:
A. Jourdan, 1897], p. 260). This eschatological expectation is also illustrated by some
testimonies, among them that of the Emir's cousin, to whom we have already referred,
and who, regarding the prodigy that took place in Baghdad, said: "We have been ex-
pecting the realization of this prophecy for many long years, and nothing appeared
when the French marched against Algiers and conquered it" (cited in "Histoire d'El-
Hadj A'bd el-K'ader," p. 421). [Translator's note: it is perhaps worth adding that there
were indeed close links between Sufism and this "redemptionist" Mahdism, and this
is what accounts for the concern of colonial authorities over possible Mahdist uprisings in the second half of the century. Depont and Coppolani's remark concerning the
"exploitation" of this Mahdism doubtless refers especially to the figures of Bu Ma'za
and Bu 'Amama. "Redemption" is not quite the right word to express the orthodox eschatological notion in question, however, as this has Christian connotations. It would
be more accurate to speak of the expectation of a "renewer" and of a "restoration." This
expectation is part of the Islamic tradition, and is not a "heresy," as certain older studies would have it; it was only accentuated excessively or abusively here and there, and
refers to the prophetic figure who will briefly restore the Islamic pattern as a mercy

account: the Ottoman yoke had induced the hope of the coming of a better age and of the coming of a liberator. It is in this atmosphere of eschatological expectation that the election of the Emir took place; he being the incarnation of the hope that animated it.

The hagiographic stories, then, quite logically included the election of the new Emir, and are efficaciously related by the European witnesses. The discovery by the western tribes (the Hashim, the Bani-Amr, and the Ghraba) of the strength of the French Africa Army and its will to extend its conquest over the entire south of the Regency had led their leaders to quickly organize an armed resistance—a necessity all the greater in view of the anarchy that was spreading over the entire country. In the autumn of 1832, in Ersebia in the plain of Ghriss, the main tribes, at the initiative of the Hashim, to whom Sidi Muhyi ad-Din was affiliated, held an emergency meeting in an extraordinary assembly in order to elect a leader. It was a solemn event, in accordance with the causes that motivated it. Sidi Muhyi ad-Din was offered the command. Respected throughout the province of Oran, he possessed, in the eyes of the local aristocracy and the populace, the necessary title and qualities to unite the community of the Muslims against an adversary that threatened their territorial and religious integrity. Sidi Muhyi ad-Din excused himself on account of his old age and, owing to the insistence of those present, proposed instead one of his sons, Abd el-Kader, who had already acquired a certain reputation for bravery after the first skirmishes during the spring of 1832. But certain members present remained doubtful regarding his ability to lead, convinced that he "had passed his life reading holy books and had not learned the art of leadership."[9] Here again, it was signs of marvels that sealed his destiny: Sidi Laaradj,[10] an elderly sage who enjoyed a great reputation in the region of Mascara, declared having seen in a dream "Abd el-Kader seated on a seat of honor and dispensing justice." The narrative of the dream continues: "Thy son, or thyself, must be the sultan of the

immediately prior to the arrival and very short reign of Antichrist. As in the Christian tradition, Muslims believe that it is the second coming of Christ which ends the reign of Antichrist and also brings to its end this human cycle.]

9 Alexandre Bellemare, *Abd-el-Kader*, p. 36.

10 According to the legend and to the military chronicle, this person played a very important role, to the point that he was included in the painting of Horace Vernet, *Prise de la smalah d'Abd-El-Kader à Taguin. 16 mai 1843*, National Museum at Versailles.

Arabs. If thou acceptest the power for thyself, thy son will die; if thou acceptest it for him, thou wilt soon die."[11] Now, the young man's father himself had had a similar dream. This coincidence of visionary dreams was judged sufficiently convincing to confirm the triumphal election of Muhyi ad-Din's son. On the 22nd of November 1832, under a tree,[12] according to tradition, the dignitaries and notables of the region filed before the new Commander of the Faithful[13] in order to pledge allegiance. The allegiance was confirmed five days later before the assembly of the faithful at the great mosque of Mascara.

His affiliations to the religious aristocracy and the Qadiriyya *tariqa* placed the new Emir under the seal and protection of the Prophet Muhammad and of the saint of Baghdad, Sidi Abd al-Qadir al-Jilani. This double patronage legitimated his temporal power, but also intensified his spiritual aura, which in its turn had political efficacy. Édouard de Neveu, who furnished one of the first studies on the Sufic brotherhoods in Algeria, emphasizes this with the illustration of a belief held by the Muslims, which expresses well the part that marvels had in the political genesis of Muhyi ad-Din's son. "Henceforth," said the Arabs, "not a day passed without Mulay Abd al-Qadir [al-Jilani] coming to visit his protegé, the son of Muhyi ad-Din. . . . No important decision: treaties with the French, declarations of war, construction of new cities, movement of tribes, levying of taxes, etc., was undertaken by Abd el-Kader without it being placed under the safeguard of his homonym of Baghdad."[14] This example illustrates well the belief of his people concerning the position as intermediary of their Commander between the contingent world and the world of mystery (*'alam al-ghayb*; lit. the "invisible world"). According to Muslim tradition, such a position pertains to the holy man (*wali*), to whom are granted all manner of

11 Alexandre Bellemare, *Abd-el-Kader*, p. 36. Was this narrative prior to or posterior to the *Mubaya'a**? Whatever the case may be, Sidi Muhyi ad-Din would die in 1833.

12 Certain sources say that this tree was an ash, *ad-Dardara*, whereas according to the written testimony of Husayn, the Emir's cousin, it was a "royal" black locust tree, named for this event "Karubet as-Sultana" by the Hashim Sheraga.

13 It is interesting to note that this *Mubaya'a* recalls, to some extent, that of the Prophet, related in the Sura *al-Fath*, "The Victory." This resemblance between the two men surely occupied a considerable place in the popular imagination. The official election was confirmed by a new ceremony, a little more than two months after the first.

14 Édouard de Neveu, *Les Khouans*, p. 29.

particular virtues and charismatic gifts, and which the Emir clearly seemed to personify.

Like an 'Ali ibn Abi Talib, one of the successors of the Prophet, Abd el-Kader possessed the gift of eloquence. Dr. Frankl, following his meeting with the Emir in Damascus in 1856, wrote: "He has acquired great influence in the East, owing to a reputation for courage and eloquence which often is regarded as prophetic."[15] His eloquence had a quality which in certain aspects seemed prodigious. It gave his discourses and preachings an incantatory force which, according to his secretary, caused "tears to well from everyone's eyes, and [softened] the hardest hearts."[16] This gift assuredly was part of the "extraordinary fascination that he exercised upon all who came near him."[17] Among these personalities was Léon Roches, one of the rare European witnesses to live in the intimacy of the Emir, whose secretary he became after his conversion to Islam. It is in his Memoirs that are found the most eloquent testimonies concerning the charisma of Abd el-Kader among his compatriots: "I have seen the Emir pray before more than 2,000 Arabs who believed that God heard them more favorably when united to a man as holy as the sultan."[18] During an expedition lead by the Emir against the Saharan fortress of Ain Madhi,[19] the Frenchman, suffering from fever, exhausted and undergoing the effect of an "excitation of nerves," found himself in the tent of the Emir whom he begged to cure him. He recounts: "He calmed me, had me drink an infusion. . . . He placed his hands on my head . . . and under his gentle touch I was not long in falling asleep. . . . After this night I no longer had a single bout of fever and I had healed my dysentery by eating a pomegranate with

---

15 Cited in R.P. Beaton, *The Jews in the East, from the German of Dr. Frankl* (London: Hurst & Blackett Publishers, 1859), pp. 282-290.

16 Charles H. Churchill, *La Vie d'Abd-el-Kader*, p. 162. The secretary of the Emir was Qadur ibn Roula, whose full text, which is included in the military regulations of the Algerian troops, has also been considered as a viaticum and a model of behavior for one in charge of command.

17 Ibid., p. 287.

18 Léon Roches, *Trente-deux ans à travers l'islam*, vol. 1, p. 176.

19 Shaykh Ahmad Tijani, master of an important Saharan brotherhood, had rejected the Emir's repeated appeals for unity, which unleashed a military campaign against the brotherhood at Ain Madhi. After a long and costly siege, the city was finally taken and the master of the place banished from its territories.

its skin grilled over a campfire."[20] This anecdote inspired the author to a conclusion worth taking into consideration: "What is certain is that, in the entire camp of the Emir, my healing was attributed to the power of his intervention with the Most High." "The king toucheth thee, God healeth thee," by this consecrated formula the sovereigns of France formerly received those who appealed to their function as thaumaturges. According to those around him, Abd el-Kader had received this divine favor which, among others, made of him a saint.

Despite the considerable forces engaged by France during the fifteen years of battle, the Emir Abd el-Kader was neither killed nor captured. Yet he had participated in all the campaigns and would hurl himself into the midst of the battles, fearing neither artillery nor hand-to-hand combat, willingly risking his life, to the point that many of his horses were killed under him. If this bravery aroused the admiration of his adversaries, it also increased his aura among his coreligionists, convinced that his invulnerability and his "ungraspability," were proof of his divine election. Already in the spring of 1832, when he was only a cavalryman among others, the young Abd el-Kader, placed under the command of his father, had distinguished himself beneath the walls of Oran against the French garrison. While bullets from the enemy soldiers were raining down, he recovered the body of his cousin, slain that day, and despite several wounds returned safe and sound to his people. This caused Léon Roches to say that "the Arabs are convinced that the son of Sidi Muhyi ad-Din is invulnerable, as was his father."[21] On the subject of this "ungraspableness," Abd el-Kader said: "When standing on the shore and watching the fish swim freely in the sea, it seems that one has only to reach out to grasp them; and yet one needs all the art and the net of the fisherman to obtain and master them. Some Arabs are like that."[22] This reputation, corroborated by subsequent events, would take on a prodigious character after the breaking of the treaty of Tafna, in 1839, and the intensification of the African Army's operations. At the beginning of 1841, when the war was at its height, the Soult-Guizot government tried to destroy the support of Abd el-Kader's followers. Considerable means were placed at the disposal of Gen-

---

20 Léon Roches, *Trente-deux ans à travers l'islam*, vol. 1, p. 211.

21 Ibid.

22 Cited in Paul Azan, *L'Émir Abd el Kader, 1808-1883. Du fanatisme musulman au patriotisme français* (Paris: Librairie Hachette, 1925), p. 137.

eral Bugeaud and the press closely followed what was then considered to be a veritable manhunt. An observer wrote that of the 106,000 men which had taken to Africa, "Abdelkader alone exacts an annual tribute of 100 million and 10,000 soldiers." For eight years, from the renewing of the war in the autumn of 1839 until his voluntary surrender in December of 1847, the Emir was ceaselessly tracked by French troops. The best generals and the most seasoned officers were mobilized to put in place a system of active units intended to annihilate the infrastructures of his embryonic State and to capture him. "One may wonder," comments Alexandre Bellemare, what is more admirable, these intrepid soldiers in combat . . . or this man who, having started from Morocco at the head of 1,500 to 1,800 cavalrymen, advances, and along the way raises contingents of tribes, from which he makes a provisional army, holding breathless an army of 106,000 men."[23]

More than once, the bulletins from Africa announced the imminent capture of the Emir, even his surrender, before finally publishing a retraction. The unseizable character of Abd el-Kader feathered the nests of the editorialists and inspired the imagery of Épinal as well as that of popular song writers.[24] In the eyes of his partisans, the Emir was *mahfudh*, the beneficiary of divine protection, or also possessed of a special favor, *karama*, granted by God to some of his elect and his saints. For the French generals, this ability to escape the traps that had been cunningly laid, illustrated the genius of the Arab leader. Certain officers nevertheless acknowledged their perplexity before these feats, and Bugeaud avowed that "a magician would be required to divine his movements, and our soldiers would need wings to reach him."[25] General Arbouville went so far as to ask whether this uncatchable adversary were not endowed with the gift of ubiquity! During the course of

23 Alexandre Bellemare, *Abd-el-Kader*, p. 304.

24 "Even a madman committed in Bicêtre hospital would have his favorite fancy consist in having invented an infallible system to capture the enemy" (O. Delepierre, *Histoire littéraire des fous* [London: Trübner & Co., 1860], p. 48). The "ungraspableness" of the Arab chief also inspired songwriters, as in these anonymous words written after his surrender: "For fifteen years he was tracked, this famous Abd el-Kader, he could turn himself into air and return to his camp; they tried catch, but couldn't find the Emir" (cited in A. Ruscio, *Que la France était belle au temps des colonies* (Paris: Maisonneuve et Larose, 2001), p. 517.

25 Memoir of Marshal Bugeaud, the Minister of War, November 24, 1845, in B. Etienne and F. Pouillon, *Abd el-Kader le magnanime* (Paris: Gallimard, 2003), p. 100.

the year 1847, pursued across the entire Algerian territory, the Emir took refuge in eastern Morocco. Since the signing of the Treaty of Tangiers, September 10, 1844, which made him an "outlaw" across the entire extent of the Moroccan territory, Abd el-Kader and his followers were not secure anywhere. In the spring of 1847, the *deïra** camped in the environs of the Malouiya. The attempt to assassinate the leader of the resistance probably goes back to this period. Churchill gives a somewhat romanticized version of the event: "One night, while the Deïra were still camped at Ain Zohra, an assassin slipped stealthily into the tent of Abd el-Kader. The Sultan was reading. At the sound of steps, he raised his eyes and saw standing before him a black man of impressive stature, a dagger held raised in his arm. Suddenly, throwing his weapon on the ground, the man threw himself at his feet. 'I was going to strike thee, he cried, but from the moment I saw thee, I was disarmed. I see, around thy head, the halo of the Prophet.'"[26] This story, aside from its marvelous character, reinforced the likeness of the Emir with his eminent model. Henceforth, in placing his steps in those of the Prophet, the Emir Abd el-Kader acquired an immense prestige among his followers which remained intact well after the end of his involvement in politics.

His surrender in December 1847, far from plunging him into oblivion, paradoxically amplified his memory; as if, rather than dissolving his aura, his physical absence instead sublimized it. The man had disappeared, but his blessed influence, his *baraka*, continued to haunt the places he had passed through. In Mostaghanem, in the 1850s, a delegation of Saharan chieftains who had defected were being conducted to the French stables of the city. The Africa Army officers who accompanied them were suddenly surprised by the abrupt movement of their guests upon seeing a black stallion toward which they ran wildly, embracing its neck, its shoulders, and even its hooves. This stallion had been a former war horse of Abd el-Kader. "He carried him!" was the repeated exclamation, which expressed their irresistible feelings, and it was with great difficulty that they were pulled away.[27] Such a scene shows the charisma which the Emir continued to have in Algeria.

26 Charles H. Churchill, *La Vie d'Abd-el-Kader*, p. 263.

27 Ibid., p. 288. The fact is also mentioned in the work of Msg. Dupuch, *Abd el-Kader au château d'Amboise* (Paris: Ibis Press, 2002), p. 27.

His aura, which Charles Henry Churchill termed the "magic of the name,"[28] was nonetheless not diffused solely among Abd el-Kader's countrymen and partisans. In France, his legend circulated in the press and his name became popular to the point of making him a living legend, whose lasting quality is in part due to the testimonies of his French adversaries; paradoxically, it was those whom he fought who brought it to light most eloquently.

In the Mirror of the Enemy

At the outset of the conquest, military propaganda focused on disparaging the enemy. Abd el-Kader was described with the features of an "ogre from the desert," or as a kind of "Bluebeard."[29] In response, the press, fed on a biased image of the young Arab leader, made him out to be "ambitious," as well as a "fanatic." However, and it is not the least of the paradoxes induced by the Emir, the facts would not only contradict these assertions, but would compel viewing him as a noble figure. The Africa Army was not long in acknowledging the military qualities of its formidable adversary. His daring which, starting from nothing, took charge of a nascent army comprised basically of ill-equipped civilians, in order to face the foremost army in the world; his sobriety after a victory; his ability to "rebound after he seemed to have been definitively defeated";[30] his extraordinary determination "when things seemed hopeless"; finally, his political genius: all these reasons explain in large measure the admiration that he aroused within the ranks of his adversaries among the higher officers as well as among the soldiers. In a letter of December 1842, General Bugeaud wrote concerning the Emir: "He fights against his ill fortune with great energy and great intelligence. He is truly a masterful man, worthy of a better lot." It is interesting to note that the best and oldest biographies were all written by military men: Alexandre Bellemare, Colonel Charles Henry Churchill, and Colonel Paul Azan. General Duvivier honors his enemy in the fol-

---

28 Regarding the Emir, the Governor-General of Algeria, General de Martinprey, in a confidential report, emphasized "the prestige still held by his name" (cited in B. Etienne, and F. Pouillon, *Abd el-Kader le magnanime*, p. 274).

29 L.-A. Berbrugger, "Voyage au camp d'Abd-el-Kader," *La Revue des Deux Mondes du 15 août 1838* (Toulon: Impr. E. Aurel, avril 1839), p. 48.

30 Paul Azan, *L'Émir Abd el Kader*, p. v.

lowing poem: "Poor son of the desert! Having for riches only thy Koran, thy saber, and thy horse, for arms only thy genius and thy word, thou shalt perhaps fall like the tall palm under the strain of the desert wind *simoon*, but future generations will honor thy name."[31] A legionnaire's letter manifests his infatuation for the Emir, by "I like him; I admire him."[32] As the Christian poets and chroniclers had held Salah ad-Din al-Ayyubi, the Saladin of the Crusades, as a model of the chivalric virtues, so too the Emir was held as a magnanimous adversary. If his bravery and tenacity, very military qualities, are often brought-up by the pens of the French historians, his religious and moral qualities are also emphasized from the first encounters of Africa Army officers with their adversary. These testimonies revealed a nuanced picture of the personality of Abd el-Kader, as complex as it was paradoxical. Despite what we could term a rupture in his destiny, upon being immersed in the temporal sphere, the Emir kept all the distinctive features of the religious aristocracy. This double filiation can be recognized in the writings and drawings which appear soon after the signing of the Treaty of Desmichels in 1834, and still more so again after the Treaty of Tafna of 1837. They juxtapose two figures of the Emir which at first sight seem antinomian: the warrior and the ascetic.

By the year following his election, thanks to his being an efficacious politician, the young Emir had extended his sphere of influence to the entire province of Oran. His success with the tribes who at first refused to follow his banner, his action to put an end to the anarchy and to the sporadic quarrels that prevailed among them, resulted in a clear lessening of insecurity. The reestablishment of moral order and security in all the territories under his administration made his supporters say that "a young girl could cross the country without fear while wearing a gold crown on her head"; all of which explains to a great extent the prestige he acquired among the people of the province. He progressively established himself as the chief interlocutor with the French Africa Army; and paradoxically, it was one of its commanders-in-chief, General Desmichels, who raised Abd el-Kader in the eyes of his men by making him the privileged interlocutor in a negotiation which led

---

31 General Duvivier, "Quatorze observations sur l'Algérie: Abd el-Kader," *Le Magasin pittoresque* (n.p.: E. Charton, 1848), p. 25.

32 Clemens Lamping, *Souvenirs d'Algerie, 1840-1842* (Paris: Bouchène, 2000), pp. 146-147.

to a peace treaty. The Treaty of Desmichels, signed February 26, 1834, in effect recognized the sovereignty of the Commander of the Faithful over the greater part of the western territories. By this act, the French general expressed both his desire to reestablish peace in the province of Oran as well as to confine the influence of the Emir solely to that region of the country. The fact of treating the young leader as an equal, as well as supporting him against his toughest rivals, caused a number of French commentators at the time to say that General Desmichels favored the ambition of the Arab leader. Indeed, the treaty consolidated the Emir's administration and contributed to the creation in Mascara of a nucleus of a professional army, to which were joined "when necessary" auxiliary forces sent by the tribes. For all these reasons, the agreement ultimately would be judged too advantageous for Abd el-Kader's side. The discovery of secret clauses emphasizing this advantage[33] would provoke, at the demand of the governor-general Drouet D'Erlon, the recalling of General Desmichels and his replacement by General Trézel, a change which signified the breaking of the treaty and the resumption of hostilities.

The truce which followed the Desmichels Treaty allowed the dispatch of French official missions into the camp of the Emir Abd el-Kader. These gave rise to the first direct testimonies concerning the young Arab leader and to more nuanced descriptions favorable to him, and had the consequence of raising his reputation and modifying his image among the French. One officer, having arrived at the enemy camp the month after the signing of the treaty, gives an essentially physical description of the Emir, describing him as "very handsome, dignified, and very distinguished in his manners."[34] A year later, another officer was with Abd el-Kader and sketched a quite different and more edifying portrait. Captain de Saint-Hippolyte,[35] clearly charmed,

33 Articles 1 and 3 foresaw a "freedom to possess war munitions" for the Emir's camp, which moreover exercised total control of the port of Arzew, from which all export merchandise was shipped.

34 L.-A. Desmichels, *Oran sous le commandement du général Desmichels* (Paris: n.p., 1835), p. 131.

35 The captain of the Saint-Hyppolite was sent on mission with him by order of the governor general in order to authenticate the copy of the Desmichels Treaty which was in the Emir's possession. In was during the course of this investigation that a "secret" treaty was discovered.

wrote: "The Emir is a remarkable man. His is a moral state unknown to Europe. He is a being detached from the things of this world, who believes he is inspired, and to whom God has given the mission of protecting his coreligionists. . . . His ambition is not to conquer; glory is not the motive of his actions; personal interest does not guide him; the love of riches is unknown to him; he is not attached to the earth save for that which involves carrying out the will of the Almighty, of whom he is merely the instrument."[36] This nuanced moral portrait established the Emir as an ideal of religious nobility—a dimension, until then unknown among the French, and that would be affirmed in most subsequent descriptions.

The defeat of the troops led by General Trézel at Makta, in June of 1835, led to a hardening of the conquest, which was supported by the sending of new contingents and new men at their head. In addition to the rotation of the officers in charge of the contingents, between July 1834 and the resumption of hostilities at the end of 1839, no less than four governor generals succeeded in Algeria: Drouet d'Erlon, Clauzel, Damrémont, and Valée. This new policy of the stick confronting an unpredictable and tenacious enemy was particularly well incarnated by Marshal Clauzel and General Bugeaud, who arrived in Algiers in the spring of 1836. In the space of two years, the fledgling State constituted by Abd el-Kader would suffer several defeats and lose its main strongholds, including the island of Rachgoun and his capital, Mascara, on December 6, 1835. The loss of his capital, partly due to a desertion of his followers, for a while made the Emir consider exiling himself to Morocco. However, pressured into remaining by the inhabitants of Mascara, he continued to fight. After another defeat in January 1836, at Tlemcen, where he had to battle troops commanded by Marshal Clauzel, Abd el-Kader regained the advantage in April over General Arlanges' troops, which he blocked for several weeks at the mouth of the Tafna river. In July of the same year, the troops of General Bugeaud—whom the Emir confronted for the first time—inflicted a crushing defeat on the Emir on the banks of the Sikkak river. Despite this accumulation of setbacks, the Arab leader did not allow himself to become discouraged. As Paul Azan recounts, "three times, after the capture of Mascara, then of Tlemcen, and after the battle of the Sikkak,

---

36 Cited in S. Aouli, R. Redjala, and P. Zoummeroff, *Abd el-Kader* (Paris: Fayard, 1994), pp. 153-154.

Abd el-Kader was deserted by all. A less energetic man, one weaker in belief, less inspired, might have allowed himself to fall into discouragement. Each time, he emerged triumphant from the trial, having lost none of his prestige in the eyes of his followers."[37] This steadfastness in battle and his bravery before an increasingly powerful enemy do not alone explain the admiration that the Emir aroused in the ranks of his adversaries. Adolphe Vilhem Dinesen, a Danish officer of the Africa Army, is a typical witness. In a story[38] published in 1840, he supplies a more complete and finely shaded idea of why the French military had been led to praise an enemy whom some had even held up as a model.[39]

Dinesen landed in Algiers at the beginning of 1837, enlisted as a volunteer in the French army, and earned for his dedication the Legion of Honor. This did not prevent him from being very critical of the army in which he served: "It is, moreover, typical that wherever the French pass in Africa the trees disappear, the springs dry up, the inhabitants flee, and there remains only a desert. The French know how to conquer, but they do not know how to preserve."[40] However, his judgment is more indulgent towards the Muslim populations, which seems to be inspired by the figure of the Emir. This officer at the outset acknowledges his "lively admiration for the personality of a man who has revived a people's patriotism."[41] He emphasizes the immensity of the task which the Emir had to confront in order to put an end to the ancient rivalries between the tribes and unite them into a single entity—a policy furthered by "scrupulous respect for the law," the foundation of which is humanity and justice.[42] The Dane also emphasizes the qualities of Abd el-Kader which according to him characterize

---

37 Paul Azan, *L'Émir Abd el Kader*, p. 87.

38 A.V. Dinesen, *Abd-el-Kader et les Relations entre les Français et les Arabes en Afrique du Nord* (Algiers: Éditions Anep, 2001), p. 157.

39 This emerges, for example, from the testimony of a French legionnaire: "His friends call him prophet, defender of Islam, and even his enemies cannot deny his courage and generosity, these two cardinal virtues which make a hero. Truly, the tenacity and intelligence with which he has been leading this murderous fight for ten years deserves better success" (Clemens Lamping, *Souvenirs d'Algérie*, p. 147).

40 A.V. Dinesen, *Abd-el-Kader*, p. 44.

41 Ibid., p. 17.

42 Ibid., p. 82.

superior men, and most particularly the mastery of their inner states regardless of circumstances: "Nothing is more foreign to his character than cruelty. He rarely loses his temper and is always able to control his mood."[43] It is this self-mastery that enables him to overcome his fear and go "smiling . . . to meet death,"[44] as is attested to by the disdain of the Emir before the cannonballs,[45] a fact which restored the will to fight of his soldiers and forced the admiration of the French artillery. The Duke of Orléans wrote regarding a battle which preceded the taking of Mascara, and in which the Emir, surrounded, saw his men fall around him, slaughtered by artillery fire: "The effect of it was terrible . . . above all around the Emir; his secretary and his standard-bearer fell at his sides; but he himself, proud of being the aim of all the fire, rode his black horse pacing slowly, and defied with his confident fatalism the skill of the gunners, who were forced to admire his bravery."[46] The attitudes enumerated by Dinesen are all expressions of eminently spiritual virtues in which the young Abd el-Kader had been educated: breaking the logic of discord, "worse than murder" (Koran 2:191) between rival tribes and reconciling individuals, mastering his anger while cultivating courage, overcoming his fear by putting his trust in God, who alone in His unfathomable wisdom, decides the moment of last breath. Dinesen gives priority to the religious intention of the Emir and to the strength that he draws from his faith in order to explain the determination in his political purpose. After the death of his father, in 1833, the Emir was left "alone with God and the genius he had received from Him. This conferred upon his will and his acts a strength and steadfastness without which nothing great can be accomplished."[47] Where other witnesses had been satisfied by explaining "this strength and steadfastness" by an excessive ambition, Dinesen believes on the contrary that Abd el-Kader was sincere, and guided by the "conviction that his fight was inspired and directed by a superior will, which gave his acts that unshakeable perseverance that enabled the success of almost all his undertakings. This is why these great men are called

43 Ibid.

44 Ibid., p. 54.

45 Ibid., p. 37.

46 Cited in Paul Azan, *L'Émir Abd el Kader*, p. 62.

47 A.V. Dinesen, *Abd-el-Kader*, pp. 42-43.

exalted."[48] At this point in his testimony, Dinesen perspicaciously penetrates the Sufic dimension of the Emir: "The impression of religious authority, stemming from his position as marabout, is much more evident than that of war chief. It is not a mistake to compare him to the descriptions of Christ transmitted to us by tradition."[49] For Dinesen, the religious impression radiated by the Emir prevails definitively over his political function, to the extent of the unexpected comparison with Christ, all the more paradoxical in that it emanates from the enemy camp and in the context of war. The tension between these two dimensions, temporal and spiritual, assumed by Abd el-Kader, will be at the heart of all subsequent French testimonies.

On the verge of new negotiations that would lead to a new peace treaty, the Emir was definitively recognized by his adversaries as an indispensable interlocutor. Henceforth, his steadfastness in battle, his bravery and his genius before an increasingly powerful French army, his magnanimity, were known to all and forced the admiration of General Bugeaud, his most emblematic adversary. In the spring of 1837, the victor of the battle of Sikkak was about to accomplish what General Desmichels had tried in vain to do before him: to meet the Emir Abd el-Kader. In his work, Dinesen emphasizes the admiration shown by the former commander-in-chief of the garrison in Oran[50] for his young adversary: "General Desmichels had long wanted to meet Abd el-Kader. He desired to personally know this renowned young Arab leader and speak with him on matters of common interest."[51] But the Emir was not able to consider such a meeting owing to the "fear of arousing some difficult point of etiquette," as Bellemare put it.[52] An encounter with a representative of the enemy army would certainly have provoked opposition within his own camp and would have broken the fragile unity between the disparate tribes which Abd el-Kader had forged with so much difficulty.

---

48 Ibid., p. 43.

49 Ibid., pp. 136-137.

50 General Desmichels knew the Emir through the exchange of letters and the reports of officers (Thorigny, accompanied by M. de Forges and by Dr. Collin, who arrived at the camp of the Emir in March 1834, and Gaudens Tatareau, who arrived the following year) whom he had sent on missions to him.

51 A.V. Dinesen, *Abd-el-Kader*, p. 67.

52 Alexandre Bellemare, *Abd-el-Kader*, p. 178.

After the rout at Sikkak, things would patently change. Facing severe trials owing to repeated defeats, Abd el-Kader was aware of the need for a truce to restore his administration. For their part, the French political authorities had not always opted for a clear policy towards their new "possession." In the Chamber of Deputies, there were lively discussions over the question of the Algerian establishments; the supporters of a restrained occupation, even of an evacuation of this "legacy of the Restoration," made their voices heard. The Emir, who regularly received French newspapers, was perfectly aware of France's ambivalent position; the parliamentary debates were translated for him. The defeat at Constantine in November 1836 had provoked the recall of Marshal Clauzel, replaced by General de Damrémont. The preparation of a new campaign required firstly the pacification of the western province. It was just at this time that General Bugeaud, on April 5, 1837, sailed to Oran. By January 1837, the Emir, more open to negotiations with the enemy and supported by his followers in this,[53] entered into contact with General Brossard, the new commander-in-chief of the garrison at Oran. In March, General Bugeaud was "authorized to use all means to induce Abd el-Kader to make overtures of peace."[54] Negotiations then began, and resulted in the signing of the Treaty of Tafna in the spring of 1837.

General Bugeaud was a good deal more infatuated with himself than General Desmichels. His brilliant military career, his position as deputy, and his privileged relationship with the French king, authorized him to manifest a spirit of independence, including his relationship with his superiors, which would not fail to arouse censures. Reinvigorated after the victory of Sikkak against an adversary whose genius he acknowledged, he intended to interpret in his own way the instructions from his supervisory ministry and assume the full consequences. The day before signing the treaty, he wrote to the head of the government: "I will be answerable for the Emir, and will prove the faith I have in his word by the great responsibility that I take upon myself."[55]

---

53 Abd el-Kader had wanted to take a collegial decision. An assembly of all the notables of the great tribes of the west met one week prior to the encounter at Tafna. It approved the clauses of the treaty and promised its support to its chief.

54 Service Historique de l'Armée de Terre (SHAT), Fonds Serie 1H46, Dossier 2, Province d'Oran (March 1837).

55 Letter of May 28, 1837 to Count Mollé, cited in Paul Azan, *L'Émir Abd el Kader*, p. 94.

Despite the desire shared by both sides to reach an agreement, the negotiations were protracted and several times on the verge of being discontinued. However, on May 30, 1837, the Treaty of Tafna, named after an important water course in the province of Oran, was signed and was definitively ratified on June 15, 1837, by King Louis-Philippe. In addition to the consolidation of the Emir's authority over the entire province, it anticipated extending his administration to the province of Titteri, and beyond it, up to the limits of Constantine.[56] This second treaty began a period of peace and prosperity which benefitted both parties. For two and a half years, Abd el-Kader worked towards the consolidation of his State, whose new capital was Tagdempt. Bearing the stamp of its chief, it was a centralized and hierarchized State marked with the seal of the religion. The Emir established a professional army, a system for collecting taxes, and a system of courts. In creating such an administration, which unified and regulated the functioning of disparate tribes, the Emir foresaw the establishment of a national entity. Now, this future union, capable of "raising up a formidable power," worried the French opponents of the treaty. On the days following its signing, it received a lukewarm welcome in France: General Damrémont, the governor-general, after his ratification by the king, declared: "The treaty is not advantageous, for it makes the Emir more powerful than a decisive victory would have, and places us in a precarious position, without guarantees, enclosed within adverse limits."[57] Considered by a number of observers as a diplomatic victory for the Emir and his burgeoning national entity, this treaty was soon viewed with frank hostility, particularly after it was discovered that it had led to the corruption of French officers.[58] In the meantime, on the eve of signing the treaty,

---

56 The French and Arab versions of the Treaty of Tafna were drafted, either through error or deliberately, in such a way as to allow doubts to persist regarding the exact limits of the territories administered by both sides, especially in the case of the territory of Constantine: moreover, a translation "error" in Article 2 would be the origin of a renewal of hostilities.

57 Cited in Alexandre Bellemare, *Abd-el-Kader*, p. 189.

58 Generals Brossard and Bugeaud appeared before a military court for a dark affair of money mingled with the negotiation of the Treaty of Tafna. The trial, which had national coverage, was concluded with a conviction and the belated remorse of General Bugeaud: "I declare, loudly and clearly, for the young officers who hear me, that I have committed an act unworthy of the nobility and dignity of my command" (cited in Charles-André Julien, *L'Histoire de l'Afrique du Nord* [Paris: Payot, 1931], p. 596).

and in order to make official and clarify certain points, a meeting between the Emir Abd el-Kader and General Bugeaud was arranged on
June 1st, 1837, on the banks of the Tafna.

Having arrived in the morning, as previously arranged, at the site
of the rendezvous, the general was quite annoyed by the delay of the
Arab army. The sun was sinking towards the horizon, and it was not
until around four in the afternoon that the French officer, accompanied by his chief-of-staff and a small detachment of the Africa light
cavalry, met with Abd el-Kader, accompanied by the dignitaries of the
main tribes. The occasion was solemn, the impressive silence broken
only by the two negotiators and the whickering of the horses. A kind
of palpable tension reigned among the French soldiers; their army was
staying a few kilometers behind and they knew that they were at the
mercy of their adversaries. The Arab horsemen, seated on their su-
perbly outfitted horses, were impressive. Captain Amédéé de Muralt,
who participated in the encounter, writes: "I did not know where to fix
my gaze, Abd el-Kader, his chieftains, his army were there before us,
and captivated our attention."[59] The general himself, usually sober in
his compliments, seemed impressed: "I saw the Emir's escort advancing towards me: their appearance was truly imposing; there were 150 to
200 marabout chieftains of remarkable appearance, all the more high-
lighted by their slow pace. They were mounted on magnificent horses
that they made strut and which they handled with much elegance and
skill."[60] However, it was on the Emir that gazes converged. If the general appearance of the Arab leader did not seem to have struck the
French witnesses who qualified it as "simple" and even "ordinary," that
was not the case as regards his face and his facial expression. The general attested: "He is pale, and rather resembles the portrait often given
of Jesus Christ. On the whole his face is that of a devout person." Here
it is the ascetical dimension that inspired the comparison with Christ.
Other participants at the meeting at Tafna were struck, like Dinesen
and Bugeaud, by this resemblance, and other witnesses affirmed it
later. Dr. Bonnafont concluded likewise that his physiognomy, which
appeared sickly, somewhat resembled that of Christ at an age of 30.[61]

59 Cited in S. Aouli, R. Redjala, and P. Zoummeroff, *Abd el-Kader*, p. 210.

60 Extract of a letter to the Head of Government and Minister of Foreign Affairs,
Count Mollé, cited in Paul Azan, *L'Émir Abd el Kader*, p. 95.

61 Jean-Pierre Bonnafont, *Douze ans en Algérie, 1830 à 1842* (Paris: E. Dentu, 1880),
pp. 275-277.

After the Emir's surrender in 1847, the Duke of Aumale, at that time the governor general, declared: "The overall impression of his figure is austere; it recalls the traditional figure of Christ."[62] The recurring surprise at this resemblance is such that one tries to understand its significance.

The son of Muhyi ad-Din, as we have said, was trained during his youth to become a "man of the rosary." It is the political events that decided the matter otherwise. It was out of obedience to this father, and probably reluctantly,[63] that the young Abd el-Kader accepted to be raised to the title of Commander of the Faithful. His personality was by then so impregnated by the Sufi tradition that his new temporal function did not impugn his first vocation. If his commitment to the *jihad* answered to a religious duty, it was at the same time the expression of an inner attitude. In the spiritual tradition of Islam, there exist two forms of *jihad*. *Al-jihad as-saghir*, the "lesser holy war," designates the fight conducted against an outward enemy who attacks the territorial integrity of *Dar al-Islam*. On the spiritual plane, one speaks of the *jihad al-akbar*, the "greater holy war" or the "greatest holy war," which takes place in one's inner self, against one's own passions and the natural impulses that man shares with animals. In a *hadith* transmitted by al-Bayhaqi, the Prophet, returning from a military expedition, declared: "We have returned from the lesser *jihad* in order to proceed towards the greater *jihad*." His companions asked: what is this "greater *jihad*"? The Prophet replied: the fight against the passions." Another version says: "that of the heart." This latter form of *jihad* the tradition considers to be the most important and the most difficult to undertake; in every way it conforms to a work of ascesis.[64] It is precisely this spiritual

---

62 Cited in A.E.H. Carette, *L'Univers pittoresque* (Paris: Firmin Didot Frères, 1850), p. 346.

63 Abd el-Kader would often return later on to the reason that urged him to accept the charge of Commander of the Faithful. In the autobiographical essay which he wrote in captivity, he writes soberly that he had accepted this charge "to not contradict his father" (*Autobiographie*, p. 74)

64 This double aspiration, to free oneself from an outward and an inward enemy, is ancient. The *ribat al-fath*, literally, the "fortresses of victory," had the double function of being, on the one hand places of devotion and ascesis and, on the other hand, in times of war, to serve as rearguard bases of resistance to crusading armies (the word *fath* moreover signifies at once "victory" and "spiritual illumination"). Present in the East during the Crusades, they are also to be found starting from the sixteenth century over the entire coast of North Africa, in order to fight against the incursions of Spanish armies. Grouped together by Sufi brotherhoods, these "brothers in God," *ikhwan*, were

dimension of the war leader that was apparent to the French, and that they would contribute to bring to light.

After the agreements at Tafna, the political situation became favorable to exchanges. The first European travelers were authorized to visit the territories administered by Abd el-Kader, which henceforth extended over two-thirds of the country. Of all the persons who met the Emir, we shall retain the testimonies of three, particularly important ones. Louis-Adrien Berbrugger, curator of the library and museum of Algiers, and the physician, Dr. Bodichon, were both part of the research mission that went to the Emir's camp at the beginning of the years 1837 and 1838. The two men were part of a caravan which comprised a dozen persons, including the Mr. Gavarini, the consul-general of the United States, an attorney; the secretary public prosecutor; a businessman, and an interpreter. Both Berbrugger and Dr. Bodichon considered the Emir to be the main obstacle to France's plan for Algeria; the doctor, having a very harsh opinion concerning "the natives," would later even support the total or partial "extermination" of the Arabs in Algeria. The other person is Léon Roches, whom we have already mentioned, and who at this point was an enthusiastic supporter of Abd el-Kader, even though he had never met him previously.

Dr. Bodichon, like his traveling companion, was not unaware that the Emir pertained to the religious aristocracy, but it was above all the war leader that he had in mind when they met. Upon seeing him, he discovered his other face: "In the person of Abd el-Kader, his attitude, his gestures, the inflections of his voice, the formulations of his speech, his look, the expression of his face, the form of his forehead, all denote a deeply religious man. It is the head of a young anchorite with an ascetic and dreamy face."[65] Louis-Adrien Berbrugger, for his part, stresses the "altogether religious nature" and the "ascetic figure" of the Arab leader, which remind him of the "beautiful heads of monks whose type has been bequeathed to us by the Medieval Age; of those warrior-monks, however, who most often are found in the midst of the tumultuous clash of the battlefield rather than in the tranquil obscurity of cloisters."[66] Unable to explain the gap between what he used to

also designated by the term of *murabitun*—hence the derived "marabout"—"those who live in a *ribat*," a term whose etymology makes reference to the fact of being attached or tied to.

65 Dr. Bodichon, *Études sur l'Algérie et l'Afrique* (Algiers: n.p., 1847), p. 23.

66 Louis-Adrien Berbrugger, "Voyage au camp d'Abd-el-Kader," *La Revue des Deux*

know of the Emir and what he discovered, Berbrugger draws from the medieval Christian imagery of the warrior monk who combined both domains which for Berbrugger were opposites, astonishingly united in the Emir. Certain authors of accounts of travels in Algeria in the nineteenth century describe the "biblical" atmosphere of the country, in particular its landscapes, the physiognomy and dress of its inhabitants, its pastoral scenes, etc. This explains in part that the French saw in Abd el-Kader a figure close to that of Christ. The testimony of Léon Roches is very close to that of his two countrymen. However, the enthusiasm that Abd el-Kader inspired in him, gives his account a particular accentuation, upon seeing him for the first time: "At last I have seen Abd el-Kader, and I write you while under the charm this champion [of Islam] exerts upon me . . . for I have neither seen nor wished to see anyone but Abd el-Kader."[67] He too has recourse to the image of the monk: "If an artist wished to paint one of those inspired monks of the Middle Ages, whose fervor led them under the standard of the Cross, it seems to me that he could not choose a fairer model than Abd el-Kader. A mixture of warrior energy and asceticism spreads an indefinable charm over his face."[68] The fascinated portrait of Léon Roches renders an account of the harmonious contradiction that the Emir presented as a paradoxical figure: "When he prays, he is an ascetic. When he commands, he is a sovereign. When he speaks of war, his features light-up; he is a soldier."[69] But in this astonishing coexistence, it is the spiritual dimension which seems to prevail: "I have seen him in prayer and have been struck by his mystical fervor, but that night he seemed to me to be the most gripping image of faith. It is thus that the great saints of Christianity must have prayed."[70] His biographer, Alexandre Bellemare proposed a no less astonishing comparison when describing him as a "Peter the Hermit of [Islam]."[71]

Mondes du 15 août 1838 (Toulon: Impr. E. Aurel, 1839), p. 48.

67 Léon Roches, *Trente-deux ans à travers l'islam*, vol. 1, chap. 21.

68 Ibid.

69 Ibid., chap. 39.

70 Ibid., chap. 45.

71 Alexandre Bellemare, *Abd el-Kader*, p. 151. A similar comparison had aroused the criticism of certain Catholic journals of the time. Cf. *Bibliographie catholique. Revue critique*, vol. 24, January to June, 1863 (Paris: Au bureau de la bibliographie catholique, 1863).

These testimonies as a whole highlight a trait of Abd el-Kader which until then had remained unknown: the determination and steadfastness which characterized his political action served neither an immediate interest nor a personal ambition; Alexandre Bellemare is clear on this point: "a more noble, more lofty, motive directed his conduct: it is from this that he drew his faith. This alone could explain the superhuman tenacity of Abd el-Kader, his resignation in misfortune, his hope, even when hope no longer seemed to make sense. However great it may be conceived, the love of power could never be great enough to enable a man to bear trials such as those undergone by the Emir."[72] Even though he fully assumed the political responsibilities as head of a country and had been the originator of a national consciousness, the Emir was not, properly speaking, a man of power.[73] A man of the purest tradition of Islam, he had not sought temporal authority, it had been thrust upon him, and he submitted to it out of a spirit of duty. This explains his systematic refusal of the title of sultan, which would have made him the equal of the king of Morocco, Mulay 'Abd ar-Rahman, under whose authority he wished to remain as long as events allowed him to do so.[74] And it was precisely this detachment—Father Suchet said that Abd el-Kader was "embarrassed by his greatness"[75]—which paradoxically had rendered such endurance possible. The austerity of his appearance and the simplicity of his manners were those of a man submitted to an ascetic discipline, notwithstanding his official function. The Sufic sayings which warn against power and those who hold it were not absent, and the Emir seems to have been at once a "prince," *amir*,[76] who also wished to be one of the "poor in God," *faqir*.* After his exile to Damascus, and still today, the Emir is named the "Saint among the Princes, the Prince among the Saints."

72 Alexandre Bellemare, *Abd el-Kader*, pp. 454-455.

73 Ernest Renan seemed to consider the political role of the Emir as accidental: "The most illustrious representative of the Semitic race of our day, Abd el-Kader, is a scholar, a man of religious meditations and strong passions, in no way a soldier" (*Études d'histoire religieuse* [Paris: Michel Lévy frères, 1862], p. 89).

74 In his *Autobiographie*, Abd el-Kader specifies that he had asked that "his name not be cited in the prayers of the mosques, except after the name of Mulay 'Abd ar-Rahman" (p. 74).

75 Abbé Suchet, *Lettres édifiantes et curieuses sur l'Algérie* (Tours: Mame, 1840 [1842]).

76 The Arabic term *amir*, from which "emir" derives, has the meaning of "Commander" and of "Prince."

CHAPTER 4

A Liberating Ascesis

Man is like a mirror: a mirror cannot reflect the image of the sky
unless it is clear: the spirit cannot nourish great thoughts unless it is free. In
the state of captivity in which I am kept, I cannot nourish any
other thought than that of my pain.
Abd el-Kader to Count de Falloux, 1848

Amongst all the veils, thine existence and thy soul are assuredly the thickest.
However, it is only through them that thou canst know thy Lord when, pre-
cisely, they have ceased being veils in order to become mirrors.
The Book of Halts, Mawqif 166

Dig into the ground of thy heart until the water of wisdom springs forth.
Abd al-Qadir al-Jilani

Fidelity to the Religious Heritage

"O ye who believe! What aileth you that when it is said unto you: Go
forth in the way of God, ye are bowed down to the ground with heavi-
ness? Take ye pleasure in the life of the world rather than in the Hereafter? The comfort of the life of the world is but little in the Hereafter"
(Koran 9:38). Mistrust of the world here-below, the place of "fleeting
enjoyment" (Koran 57:20), and the permanence of the Hereafter are
recurring themes in the religious literature and in particular that of
tasawwuf. In it, man is considered as merely a passer-by on earth, as
taught by the following *hadith*: to a companion who suggested that the
Prophet use a rug so that his sleep be more agreeable, Muhammad replied: "What have I to do with this lower world? I am only a rider who
goes into the shade of a tree and then leaves it behind and goes on his
way"; thus man must take care not to be attached to beings and things,
on pain of forgetting why he has been created. It is a question of living in this world with the awareness of its ephemeral nature, existence
having a meaning only if it is entirely dedicated to advancing towards
the Hereafter,[1] the place of permanent abode, an idea of life which in

---

1 According to the *hadith*: "Work in this world as if you had to stay in it eternally, and
for the next as if you had to die tomorrow."

his work, *Miqradh al-Hadd*, Abd el-Kader summarizes in these terms: "Man's greatest happiness is for his ultimate aim to be the meeting with God." The Emir here refers to man's fundamental state of servitude before God (*'ubudiyya*) which is, according to a Koranic verse, the very reason for man's existence on earth.[2] The means to achieve this objective are at once acts of worship (*'ibadat*), the five pillars of Islam,[3] which are meant for all the faithful, and the ascetic practices of renunciation of the world (*zuhd*) at the heart of the teachings of the Sufic paths. It is to all these practices that the young Abd el-Kader had been initiated by his father. Concerning the works of obligatory worship, the saint of Baghdad said to the disciples: "True prayer makes you cover half the path, the fast places you before the door, and the tithe lets you into the house."[4] Regarding ascetic renunciation, he said: "You will not be able to enjoy His love if you do not lose everything."[5] Or again: "This entire Way is effacement and extinction."[6] Regardless of the forms that they take, these ritual practices—obligatory (the prayer, the fast, the tithe) or otherwise (recitation of the Koran, litanies, spiritual retreat)—have as their sole end the remembrance of God and seeking His nearness. Turned inward, the aim of this strict discipline is the progressive transformation of the soul in view of its elevation—freeing the disciple from the grip of his lower needs—and its purification, by which the soul will then become a mirror of the divine light. On the outward plane, its end is to ennoble the character by developing the virtues. Because he had been initiated into this discipline from childhood, for the son of Muhyi ad-Din it was fused with his memories of play and learning. With the years, it had become a need, like eating, drinking, or sleeping. Abd el-Kader's faithfulness to the religious and spiritual legacy of his father had been exemplary. What distinguished him were the extremely varied contexts in which this initiatic practice had been expressed.

In the autumn of 1832, the life of Muhyi ad-Din's son changed drastically: from the modest teacher of a *zawiya*, he became the Com-

---

2 "I have created the jinn and men only that they may worship Me" (Koran 51:56).

3 The testimony of faith (*shahada*), the prayer (*salat*), the legal alms (*zakat*), the fast (*siyam*), the great pilgrimage (*hajj*).

4 Sidi Abd el-Qader al-Jilani, *Enseignements soufies (Al-fath al-rabbani wa-l-faydh al-rahmani)* (Beirut: Dar al-Bouraq, 1996), p. 465.

5 Ibid., p. 76.

6 Ibid., p. 457.

mander of the Faithful. His election to this title by a federation of western tribes was made on the basis of religious legitimacy. It instituted him as guarantor of the religious law (*shari'a**), which defines both a legislative system and a moral code. Thus, the new emir would naturally endow his fledgling state with a theocratic structure of which the governing principle is respect for the religious law, and he named men of the religious nobility to posts of responsibility. The defensive war against the French Africa Army was also conducted in the name of religion: the *jihad* had been proclaimed after having been validated by an assembly of *ulemas*.* The imprint of the religion is present at all levels of the new administration, and the son of the *zawiya* even clothed the instruments of the temporal power with spiritual references. The principal coin was named *Muhammadiyya*, in reference to the Prophet, and Louis-Adrien Berbrugger informs us that on the officers' uniforms could be read, "on the right sleeve, in silver letters: 'Patience is the key to victory.' On the left sleeve: 'There is no god but God, and Muhammad is his messenger.' On the right side of the jacket at the level of the breast: 'Allah' (God). On the left side, below the heart: 'Muhammad.'"[7] As for the sentries, they uttered "God is eternal" in order to authorize passage.[8] For the Emir, it was a matter of anchoring power in religious legitimacy, while developing an effective spiritual pedagogy of the remembrance of God,[9] and in accordance with the same logic he placed the *zawiyas* at the center of this administration.

In the midst of this societal project, the young chief offered himself as an edifying model of strictness. Alexandre Bellemare emphasizes this salient feature of his personality: "Those who have been in a position to approach him, to share his intimate life, can say with what faith and recollection, with what scrupulous exactness the Emir fulfills not only the prescriptions of his religious law, but also the prayers or devo-

---

7 Louis-Adrien Berbrugger, *Négociation entre Mgr l'évêque d'Alger et Abd el-Kader pour l'échange des prisonniers* (Paris: J. Delahaye, 1844), p. 32.

8 Louis-Adrien Berbrugger, "Voyage au camp d'Abd-el-Kader," p. 35.

9 Similarly, the composition of the battalions of the Emir's army (one unit of 100 men, composed of a superior officer and three sections of thirty-three men each) is the same as that of the Muslim rosary (*tasbih*), which contains the same number of beads distributed in the same way. It would also be interesting to study the cosmogonic, not to mention the metaphysical, structure of the *smala*,* based on the circle. Concerning this see Bruno Étienne, *Abdelkader, isthme des isthmes* (*barzakh al-barazikh*) (Paris: Librairie Hachette, 1994), p. 192ff.

tional acts which are merely recommended as supererogatory works."[10] The testimony of Léon Roches, which is all the more precise in that it comes from an individual well acquainted with Islam, having been a Muslim himself, conveys the same idea: "We had penetrated into Djebel Amour when we were assailed by a snowstorm which fell so heavily that soon the snow on the ground exceeded thirty centimeters. The cold was unbearable. Despite the severe temperature, when the hour arrived, Abd el-Kader dismounted his horse, made his ablutions with snow, and recited his prayer as if he were in his tent. Very few were those who imitated him."[11] Prayer, the heart of religious *praxis*, is a "bond," a privileged means of binding oneself to the Creator. It is cyclical[12] and codified according to a precise series of gestures: from the initial standing position to the final prostration, everything in it symbolically evokes the relationship of the servant to his Lord. The call to prayer, so dear to Islam, is merged with the remembrance of God (*dhikru 'Llah*), which in a movement of return towards the One enables man to tear himself away from forgetfulness, the source of all evils; for he who forgets God exposes himself to being forgotten by Him. To protect oneself against this dreadful pitfall, the disciple practices vigilance and examination of conscience; placed under God's gaze, he must take care not to deviate, either by his acts or by his words, from the limits fixed by the religious law and the rules of propriety (*adab**). "The Way is nothing other than propriety," goes a well-known saying amongst the Sufis. In other words, the spiritual Way is not limited to particular moments or domains: time management, the choice of clothing and food, behavior within the community, the manner of expressing oneself, are all so many means and occasions for putting into practice, "standing, sitting, or lying down" (Koran 4:103), the principles that have been taught. This spiritual education, which molded the Emir, recalls with gravity that the time given to man can either bring him closer or else distance him from God, depending upon

---

10 Alexandre Bellemare, *Abd-el-Kader*, p. 451.

11 Cited in S. Aouli, R. Redjala, and P. Zoummeroff, *Abd el-Kader*, p. 478.

12 The daily prayer is repeated five times daily; the collective prayer takes place on Fridays. Certain prayers (the prayer of the two main feasts of the Muslim calendar) take place once a year. Finally, the prayer of the *tarawih* takes place every evening after the setting of the sun during the entire month of Ramadan (ninth month of the lunar calendar).

whether he consecrates his quest or not; the time given to worship is time gained over death, a time that is inscribed in eternity. According to this principle, so as to lose none of this precious gift, each moment must be occupied with the remembrance of the divine, the means *par excellence* of reminding man of God and God of man. "Remember Me, I will remember you" (Koran 2:152): it is by this process of reciprocity that the divine Presence is actualized.

The battles led against the French Africa Army enabled the Emir to test the spiritual values which he had inherited and intensify his *praxis*. With death liable to occur at any moment, the *dhikr* becomes more regular and fervent, thus preparing the combatant to consecrate his last breath to the invocation of the Name of God. Once the threat has been removed, weapons sheathed, the Emir again takes up his black rosary which never leaves him, and which, according to Léon Roche, he counts "rapidly and, as he listens, his lips go on repeating the words consecrated to this kind of prayer."[13] The mental recitation of the divine word, considered as a form of prayer, becomes a second breathing. In the course of long rides across the country, the recitations of the Koran and litanies are chanted to the rhythm of the horse's trot. Abd el-Kader could remain in the saddle up to thirty-six hours at a stretch, dismounting only to make his ablutions and perform his prayer. During periods of truce, his heavy responsibilities as head of his nascent State left him little respite. It was at the end of the day, after the last canonical prayers, that he could retire to the solitude of his tent to dedicate himself to the study of the Koran.[14] Like his father, whom he had often seen prostrating at night, he had assimilated the tradition according to which the divine Presence is nearest during the last third of the night.[15] Léon Roches evokes this nocturnal devotion: "The smoky wick of an Arab lamp barely illumined the large tent of the Emir. He was standing three steps away from me; he thought I was

13 Léon Roches, *Trente-deux ans à travers l'Islam*, vol. 1, p. 154.

14 Regarding the zeal of the Emir in studying, Charles H. Churchill writes: "During the night, he remains standing for seven straight hours repeating by heart all the verses of the Koran, from the first to the last" (*La Vie d'Abd el Kader*, p. 266).

15 There are numerous Koranic verses referring to the excellence of prayer during the night (17:79; 25:64; 32:16; 39:9; 101:17), as well as *hadiths*, such as that related by Abu Hurayra: "Our Lord comes down each night from Heaven during the last third of the night and says: 'He who invokes Me, I will answer his invocation; he who requests of Me, I shall grant what he wishes, and he who asks forgiveness of Me, I will forgive.'"

asleep. His two arms lifted to the height of his head, opening his burnous and his milk-white haik which fell in superb folds. His beautiful
blue eyes, outlined with black eyelashes, were raised, his lips seemed to
still recite a prayer and yet they remained motionless; he had reached
a state of ecstasy. His aspirations towards heaven were such that he
seemed no longer to touch the earth."[16] Is this a description of a *jadhba*, that ecstatic state reached by the Sufi who, at the summit of his
spiritual aspiration, is torn from himself and from time to subsist in
God? Or is it simply a prayer in the middle of the night which, in the
enthusiastic view of a romantic witness, takes on the appearances of
an ecstasy? The question remains. However, it must be noted that this
testimony, which took place in the Emir's thirtieth year, is in harmony
with his future ecstatic experiences.

During his years of combat, the religion constituted a constant
help and support for Abd el-Kader. In a letter to General Desmichels,
he evokes the strength that he draws from his faith: "If we are outwardly weak, our faith is in God; for He has said: 'Your strength lies
in your very weakness; trust in Me, and ye will succeed in your actions; observe your religion, your victory will be assured, and if ye lack
strength ye shall find it in your beliefs.'"[17] According to what those near
him report, the Emir never complained; out of modesty, certainly, for
in reality he complained only to God, which is well illustrated by this
complaint attributed to him: "The nights are long, O my friends! The
One, the Eternal alone knoweth my state."[18] The invocations intensified as the difficulties multiplied. The number of testimonies emphasizing how his spiritual *praxis* was sustained allows us to suppose that
he placed all his decisions under the auspice of prayer: action, blessed
and guided, freed him from fear and from inordinate regrets in case
of defeat.

In his appearance as well as in his conduct, Abd el-Kader, con-
sciously or not, reproduced the model of his father. Everything in
Muhyi ad-Din breathed sobriety; no pomp, even though his aristocratic origins allowed it. To this detachment were joined moderation in
his gestures and words; a manner of being in the world which recalled
in all circumstances the state of one who is "poor in God" (*faqir*), the

16 Léon Roches, *Trente-deux ans à travers l'Islam*, vol. 1, pp. 319-320.

17 Cited in S. Aouli, R. Redjala, and P. Zoummeroff, *Abd el-Kader*, p. 121.

18 Ibid., p. 111.

name given to the disciples of the Qadiriyya, which in numerous sayings urge poverty and humility. Regarding a spiritual dream in which he had seen himself before many doors of Paradise, Sidi Abd al-Qadir al-Jilani recounts: "Everywhere I encountered crowds of people. Then, I went to the door of humility and poverty, and I found it open. So I entered and called out: 'Come this way!'"[19] Poverty and humility are described as one and the same door opening onto the everlasting abode.

Simplicity and the ordinary impregnated the youthful years of Abd el-Kader and fashioned his character to the point of becoming second nature. Once he became the Commander of the Faithful, neither titles nor power changed his manner of being. He continued to wear clothing sewed by his family and to nourish himself with the products of the land inherited from his father. The simplicity of his dress is one of the features that seemed to have most struck the first French witnesses that came into contact with him. General Bugeaud, in a somewhat condescending tone, writes regarding him whom he will fight fiercely, that he "presents no difference from the most common Arabs. . . . All his clothing was soiled, coarse, and three quarters worn away; it can be seen that he affects the rigor of simplicity."[20] Yet austerity was also demanded by the context: *jihad* in the face of a powerful enemy demanded the acquisition of horses, saddlery, and arms, aside from which, in the eyes of the Emir, all other expenses were unjustified, and above all for those closest to him. The chronicle thus reports that he had, before witnesses, cut off two gold trimmings from the burnous of his brother Mustafa,[21] and that he had substituted for the fabrics and valuable objects with which his wife had decorated his tent, cushions covered with gazelle skin and straw matting from Mascara.[22] If these

19 Sidi Ahmed Ibn 'Ajiba, *L'Autobiographie (Fahrasa) du Soufi Marocain Ahmad Ibn 'Agiba*, p. 80.

20 Paul Azan, *L'Émir Abd el-Kader*, p. 95.

21 In *Rappel à l'intelligent, avis à l'indifferent*, translated by Gustave Dugat (Paris: B. Duprat, 1858); now in the volume *Lettre aux Français, notes brèves destinées à ceux qui comprennent pour attirer l'attention sur les problèmes essentiels* ("Letter to the French, Brief Notes Intended For Those Who Understand In Order to Draw Their Attention to Essential Problems"), translated by René Khawam (Pris: Phèbus, 1977, re-edited in 2007), the Emir specifies in what way gold and silver must have only an economic function: "God created them that they may pass from one hand to another, fulfilling their function of equitable judges. They are the standard of all wealth."

22 Léon Roches, *Trente-deux ans à travers l'Islam*, vol. 1, p. 369.

zealous gestures served as an example to his subjects, he himself indisputably disdained material comfort to the point of extreme frugality. "Often, after a forced march in the desert, he could be seen satisfied with a handful of grains of wheat as nourishment for an entire day."[23] Banishing "every kind of refinement," this frugality at times took an excessive turn: "He rarely allowed himself the enjoyment of coffee. Once he had seen that he was making a habit of it, he deprived himself of it for several days."[24] This privation is typical of a mind concerned with freeing itself from the diverse forms of habit, considered as an obstacle to spiritual progress. Abd el-Kader had the conviction, inherited from his ancestors, that the root of all concupiscence lay in excess of food. When he became aware that the discouragement of his followers was linked to the shortage of food stocks, which had been looted by the French troops, he said, with a tone of disdain: "The belly! The belly! This is what causes men to be lost."[25]

This austerity was tempered by a concern for justice and a great generosity. The chronicle has retained several edifying examples in which abnegation and generosity are combined. During the summer and fall of 1838, after the siege and the taking of Ain Madhi, the fief of the Tijaniyya brotherhood, the Emir and his troops returned to their capital at Tagdempt. Some time later, when the cold had begun to settle in and there were signs of the first snows, he had to go to his camp, one hundred and fifty kilometers away. Léon Roches was among the several cavalrymen who accompanied him, and witnessed a scene which he noted: "We met with some unfortunate Arabs who were nearly dying of cold; the Emir removed one of his burnouses and tossed it to one of them."[26] His choosing to share his clothing and his food with the humblest of his men certainly had an effect of efficacious emulation, and contributed to extending his popularity in a traditional milieu in which respect for individual and public morality was a sign of probity and nobleness. To Colonel Daumas, who mentioned the corruption of the Arab chiefs in Algeria, the Emir replied: "If I had been like them,

---

23 Mgr Dupuch, *Abd el-Kader au château d'Amboise*, p. 85.

24 Léon Roches, *Trente-deux ans à travers l'Islam*, vol. 1, p. 283.

25 Alexandre Bellemare, *Abd-el-Kader*, p. 233.

26 Léon Roches, *Trente-deux ans à travers l'Islam*, vol. 1, p. 368. The gesture of the Emir recalls that of St. Martin offering a beggar the lining of his coat: an act which earned the future bishop of Tours the vision of Christ.

would the Arabs have kept on fighting as they have and have sacrificed everything to follow me?"[27]

After the resumption of hostilities in the fall of 1839, and aside from some military successes, the Emir's setbacks multiplied. His territories were devastated and his villages systematically destroyed. The situation obliged him to be mobile in order to escape the traps set by the "active colonialists" of the new governor general. The raid and sacking of Abd el-Kader's encampment or *smala* by the Duke of Aumale, in the spring of 1843, was a harsh blow. Absent from his mobile capital when the news arrived, Abd el-Kader was at first utterly crushed. The pillage which accompanied this major episode in the annals of the conquest had not spared his important library. Charles H. Churchill estimated at five thousand the number of manuscripts.[28] Nevertheless, according to the same author, he learned with serenity of the loss of the thousands of manuscripts he had patiently collected: "May God be praised . . . all those objects which I prized so highly, which were so close to my heart, and upon which I lavished so much care, did no more than impede my movements and turned me from the right path."[29] Each difficulty harbors a benefit, declares the Tradition, and it is on this wisdom that Abd el-Kader had been nourished. In a general way, all that which leads man to free himself from the world and reinforces his bond with the next is considered to be a grace, which the Divine Wisdom may dissimulate under the appearance of a trial. The successive setbacks suffered during the 1840s had certainly eroded, little by little, Abd el-Kader's attachment to the world; a process that led him to a political and military surrender which in many respects was like a symbolical death.

The Surrender: A Symbolical Death

"And God undoes what my hand has done."[30] It is with this fictitious saying attributed to him by a French chronicler that the Emir would have welcomed the news of his surrender after fifteen years of fighting.

---

27 Alexandre Bellemare, *Abd-el-Kader*, p. 351.

28 Charles H. Churchill estimated at five thousand the number of manuscripts (*La Vie de Abd el Kader*, p. 235).

29 Ibid., p. 236.

30 *Abdelkader en France* (Paris: Porreau, L.C., 1848), "Adieu à sa patrie."

What he had organized, built, sown at the cost of so many efforts and patience was irremediably undone. Betrayed by some of his own followers, placed under the blow of a decree of the Moroccan sultan Mulay Abd ar-Rahman, which made him an outcast throughout his entire realm,[31] exhausted by the pitiless policy of Marshal Bugeaud, the Emir, in this year of 1847, was in a critical situation. From having so often reminded his men of it, he was not unaware that desolation emanates from the same superior will as consolation: a fathomless will driven by an equally unknowable wisdom, which make human destinies unforeseeable. This is what he had written to Bugeaud previously: "You forget that the things of life are changeable. Regarding this, I know more than you do. I am convinced that nothing can endure on this earth, from the creation of Adam until the extinction of mankind."[32] In 1847, when he had learned of the resignation of his adversary, then the governor general, the Emir believed matters would turn around. However, despite this major event, the winds of fortune did not appear favorable towards him. After the onset of this fateful year, the Algerian camp underwent the surrender of two more prestigious leaders: in February, that of Ben Salem, "the faithful, the reliable, the devoted,"[33] who was the lieutenant of the Emir for the area of the Sebaou valley, and two months later, that of Bou Maza, "the goat-man," another great figure of the resistance to the conquest. The surrender, on the 16th of December, of his own brother, who had negotiated safe-conduct for himself with the French, had surely evoked the darkest forebodings in the Emir. To this is added the fury of the Moroccan troops in hunting down the *deïra*, the little tent city in which the family of the Emir and his last men was gathered, camped on Moroccan territory. Despite very unequal forces, around 1,000 cavalrymen against 5,000 Moroccans, the Emir tried to protect the *deïra*: "On the night of the 20th to the 21st of December, began the fording of the Moulouya. At sunrise, the Moroccans appeared on the heights: it was necessary to give a final battle so as to cover the retreat of the *deïra*. The regulars committed themselves. Abd el-Kader was in

31 After the Treaty of Tangiers of September 1844, imposed by France in Morocco, the French bombing of the cities of Tangiers and Mogador, and the defeat of the troops of Mulay 'Abd ar-Rahman at Oued Sly, the articles of this treaty made the Emir Abd el-Kader an "outlaw."

32 Cited in S. Aouli, R. Redjala, and P. Zoummeroff, *Abd el-Kader*, p. 377.

33 Charles H. Churchill, *La Vie de Abd el Kader*, p. 377.

their midst . . . his garments riddled with bullets, and three horses were shot from under him. At the end of the day, the goal was attained; the *deïra* reached Algerian soil."[34] Despite this final military exploit engaging the Moroccan troops, the Emir sensed that the *jihad* was coming to an end.

Although he had already experienced other extreme situations, at the end of the year 1847 all the events converged towards the same fateful outcome. On the 22nd of December, 1847, he held a council composed of his last companions-in-arms. Although most of them had been wounded during the last battles and had lost a number of their family members, including one of the most faithful, Agha bin Yahya, and that the *deïra* was in an almost desperate situation, they said to Abd el-Kader: "Let the women and children perish, ours as well as thine, so long as thou art well and able to carry on God's battle. Thou art our head, our sultan; fight or lay down arms, as thou wishest. We shall follow thee wherever it seemest to thee good to lead us."[35]

At the conclusion of the meeting, he decided to end his military commitment and, according to Charles H. Churchill, announced: "Believe me, the fight is over. Let us resign ourselves. God is witness that we have fought as long as we have been able to. If He has not given us the victory, it is because he has judged that this land must belong to the Christians."[36] Negotiations began the very same day with the commander-in-chief of the region of Oran, General Lamoricière. The Emir demanded "the pledge of the French that could neither be diminished nor changed."[37] The reply of the French officer could not be clearer: "I have received your letter and understood it. I have the order of the King's son to grant you the mercy you have requested and to grant the passage of the Djemma-Ghazaouet to Alexandria or to Akka; you shall be taken to no other place. Come when it suits you, whether by day or night. Do not doubt this promise: it is positive. Our sovereign will be generous towards you and yours."[38] It is only after having received this

---

34 Paul Thureau-Dangin, *Histoire de la monarchie de Juillet* (Paris, Librairie Plon, 1892), vol. 7, p. 313.

35 Charles H. Churchill, *La Vie de Abd el Kader*, p. 271.

36 Ibid., pp. 271-272.

37 Paul Thureau-Dangin, *Histoire de la monarchie de Juillet*, vol. 7, p. 314.

38 Paul Azan, *L'Émir Abd el-Kader*, p. 234.

letter, with the seal of a superior officer and the sword of General Lamoricière, which constituted an official guarantee, that on December 23, 1847 the Emir with followers headed towards the port city where the headquarters of the Africa Army was located. The terms of the treaty were clear: in exchange for his surrender, the Emir Abd el-Kader and those of his camp who wished to join the Emir in his fate, would be transferred to Alexandria or to Saint Jean-d'Acre. Concluded on the 23rd of December, the treaty was signed by General Lamoricière and ratified by the new governor-general, the Duke of Aumale. This double guarantee determined that the fate of the Emir and his followers was placed in the hands of the French authorities. The *deïra*, preceded by the Emir and his last cavalrymen, headed towards the port city of Jam' Ghazouet where the Duke of Aumale was to arrive from Oran. En route, they met a detachment of cavalry led by Colonel de Montauban which escorted them to Sidi Brahim. (It is here that the Emir obtained one of his most striking victories. In September of 1845, his troops had surprised the men of Lieutenant Colonel de Montagnac. After a hard battle, some of the French soldiers who had sought refuge in the area of the mausoleum, had resisted to the end in the hope of seeing reinforcements. Upon their refusal to surrender, the Emir attacked, and all of them died.) While awaiting the arrival of General Lamoricière, the Emir asked to remain alone inside the mausoleum of Sidi Brahim. His English biographer gives a perspicacious interpretation of this episode: "He dismounted his horse and, at the moment of entering the doorway, he drew his sword and gave it to one of the men of his entourage. His career had come to an end. Until then, his life had been dedicated to God and to his homeland. Henceforth, it would be dedicated to God alone."[39]

Subsequent events would confirm the eminently symbolical character of this reversal of destiny. Upon arriving at the port city, where there reigned an atmosphere of mixed stupefaction and incredulity, the Emir was introduced at six o'clock in the evening to the Duke of Aumale. *Le Moniteur algérien* recounts: "In accordance with his steps leading to his present situation, he humbly left his sandals at the threshold, awaited a sign, and uttered the following words, translated by the main

39 Charles H. Churchill, *La Vie de Abd el Kader*, pp. 274-275. It is interesting to note once again the power of the symbols, and to recognize a clear sign in the successive deprivations (strippings away) that the Emir was undergoing.

interpreter Mr. Rousseau: 'I would have wished to do earlier that which I do today; I have awaited the hour set by God.'"[40] The shedding of his sandals, the renunciation of power, the reference to the divine decree, conferred on this moment an initiatic dimension. But it was the day after this first interview with the King's son that the reversal was completed: in giving his horse as a sign of submission, the Emir made a gesture which in every respect represented a sacrificial act.

The gift of the war horse, according to the code of honor customary in Algeria, signifies the full acknowledgment of a defeat by the vanquished. The importance of this ritual resides above all in the fact that the horse is considered a noble animal in Islam.[41] In the Maghreb, where the equestrian art is ancient, numerous legends lend quasi-supernatural qualities to the horse, which justify, according to the Emir, "the immense love of the Arabs for the horse, an instinctive love that is transformed into religious duty."[42]

The symbol of pride, courage, beauty, and freedom, the horse is an ever-present actor in epic narratives, wherein the virtues of the knight are fused with those of his steed. The accomplished knight is he who attains a perfect symbiosis with his horse to the point of making one body with him, and it is known that the Emir was an outstanding horseman: a relationship which, on the plane of metaphysics, evokes the relationship of man with his soul. In this connection, it is interesting to recall a remark of a witness, who wrote: "Abd el-Kader was magnificent on the horse with which he seemed to be one."[43] As with the fickle nature of the horse, with man it is a matter of taming the rebellious soul and leading it with patience and determination towards a state of pacification.[44]

---

40 This excerpt from *Moniteur algérien* was included in *Revue de l'Orient, de l'Algerie et des Colonies*, "Derniers efforts soumission d'Abd-el-Kader," vol. 2, 1847, p. 476.

41 See the Sura "The Coursers" which witnesses to men's ingratitude (Koran 100:1-6). Like the one following, there are several *hadith* which attest to the place accorded to horses by the Prophet: "The good is attached to the manes of horses until the day of Resurrection."

42 Charles H. Churchill, *La Vie de Abd el Kader*, p. 12.

43 See Eynard Papers, Bibliothèque universitaire de Genève, Ms. suppl. 1910-f. 99-100.

44 According to the verse, "But ah! thou soul at peace! Return unto thy Lord, content in His good pleasure! Enter thou among My bondmen! Enter thou My Garden!" (Koran 89:27-30).

The morning of Friday, the 24th of December of 1847, Abd el-Kader decided to mark this event with a powerful gesture. After riding his black mare for a few meters, he went towards the Duke of Aumale and his chief of staff. At some steps from the prince, he dismounted, handed his battle horse to the chief and announced: "I offer thee this horse, the last one which I have ridden; it is a testimony of my gratitude, and I desire that it bring thee happiness." Solemnly, the prince replied: "I accept this as an homage paid to France, whose protection shall cover thee henceforth, and as a sign of forgetting the past." General Cousin de Montauban, who attended the event, testifies: "This meeting was very moving: indeed, could one not sympathize with the great misfortune of this illustrious man, who for eighteen years held in check our African army, who had once been the ally of the King of France, before whom he comes today to humble himself, and who perhaps forever will leave this land of Africa which he had ruled, defending his land and his religion, and wherein his ancestors rest?"[45] In the *post scriptum* dated the same day, the Duke of Aumale gives his interpretation of the Emir's gesture: "I believe I must mention here a circumstance that is apparently of small importance, but which is very significant in the eyes of the natives. Abd el-Kader came to deliver a horse of submission: it is an act of vassalage in relation to France, it is the public consecration of his abdication." Whereas for the Emir this gesture corresponded to an aristocratic exigency and signified a full acceptance of the divine decree, the French party retained only the political meaning, which it would not fail to exploit subsequently.

Abd el-Kader occupied the afternoon to the ordering of his affairs that had laid in abeyance and to the liquidation of all his goods. Regarding the "rummage sale" of the Emir's and his followers' goods, Alexandre Bellemare specifies: "All the baggage, tents, horses, mules, camels, possessed by the Emir at the time of his surrender, were sold by order of the military administration, and yielded a sum of six thousand and some hundred francs. That was all that remained to Abd el-Kader of his fallen greatness!" In a note, he adds: "It is hard to believe that, despite his complaints, this sum was not returned to Abd el-Kader except by installments and on condition of first having to justify the use of each of them.[46] By renouncing power and its possessions, he

---

45 General Cousin de Montauban, Count of Palikao, "La reddition d'Abd-el-Kader, souvenirs," *La Revue de Paris*, juillet-août 1930, p. 782.

46 Alexandre Bellemare, *Abd-el-Kader*, p. 322.

became the witness of a process that would gradually lead him to a death to self. It marked a major break in the course of the existence of the one who henceforth would be designated as the "fallen Sultan." For what he underwent was a real deliverance from power (*sulta*). In the evening, the Algerians embarked aboard the *Solon*,[47] where they had been preceded by the Duke of Aumale and General Lamoricière. The steamship headed for the harbor at Mers el-Kebir, which they were to reach shortly before dawn. Although still at sea, midnight Mass was celebrated this night of the 24th of December. For the Muslims, Friday is a day of collective prayer, and also it was the sixteenth day of the new year, 1264 of the Hijra, a "white" day[48] which the Emir no doubt passed in fasting and recollection. The next morning, a hundred were transferred directly to the steam frigate *Asmodée*[49] which, two hours later, set course for France. A short while after having left the Emir, the Duke of Aumale wrote a letter to the king: "Abd el-Kader came to bid me his farewells. I cannot conceal from Your Excellency the emotion I experienced at the dignity and simplicity of this man who has played such a great role and who has just suffered such a great setback. Not a single complaint! Not a word of regret! He had words only to commend those who had served him to me, to assure me that he no longer thought of anything except to rest. I gave him my assurance that the past would be completely forgotten."[50] What the son of Louis-Phillipe could not imagine is that he would come to know the same fate as the Emir, and that he too would take the road of exile following the days of

---

47 Translator's note: It is significant that the Emir embarked not on just any ship, but fittingly on one named after the sagely Athenian statesman Solon, who legislated against the political, economic, and moral decline in archaic Athens, and set a worthy example of justice and conduct. After completing his work of reform, Solon surrendered his extraordinary authority and left the country. The travel writer, Pausanias, listed Solon among the seven sages whose aphorisms adorned Apollo's temple at Delphi.

48 The Muslim calendar is based on the lunar cycle. The 14th, 15th, and 16th days are termed "white" because the moon is then full. On those days, the faithful are advised to fast.

49 Translator's note: Equally significant was the name of this second ship, which was to carry Abd el-Kader to his ordeal in France: that of the demon Asmodeus, mentioned in the Book of Tobias (3:8). The exemplary behavior of Tobias and Sara saved them from the demon and offer an example for mankind.

50 Paul Azan, *L'Émir Abd el-Kader*, p. 236.

February, which would sound the death knell of the monarchy of July! For the time being, Abd el-Kader believed that France was merely a short stage before the East. The subsequent events would bitterly disabuse him of this.

Captivity: A Painful Retreat

The *Asmodée* entered the harbor of Toulon on the 29th of December of 1847. A total of ninety-seven Algerians first disembarked in Lazaret, on the peninsula of Cépet, which served as a place of quarantine. They remained there for ten days. Rooms were hastily prepared to receive their new occupants. While his companions[51] in exile voiced their concern, Abd el-Kader reassured them, attributing this halt to "the need for certain preparations."[52] During this time, the news spread like wildfire through the French press. More than once in the past the capture of the Emir Abd el-Kader had been announced mistakenly before being denied. But this time, the official dispatch excluded doubt. Sent by telegraphic dispatch to Paris, the news was immediately published and posted at the Stock Exchange. The text was concise and clear: "Abd el-Kader is in Toulon. The ex-Emir, caught between the troops of the emperor of Morocco and the cavalry of General Lamoricière, surrendered to Lord Duke of Aumale on condition that he be transported to Egypt, where he will reside."[53] After a first series of triumphalist articles, certain papers began to ask what were the exact circumstances of what was then designated as the "capture of Abd el-Kader." The discovery of the treaty of surrender, which stipulated his being sent into exile, transformed a "great and happy event"[54] into a political embarrassment. Émile de Girardin in his testimony on the surrender, and to point out clearly that the Emir had not been "taken," recalls the extract

---

51 "Exile" or "emigration" are the meanings of the term "hegira," *hijra* in Arabic. According to Khelfa Benaissa ("La Zawiya d'Amboise", an unfinished doctoral thesis, University of Aix-en-Provence), the French interpreter officers in charge of the Emir used the Arabic term *muhajirun*, "the immigrants," in order to designate the Arab captives.

52 Alexandre Bellemare, *Abd-el-Kader*, p. 321.

53 Reproduced in *Le Courrier des Alpes*, January 1, 1848.

54 *Correspondence du duc d'Aumale et de Cuvillier-Fleury*, vol. 1, 1840-1848 (Paris: Plon, 1910), p. 397.

of a dispatch of the Duke of Aumale dated December 25 and addressed to Lieutenant General d'Hautpoul: "Abd el-Kader has just made his submission to France. Surrounded by the Moroccans and by our cavalry, he could not save his *deïra*. But he still had the possibility of taking the south with some cavalry; he decided to trust in the generosity of France."

In another dispatch dated the same and sent to the headquarters of the new colony to inform them of the "great news," the Duke of Aumale shows his certitude regarding respect for the promise given to the Emir, and he concludes thus: "He has just arrived here in order to be taken to Marseille, by order of the government, which will send him to the East."[55] Commenting on this equivocal situation, a chronicler writes: "It has been said that Abd el-Kader embarrassed us even when he was in our hands. At one time no one knew where to find him; now no one knows where to put him."[56] The discussion in the two chambers of Parliament reflects the state of mind that prevailed at the time. On Monday, January 17, 1848, ten days after placing the Emir and his followers in Forts Lamalgue and Malbousquet de Toulon, a debate took place in the Chamber of Peers concerning the "taking of Emir Abd el-Kader and its consequences." The following 5th of February, the debate over the consequences of this matter took place in the Chamber of Deputies. Another debate would take place the 25th of November of 1850 in the legislative Assembly. The greatest reaction in the Chamber of Peers was aroused by the speech of the Prince of Moskowa. His long speech allowed one to perceive a certain admiration for the "illustrious defeated." After having recalled the events preceding his surrender and his "very glorious battle," he declared: "Now, one of two things: either you deem Abd el-Kader a brigand, a pirate, or else you see in him a defeated enemy general. In the first case, take him prisoner; in the second case, treat him according to the rights of men. . . . Let us not exaggerate the danger of deporting the Emir to a Muslim country. . . . There is one thing that must be taken into account above all: it is keeping faith in the promise given! (*Hear*) It must not be said that, as the gauge of its military word, the French general exchanged his sword

55 Émile de Girardin, *Questions de mon temps, 1836-1856* (Paris: Serrière, 1856), vol. 2, pp. 455, 457.

56 *La Revue des Deux Mondes*, cited in S. Aouli, R. Redjala, and P. Zoummeroff, *Abd el-Kader*, p. 390.

with that of Abd el-Kader and that France denied this commitment (*Hear! Hear!*)." A minority of peers and representatives in the two chambers who appealed to a sense of national honor and justice, were opposed by fierce opponents of the liberation of the "ex-emir," who gave the pretext of the impossibility of trusting his word and the potential threat he would pose once freed. Certain representatives went so far as to put into question the very existence of a treaty of surrender. To the appeal for respect for "law of nations," one of them expressed his surprise that rights could be granted to "pirates who are outlawed by civilized nations."[57]

Abd el-Kader, from the depths of what increasingly resembled a prison, received some echoes of these debates. Faced with the fallacious arguments that began to circulate in the press,[58] he tried to reestablish the truth by recalling to all who visited him that he had not been "captured," but that he had trusted the word of a French general, and swore his good faith upon all the holy books, "with his heart and with his tongue."[59] In vain. The French authorities remained insensible to his assurances.

Some ten days after their arrival in France, the government ordered the transfer of the Algerians of Lazaret to the two naval forts of Lamalgue and Malbousquet. The Emir angrily demanded that all his companions be reunited with him at Fort Lamalgue. The discovery of the new places of detention, where cold and humidity prevailed, demoralized the exiles still more by their lugubrious aspect. All those who were taken to Toulon were unanimous in denouncing the conduct of the authorities and their "inhospitable tactlessness."[60] The rooms of the fort reserved for captives were adjudged "inappropriate, dark and damp."[61] The French officers on duty among them were well aware of their state of health, and advised the political authorities to "place [the Emir] elsewhere than at Fort Lamalgue,"[62] for reasons of security but

---

57 *Le Moniteur universel*, November 26, 1850.

58 In particular, Abd el-Kader was mistakenly accused of the massacre of the prisoners of the *deïra*, concerning which we shall return in a later chapter.

59 Alexandre Bellemare, *Abd-el-Kader*, p. 358.

60 Article of Charles Poncy, in *L'Illustration*, May 6, 1848.

61 Ibid.

62 S. Aouli, R. Redjala, and P. Zoummeroff, *Abd el-Kader*, pp. 403-404.

also because, Colonel Daumas added, "humaneness demands it." To these warnings would be added, pathetically, that of the Commissioner General of Bouches-du-Rhone. In a letter to the provisional government, the young Émile Ollivier wrote: "It is certain that to keep Abd el-Kader in custody is to kill him."[63]

The victim of what increasingly resembled a breach of oath, reduced to helplessness, the Émir fell into a distress all the more profound in that it implicated his family and the companions who had joined their fate to his. Colonel Daumas reported this meeting with the Emir, which gives a good portrayal of his state of mind: "How could my resignation not weaken at times before the greatness of my misfortune? Despair was in my followers, in my very family. My mother and wives wept night and day and could not add their faith to the hope I try to give them. What can I say? It is not only the women who lament, but also the men. . . . And it is I who am the cause of all their misfortunes! . . . You have indeed lied to me and today I am blamed cruelly for having trusted you. Have you no court charged with hearing the complaints of the oppressed? . . . Ah! You are far from that Muslim Sultan who, having become deaf, began to weep, and replied to those who asked him why: 'I weep because I can no longer hear the grievances of the oppressed.'"[64] This oppressive situation caused a visitor to Fort Lamalgue to say that "all the vexations, joined to the continual lamentation of the Emir's family and servants, had plunged him into a despondency dangerous to his health. His attitude remained dignified and firm, but his appearance was visibly altered."[65]

The transfer order was only the first of a series of decisions that reflected the procrastinations of the French authorities and made all the more improbable the outlook for freedom and a departure for the East. Towards the end of February, from his balcony at Fort Lamalgue, the Emir learned of the overthrow of the July monarchy and the onset of a republican government. Occurring scarcely two months after his surrender, this event seems to have caused him a moment of remorse. He asked himself what might have happened had he not surrendered; would the abdication of Louis-Philippe not have favored a

---

63 Captain M. Perras and E. Boislandry Dubern, "Abd-el-Kader en exil, d'après des documents inédits," *Revue des sciences politiques*, No. 28, January-June 1913, p. 354.

64 Cited in Alexandre Bellemare, *Abd-el-Kader*, p. 359.

65 Émile de Girardin, *Questions de mon temps*, pp. 466-467.

surge of the *jihad*? To this was added the probable feeling of having been abandoned by God or at least that his choice had not been approved and that he had suffered the consequences. Nevertheless, Abd el-Kader knew with certain intuition that the divine decrees cannot be conditioned and that they elude human speculations. At this point, the fate of the Algerian captives was placed in the hands of the republican government. But despite the principles of justice and liberty declared by the young Republic, it decided, through the voice of its Minister of War, to leave the Emir Abd el-Kader "where the former government had left him, that is, as a prisoner."[66] His transfer to the town of Pau, in April 1848, and then to Amboise, six months later, convinced the former war chief that the trial would be long.

The first phase of captivity had certainly been one of the most difficult of the five years that it would last; it would also have corresponded to a major stage of the inner quest of Abd el-Kader. Colonel Daumas would be a privileged witness of this period of "anxious hope." Stationed at Fort Lamalgue to try to persuade the Emir to retract the terms of the treaty, the officer established daily official reports and wrote personal notes in a notebook.[67] In spite of his zeal, the officer was obliged to acknowledge the failure of his mission before the repeated refusals of the Emir to retract his word given several weeks earlier. In a letter addressed to the president of the Council, François Guizot, a vexed Daumas wrote: "We have nothing in France, despite our power and our riches, that can tempt him. He wants nothing, absolutely nothing of the things of this world."[68] The interim Minister of War, Lieutenant Colonel Charras, wrote to the Emir on the occasion of his transfer to Pau: "The gentleness of the climate, the beauty of the countryside will remind you of Algeria. You will be a guest of the Republic rather than a prisoner."[69] Let us also cite this caricatural commentary by Father Bourgade, which gives a good idea of the political and psychological manipulations of which the Emir was the object: "Abd el-Kader lives in

---

66 Alexandre Bellemare, *Abd-el-Kader*, p. 365.

67 We know through one of his descendents, Mr. Perras, that Eugène left a manuscript of 80 pages in large writing concerning his stay in Fort Lamalgue. Alexandre Bellemare cites long passages from it in his work. The original document cannot be found today.

68 S. Aouli, R. Redjala, and P. Zoummeroff, *Abd el-Kader*, p. 395.

69 Cited in Joseph Legras, *Abd el-Kader, Les grandes vies aventureuses. Avec un portrait* (Nancy, Paris, Strasbourg: Impr. et éditions Berger-Levrault, 1929), p. 225.

an old royal palace. Around the palace there are all kinds of pleasures: gardens bordered by roses, fields covered with flowers, fragrant forests, streams of clear water, a river, all that could recall Seville, Granada, or Baghdad. At the ex-Emir's door there are guards at his service. Next to him are his mother, his numerous family, and imams. He receives visits, and can leave for several leagues distant to walk and see his friends; for in France he has friends, and in France friends do not deceive."[70] It would appear that the Algerians, after the betrayal of the treaty of surrender, were afraid of being forced to recant their religion. The Emir also feared being used by the French government in its policy of conquest of Algeria—and the attempts to portray him as a defector were in fact not lacking during his captivity. But he did not deny his past commitment. He refused to be the "guest" of France, "generous towards her vanquished enemies" presented by politicians and journalists: "For me, so long as I am a prisoner, all of France is merely a dungeon. Since they have wished to make me a captive, leave me in my prison; I do not wish to be a victim crowned with flowers."[71] It was also out of dignity that he refused all distractions or the approved visits offered to him. He made only rare exceptions, and always out of regard for his interlocutors. On the eve of his departure for Pau, he gave in to one of these invitations and visited the arsenal at Toulon. The French authorities discovered at their expense that their former adversary preferred prison to dishonor. All the letters sent to them speak of the renunciation of the world. "I am a man dead to the world,"[72] he wrote to the Minister of War: a political argument but also the expression of an inward attitude, captivity taking on the meaning of a spiritual retreat.

A common ritual in most of the Sufi brotherhoods, the spiritual retreat is one of the means available to the disciple to progress on the Way. Practiced in isolation, it follows rules and precise requirements and generally concerns only the most advanced disciples. The Arab term *khalwa* refers to the idea of a deserted place, isolated, empty, a no-man's land; a place, but also an inner state. The disciple is placed in a state of solitude in which, faced with himself, he "dis-covers" himself.

---

70 Abbé F. Bourgade, *La Clef du Coran* (Paris: J. Lecofre et Cie, 1852), pp. 9-10.

71 Eugène de Civry, *Napoléon III et Abd-el-Kader, Charlemagne et Witiking, étude historique et politique. . .* (Paris: Martinon, 1853), pp. 284-285.

72 Letter to the Minister of War, General Lamoricière, cited in Alexandre Bellemare, *Abd-el-Kader*, p. 369.

For the knowledge of God necessarily passes through self-knowledge, according to the *hadith*, widely commented upon in Sufism, "Whoso knoweth his soul, the same knoweth his Lord." The spiritual retreat in Islam, therefore, can be an ascetic trial which reveals the disciple's degree of sincerity and determination. This practice is anchored in the tradition of the Prophet: it was during the course of a retreat in an isolated cave that Muhammad, then forty years old, was transfigured following his encounter with the archangel Gabriel. When Abd el-Kader entered into captivity, he also was forty years old. According to the Islamic tradition, that is the age of maturity, at which the individual becomes fully responsible for his choices on the plane of contingencies as well as on the spiritual plane; it is also the age of the return to God and of the spiritual initiation.[73] A *hadith* compares the world herebelow to a prison. It is only by a clear and resolute will that the faithful can expect to free himself. Thus, the successive prisons of the Emir, in Toulon, then in Pau and in Amboise, were paradoxically so many stages of inward liberation.

Although he makes no clear allusion to it in his writings or in his remarks of this period, it is very likely that the Sufi Abd el-Kader had a spiritual understanding of his condition as a captive. It would be astonishing, to say the least, given what we know of this personage, that he would stop short at appearances, satisfied with believing that he was the victim of a combination of circumstances the responsibility for which fell absolutely on his former adversaries. In the intimacy of his prayers and meditations, the former warrior assuredly understood that the *jihad al-kabir*, the "greater holy war," which is carried out within oneself, had been substituted for the *jihad as-saghir*, the "lesser holy war." This introspection—dialogue with the most intimate dimension of his being—would progressively reveal him to himself. The daily meetings and the detailed notes of Colonel Eugène Daumas in Toulon, followed by Captain Estève Boissonnet in Pau and in Amboise, enable one to discern a more fundamental spiritual reality behind the appearances of the Emir's political captivity.

---

73 The believer must therefore give a clear direction to his life. Sidi Abd al-Qadir al-Jilani used to say: "A person's will is double. There are two opposed wills: the will directed towards all that is other than God and the will directed towards God. These two wills ceaselessly fight and reconcile until the age of forty. Such is the meaning of the Prophet's saying, 'for he who attains the age of forty without the good in him prevailing over the evil, naught remains for him but to prepare for Hell'" (*Enseignements soufies*, p. 527).

It did not take long for Colonel Daumas, who arrived at Fort La-malgue in the middle of January 1848, to attest to the growing lassitude of the prisoners, including the most illustrious among them. Despite an even temper and a pleasant disposition, Abd el-Kader often entered within himself, meditating on his fate, to search, the officer supposed, for a sign of what "God willed of him in the future."[74]

During the course of numerous meetings with him, Colonel Daumas tried to find flaws in the arguments put forth by the Emir, in the hope of justifying an annulment of the treaty of surrender. He believed he had found one when Abd el-Kader confided to him his wish to end his life in Mecca. "I believe that in your requests to General Lamor-icière, you have never spoken of Mecca." The eloquent response of Abd el-Kader, the style and arguments of which would be repeated in the later interventions, sums up his underlying values and determination: "Oh, my God, what could be offered to me in exchange for Mecca? The honors, the goods, the treasures of this world? You know, Daumas, how I despise them. You yourself have seen me, mighty and praised to the skies by those who thereafter betrayed me. A tent for shelter, the simplest food, the same clothes as the least of my people, my horse, my arms, and the Holy War, that is all that I have wished of this world. I have something quite different in my heart and my head than human vanities. Indeed, if it could be done, today one could put in my bur-nous"—and at that, he removed his burnous—"all the diamonds, all the treasures of the earth, and I would cast them without regret into this blue sea that is spread out at our feet. I repeat, I no longer have any desire but to go to Mecca, read the Holy Books, worship God, and be buried after having visited the tomb of our Lord Muhammad in Me-dina. My role is finished."[75] Renunciation of honors, of goods, of power and the desire to end his days in the heart of Islam: the Emir was de-finitively oriented towards that which the Sufic tradition calls a "flight to God" (Koran 51:50), which passes through the "death to oneself," in reference to the hadith of the Prophet: "Die before ye die." His last words to Daumas were unequivocal: "Believe me, Daumas, you see me alive and yet I am dead."

On March 15, 1848, he had to confirm to the provisional govern-ment his irrevocable renunciation to play a political role. "I give you

74 M. Perras and E. Boislandry Dubern, "Abd-el-Kader en exil," p. 352.

75 Ibid., pp. 237-238.

a sacred word, which admits of no doubt. I declare, therefore, that henceforth I will no longer raise disturbances against the French, either personally or by means of letters, or by any means whatsoever. I swear this oath before God, by Muhammad, Abraham, Moses, and Jesus Christ." To his jailer he entrusted what he wrote in black on white in an official letter: "I am presently among the dead and no longer think of aught but of going to Mecca and Medina and worshipping God almighty until He calls me to Him."[76] After a second oath which confirmed that which he swore at the time of the surrender, both ignored by the government, the Emir endured another refusal, yet another humiliation from the Ministry of War, added to so many others, such as the lack of firewood, or being deprived of his personal money. It seems that the military authorities deliberately allowed the degrading lack of privacy in which the companions of Abd el-Kader found themselves, in hopes that it would affect them enough so that their leader would make concessions. At least that is what can be grasped by the official communications of Colonel Daumas, who counted on the weakening of the captive so as, he wrote, to "cast him into my arms later, perhaps obliging him to ask me for advice?"[77] But Abd el-Kader ceded neither to the French authorities nor to discouragement. Confronted daily with an increasingly desperate situation in the face of authorities scarcely concerned with questions of honor and justice, he sublimated his situation with the conviction that his fate proceeded from the Divine will. Daumas was aware of this, and wrote that his prisoner "draws all his strength from outside this world, as was proved when he was a warrior, and by the resignation he manifests in adversity."[78] However, this attitude of "resignation," a term that occurs often in the admiring testimony of the Emir's visitors and from the pens of chroniclers, had nothing in it of sanctimonious or unwholesome fatalism, nor of a capitulation, and still less of despair. Abd el-Kader never renounced the solemn oath he had sworn: in all his letters written in captivity, in his discussions with those who came to see him, he recalled his legitimate right to be free. The acceptance of his fate was an inward disposition,

76 Letter to the provisional government, dated March 14, 1848, cited in Alexandre Bellemare, *Abd el-Kader*, p. 358.

77 Report of Colonel Daumas of January 19 and 20, 1848, cited in Khelfa Benaissa, "La Zawiya d'Amboise," p. 122.

78 M. Perras and E. Boislandry Dubern, "Abd-el-Kader en exil," p. 350.

the work of "patient endurance" (*sabr*). This effort at every moment to not sink into despair rested firstly on trust in God, a cardinal virtue in Islam—"God is with the patient," says a verse of the Koran (8:46)—often conflated with faith (*iman*) itself. To a visitor who enjoined him to trust, the Emir replied: "A man supported by God can do much, I have experienced it. . . . Without God he is nothing."[79] And it is in the fire of trial that this trust was forged,[80] which made Charles H. Churchill write: "With Job, [Abd el-Kader] could cry: 'Howsoever He may sacrifice me, I will place all my trust in Him.'"[81]

In Pau, the prisoners were to be settled in the castle of Henry IV, birthplace of "good King Henry." Thanks to the care of Estève Boissonnet, the conditions of captivity improved. A discreet and meticulous artillery officer, Colonel Daumas' successor had lengthy experience in Algeria and a good grasp of its languages. Like his predecessor, he instituted regular reports for the hierarchy and, in one of them, he wondered about "the unshakeable resolve [of the Emir] not to leave [the castle]": "Is it that he wishes to manifest a constant protest against his detention, by being absolutely passive in our midst, refusing every kind of distraction? Was it the effect of an intuitive resignation to comply with our wishes?"[82] He understood that the explanation was not political: "I think that it has to be attributed to an entirely different cause. The life of Abd el-Kader is quite full; he prays and reads much. . . . He deeply loves this life of study and teaching which he asks to lead in Mecca." The holy city returns to the Emir's remarks and letters like a leitmotif, an "idée fixe," wrote Boissonnet in one of his reports. In Amboise, the attitude of the Emir remained unchanged: "Continually living confined in his apartment, he emerged only to preside over the common prayer."[83] Prayer contributed considerably to the moral resistance of the small community. By filling the day and the spirit of the captives, it relieved the pernicious effects of idleness in which they

---

79 Eynard Paper, Ms. suppl. 1984-f. 36-37.

80 "Do men imagine that they will be left (at ease) because they say, 'We believe,' and will not be tested with affliction?" (Koran 29:2).

81 Charles H. Churchill, *La Vie de Abd el Kader*, p. 287.

82 Extract from a report of Captain Boissonnet of June 11-22, 1848, cited in Khelfa Benaissa, "La Zawiya d'Amboise," p. 34.

83 Alexandre Bellemare, *Abd-el-Kader*, p. 379.

were plunged despite themselves and revived faith in the "descent" of Divine grace. The time which previously had been dedicated to dealing with political affairs and with the armed struggle was henceforth dedicated to spiritual *praxis*. To the obligatory five daily prayers were added the supererogatory ones, as well as the collective recitation of the Koran and of the *dhikr*. The Emir frequently made use of a rosary—black, the chronicle specifies—which he fingered continually, including when he received visitors; one of them specified that "while the interpreter repeated his words, he would lose interest; his eyes would be lowered and he seemed to be murmuring a prayer or some pious verses.[84] The study of the collections and commentaries of *hadiths* also occupied the Emir and his companions. These practices became more intense during the month of Ramadan, during which all visits were suspended. But Abd el-Kader did not fast only during the sacred times.[85] To the worried doctor he explained: "Fear not, by weakening the body the soul becomes stronger." This notable indifference towards any kind of comfort more than once astonished Colonel Daumas. "I wish to hold my soul in check," the Emir told him one day, "man is made of silk and iron: if he becomes accustomed to luxury, to softness, to good food, silk prevails, and he is no longer good for anything. On the contrary, if he rejects all the enjoyments of life, iron prevails, and he remains able to bear all tiredness, and to accomplish the greatest works."[86] By his abnegation, Abd el-Kader expresses the certitude that "the goods of this world never bring happiness and always deprive us of the advantages of the next." "The next world and this one are like East and West: one cannot go towards the one without going away from the other."[87] Being satisfied with what he received, he never asked anything for himself and rather rid himself of his own goods, as with the waistcoat that he offered to an ill palace guard assigned to the castle of Henry IV. No

84 A.F.P. Falloux, *Mémoires d'un royaliste*, p. 363.

85 On the occasion of one of his visits, Monsignor Dupuch had been struck by his fasting: "Thus, twice in two weeks I came upon Abd el-Kader, whose health declines little by little behind those locks, and his old uncle: they were joining their extraordinary and supererogatory fasts to long prayers, so that their prayer might be rendered less unworthy of Him whom they addressed in the depth of their hearts" (*Abd el-Kader au château d'Amboise*, p. 15).

86 S. Aouli, R. Redjala, and P. Zoummeroff, *Abd el-Kader*, p. 401.

87 M. Perras and E. Boislandry Dubern, "Abd-el-Kader en exil," pp. 351-352, 351.

doubt his interlocutors saw in all that a sign of scrupulous devotion. But this attitude, in which generosity is joined to ascesis, pertains to the greater war which frees the Sufis from the concupiscent soul.

Because renunciation must be total and must emanate from the spiritual heart, respect for the religious *praxis*, no matter how scrupulous, is not enough. Trials play a major role in revealing the true intention of the disciple. They alone erode the remains of attachment to honors and material goods, all the more pernicious in being veiled from the disciple. The political and military power that the Emir had enjoyed, his title of Commander of the Faithful, borne for fifteen years, had necessarily left traces in his being. The trial of captivity would literally "purify" him of his instinct of power so as to allow the establishment of the state of simple servant, the *conditio sine qua non* for him to be able to hope for the encounter with his Lord. If the inward process took place without his being aware of it, the Emir was nonetheless aware of the spiritual dimension that he lived, as here, by analogy with the ritual ablution that precedes the prayers: "I have washed my hands of all political instinct with soap and water."[88]

The transfer from Pau to Amboise took place during the first week of November, 1848. The period coincided with the rite of the great pilgrimage to Mecca, and it was exactly on the 8th of November, which corresponded to the "feast of sacrifice" (*'Id al-Adha*), that the captives were settled at the castle of Francis I. Thus, the longest phase of the captivity began under the sign of sacrifice. This religious celebration, which is also called the "great feast," like the pilgrimage that marks its final point, is intimately linked to the figure of Abraham. The ritual of the pilgrimage (*hajj*), is in fact a synthesis of the progression towards God, a progression of which the major stage is the sacrifice of the soul, symbolized, according to certain exegetes, by the visionary dream of Abraham, in which he saw himself immolating his only son.

General Lamoricière's attainment as head of the Ministry of War, the very one who had signed the treaty of surrender, made the Emir hope momentarily for the end of the political status quo, to which the preceding governments had limited themselves, a hope revived by the conciliatory attitude of Louis Napoleon Bonaparte, elected on December 10, 1848 to the presidency of the Republic. But disillusion soon set in: nothing changed and it was with great difficulty that the Emir and

---

88 *Al-Miqradh al-Hadd.*

his followers adapted to Amboise castle. "Royal Residence," for "the ex-emir," wrote the chronicle, proudly recalling that it had housed the exchanges between Francis I and Leonardo da Vinci. The pomp of the Renaissance was in reality quite distant and in 1848 the castle, which still bore the sequelae of the French Revolution, was in a state of advanced disrepair. Unlike the castle of Henry IV, which was next to the dwellings of Pau, it was isolated from the town, which gave it the air of an impregnable citadel. The number of sentries had been raised to two hundred. Once it is realized that the Emir and his companions, the majority of whom were women and children, were disarmed and bound by solemn oath, these measures can be explained only as the expression of an obsession with security. This same obsession led the new minister to forbid the captives from any contact with the outside world. The isolation became total.

The fate in store for "the illustrious captive" provoked a reaction from some gifted observers, such as Émile de Girardin and Victor Hugo. The latter, in a letter to the Minister of War, requested for his son-in-law an authorization to visit Amboise so that, he specified, "the false allegations spread concerning the situation of Abd el-Kader might disappear." The authorization was refused, as well as for Émile Ollivier, who carried out a campaign to awaken public opinion over the fate of Abd el-Kader.

The years 1849 and 1850 were assuredly the hardest for the captives. The damp climate of the Touraine, so different from that of their homeland, the unhealthiness of the castle, the state of isolation, slowly wore down their health. "Here the climate greatly fatigues us, it wears us down little by little; we can no longer live here without dying soon. The French doctors who visit us are convinced of this, and their apprehension makes them recommend our prompt departure,"[89] the Emir recounted in a letter to Monsignor Dupuch, one of the rare visitors during the period in Amboise. The medical reports give a precise idea of the ills suffered by Abd el-Kader and his intimates: cases of rickets in the children, scrofulous and choleric infections, rheumatism which affected the aged, including the Emir's mother, Lalla Zuhra. But it is the mental degradation that the reports emphasize, advising a softening of the conditions of detention to remedy it. At Amboise, twenty-five Algerians succumbed and were buried in the communal cemetery or

---

89 Letter dated March 1849, cited in Mgr. Dupuch, *Abd el-Kader au château d'Amboise*, pp. 104-106.

in the castle grounds. In the previously cited letter to the first bishop of Algeria, the Emir worried about their state of forced idleness: "What will become of us if God Himself does not uphold us with his almighty Arm?" Nonetheless, he remained faithful to the spirit with which, at the time of the *jihad*, he exhorted men to patience in the face of trials, for it is "God who sendeth them,"[90] and which, far from being a scourge, are a means of spiritual progress. The disciple is exhorted to bear them. As Sidi Abd al-Qadir al-Jilani wrote, "trials undergone with patience constitute the foundation of prophecy, of the Message, of Holiness, of Knowledge, and of Love. Thus, if you do not endure trials, you have no foundation, no center."[91] Stricken in his health and deprived of his goods, man discovers the humility of his condition; his recourse to God then becomes a necessity stripped of all affectation.[92]

"Only the grandeur of adversity still upholds Abd el-Kader at the Amboise castle. But he suppressed his pain to an alarming extent; for who could dare foresee or gauge what would happen if his courage were to fail at last?"[93] wrote a witness. The physical state of the Emir was aggravated by his refusal to leave his chambers in order to walk in the castle's garden. To the doctor who insisted, he always gave the same response: "Health . . . cannot come in the air of a prison. What I need is the air of freedom: it alone can cure me."[94] Freedom, he insisted, was the only remedy that could put an end to the "deep sadness in our hearts";[95] a sadness which one newspaper compared to that of "Moses despairing of ever seeing the olive trees of the Promised Land."[96]

Liberty had always been intimately linked to honor for Abd el-Kader. In the course of the year 1842, after two years of deadly warfare, unable to capture the ungraspable enemy, Bugeaud had tried in vain to

90 Charles H. Churchill, *La Vie de Abd el Kader*, p. 201.

91 As Sidi Abd al-Qadir al-Jilani, *Enseignements soufies*, p. 82.

92 According to the verse: "When We show favor unto man, he withdraweth and turneth aside, but when ill toucheth him then he aboundeth in prayer" (Koran 41:51). Sidi Abd al-Qadir al-Jilani, who often goes very far regarding the saving dimension of trials, wrote: "For He spurs thee on with trials, calamities, illnesses, and pains, that ye might seek Him and not leave His Threshold" (*Enseignements soufies*, p. 407).

93 Mgr. Dupuch, *Abd el-Kader au château d'Amboise*, p. 104.

94 Alexandre Bellemare, *Abd-el-Kader*, p. 379.

95 Mgr. Dupuch, *Abd el-Kader au château d'Amboise*, p. 104.

96 In *L'Illustration*, November 25, 1848.

bribe the Emir by offering him a golden exile in Mecca. Now, on April 4, 1849, the marshal, with the mission of finding an honorable solution to this situation which continued to be the object of debates in the press and of political tracts,[97] wrote him a letter in which he planned "to visit him in [his] retreat" and proposed that he accept "adopting France as your country and asking the government to grant you, your family, and your descendants, a fine property where you would have an existence equal to that of our most eminent men."[98] The Emir's reply was final: "If all the treasures of the earth could be gathered and put into the fold of my burnous, and my freedom placed in the balance, I would choose my freedom. I ask neither for grace, nor favor; I ask for the fulfillment of the promises made to me."[99] It is easy to imagine the annoyance of the military authorities before such stubbornness: formerly unable to capture him despite the means employed, today also powerless, despite the riches offered, to make him surrender his principles! Abd el-Kader had a lofty conception of freedom that could not suffer a compromise: a true freedom, unconditional, because in the eyes of God it would not have yielded to the loss of goods and honors. In demanding his political freedom, the Sufi Abd el-Kader also expresses his deeper need for an inner freedom. Monsignor Dupuch, in a burst of enthusiasm, wrote regarding him whose cause he had espoused, that "at times it seems that his ardent soul is elated at the thought of a new illumination, but it feels, and it is not the only one, that in order to devote himself to it he would at last need to enjoy the freedom he claims."[100] In that year of 1852, political freedom was only a few months away.

Louis Napoleon Bonaparte had never concealed his interest in the fate of the "illustrious captive." Alexandre Bellemare would even go so far as to declare that, since the month following his election as leader of the country, he had "announced to prominent persons the intention of keeping the promises given to the Emir in the name of France."[101]

---

97 Regarding a mini-cabinet called together by Louis Napoleon Bonaparte, in the month of January, 1849, to deal with the situation of the Emir Abd el-Kader, see Alexandre Bellemare, *Abd el-Kader*, pp. 371ff.

98 Ibid., p. 374.

99 Ibid., pp. 375-376.

100 Mgr. Dupuch, *Abd el-Kader au château d'Amboise*, p. 31.

101 Alexandre Bellemare, *Abd-el-Kader*, p. 371.

Returning after several years of exile, having known prison, he was all the more sensitive to the plight of the captive at Amboise in that his famous parent, Napoleon I, whom he idolized, had himself been victim of a perjury. If subsequently the Prince-President had not been able to fulfill what he deemed a matter of national honor, it was on the one hand because he did not enjoy all the prerogatives that he would have desired as head of the executive,[102] and on the other hand, because he feared stirring up tensions with the National Assembly. The liberation of the Emir depended exclusively on the all-powerful Minister of War who, like his predecessors, had served in Algeria. As for the representatives of the people, they had taken note of the appreciable amount of money that the surrender of the "ex-Emir" had entailed, and this had been argument enough for most of them to declare that the clauses of the treaty were no longer valid. In the end, the campaigns of both parties to discredit the Emir in the public opinion rendered any decision in his favor politically very costly. For the situation to become unblocked, it would be necessary to await the constitutional crisis which led to the coup d'état of December 2, 1851, the dissolution of the National Assembly, and the reinforcement of the presidential power.

At the same time, the active partisans of the Emir's liberation had not slackened in their efforts. In the spring of 1849, Monsignor Dupuch published *Abd el-Kader au château d'Amboise*, a plea in favor of the Emir's liberation dedicated to the President of the Republic. The young lawyer Émile Ollivier had been pursuing a discreet campaign, especially in the press, ever since his mission to Fort Lamalgue. The officials from the province of Béarn (the capital of which is Pau) who had had ties of friendship with the former "guest" of the castle of Henry IV, constituted a "pro Abd el-Kader" committee, the initiative for which apparently came from the Genevan Charles Eynard. However, it was England which supplied one of the most effective supports to the cause of the Algerian captive. Lord Londonderry, who had known Louis Napoleon Bonaparte during his English exile, pleaded the cause of Abd el-Kader up to the precincts of the English Parliament. At the begin-

---

102 The candidature of the old exile had been favored by the rural electorate and had had the political support of the "Parti de l'Ordre" (literally Party of Order); these two factors explain his very large victory, with more than 74% of the votes in the presidential elections. But the Prince-President was head of a government led by Odilon Barrot, none of whose members was in his camp. His victory resulted from political dealings.

ning of March, 1851, he obtained an authorization from the Ministry of War to go to Amboise. His visit to the castle did not go unnoticed, apparently almost causing a diplomatic incident. The day after this visit, the Lord wrote a letter[103] to the Prince-President inquiring about his intentions towards the prisoner. He reiterated a "final appeal" the summer of the same year, brandishing the threat of "releasing to the public and to the world" copies of the correspondence between the Duke of Aumale and General Lamoricière that established the betrayal of which the Arab chief had been the victim. "If Abd el-Kader had to die in the prisons of Louis Napoleon, it would be a blot that the waters of Lethe would never be able to wash away,"[104] he added.

The warnings concerning the health of the Emir—he in particular suffered among other symptoms from a facial neuralgia—obliged the authorities to quickly order a softening of the conditions of captivity. Visitors once again took the road to Amboise castle and some Algerians made excursions into the town and its surroundings. In the spring of 1851, Abd el-Kader consented to walk in the grounds of the castle. Subsequently, he agreed to reply to the numerous invitations of the nobility who lived along the banks of the Loire, including the Count and Countess of Villeneuve, who often received him at their castle at Chenonceau. The signs of the liberation to come multiplied during the course of the summer, culminating with the discrete mission to the castle of the Minister of War. The announcement of the coup d'état of the 2nd of December, which a year later led to the reestablishment of the Empire, was the definitive signal.

While awaiting the conclusion of the diplomatic negotiations with the Ottoman authorities, Abd el-Kader little by little emerged from his isolation. He was physically marked. Alexandre Bellemare, who saw him for a short while after his liberation, emphasized "his unhealthy pallor and the dull white of his complexion which pointed to the inner ravages caused by his captivity."[105] As with his ability to "master his situation," his absence of resentment or bitterness struck the witnesses. In a military report, Captain Boissonnet remarked admiringly:

103 Letter initially published in the *Morning Post*, subsequently published in the *Journal d'Indre-et-Loire* of Thursday, April 10, 1851.

104 Letter dated August 25, 1851, cited in B. Étienne, *Abdelkader, isthme des isthmes*, p. 462.

105 Alexandre Bellemare, *Abd-el-Kader*, p. 379.

"no matter what the vexations of the present situation, he bears them with resignation; day by day he seems less sad . . . always gracious," and concluded in another report that "confinement has not embittered his character at all."[106] Abd el-Kader gives proof of his clemency. He excuses "his enemies, those from whom he suffered the most, and does not allow anyone to speak ill of them before him." This same clemency explains the tribute paid by him to Marshal Bugeaud at the announcement of the latter's death, or again the letter written to the superior of the two police officers who were in charge of his surveillance at Amboise castle, asking "to grant them advancement and other favors related to the services they had rendered."[107]

During the course of the fall of 1852, France was on the eve of the proclamation of the Second Empire, and he who was in the process of being crowned with the name Napoleon III made a tour of France which he wished to conclude with a strong symbolic gesture. Passing through the Touraine, he advised Estève Boissonnet of his passage to Amboise castle on October 16. The future emperor was accompanied by some ministers, including General de Saint-Arnaud. Émile Ollivier, in his memoirs, specifies that the decision of the Prince-President was upheld "despite all the generals," and in particular his Minister of War. He in particular wrote: "General Daumas recounted that when Louis Napoleon mounted the stairs of Amboise castle, General Saint-Arnaud told him: 'Prince, it is necessary to make him come to Trianon.' The Prince nodded. Having reached the Emir, he announced that he was free."[108] This solemn moment, which would be immortalized by the painter Ange Tissier, would furnish material to a number of accounts and testimonies. It is that of the Emir Abd el-Kader which Alexandre Bellemare retains in his biography: "When I entered," the Emir tells us, "the Sultan (Louis Napoleon), who was seated on the couch, arose. His ministers, his officers were to his right and left. . . . The Commander was to my right. When I had deeply greeted the Sultan, he uttered some

106 Reports of Captain Boissonnet of 11-22 June and of 26 August 1848, cited in Khelfa Benaissa, "La Zawiya d'Amboise," p. 35.

107 Letter of Mr. Bruzelier, chief of the municipal Paris police, dated November 19, 1852, in A. Temimi, *Revue d'histoire maghrébine*, no. 10-11, January, 1978, "Lettres inédites de l'émir Abd el-Kader," letter no. 4, p. 192.

108 *Journal*, vol. 1, 1846-1860, text chosen and annotated by T. Zeldin and A. Troisier de Diaz (Paris: Julliard, 1961), p. 132.

words in French which I did not understand, but in the midst of which I only distinguished the word 'liberty,' 'one of those which I know best in your language, because it is the one I have repeated most often.'"[109]

The freedom regained[110] by the Emir coincides with the death of the politician which he had been for more than fifteen years of his life. No sooner freed, he requested a meeting with the Prince-President, which took place at the Saint-Cloud palace, two weeks after his liberation. Alexandre Bellemare, who accompanied the Emir wrote that a few moments before the meeting with the Prince-President, the Emir Abd el-Kader had performed the (afternoon) 'Asr ritual prayer. This was "probably the only time that the Saint-Cloud palace heard the prayer of a Muslim."[111] The Emir had long meditated on the contents of a written act which he wished to deliver personally to his liberator. This solemn oath, in addition to especially praising its recipient, clearly expresses the end of a stage of his life: "I come, therefore, to swear to thee, by the promises and the pact of God, by the promises of all the prophets and all the messengers, that I shall never do anything against the faith that thou hast placed in me, that I will never break this oath; that I will never forget the favor of which I have been the object, finally, that I will never return to the countries of Algeria. . . . When God ordered me to rise up, I arose, and I fought as hard as I could; when he ordered me to cease, I ceased, obedient to the orders of the Most High. It is then that I abandoned power and that I surrendered unto thee."[112] This oath, dated the 16th of Muharram of the Hegira calendar, thus five years to the day after his departure from Algeria, signifies in an irrevocable manner that henceforth his life would be "dedicated to God alone."[113]

---

109 Alexandre Bellemare, *Abd-el-Kader*, p. 381.

110 October 16, 1852 coincides with the new year of the Hegira calendar and corresponds to the emigration/exile (*hijra*) from Mecca to Medina of the Prophet Muhammad.

111 Alexandre Bellemare, *Abd-el-Kader*, p. 395.

112 Ibid., p. 393.

113 Charles H. Churchill, *La Vie d'Abd el-Kader*, pp. 274-275.

CHAPTER 5

An Ethic Tested by Deeds

The good deed and the evil deed are not alike.Repel the evil
deed with one which is better, then lo! he, between whom and thee
there was enmity (will become) as though he was a bosom friend.
Koran 41:34

In truth, our law is the affirmation of all the qualities, and
embraces all the virtues as a necklace embraces the neck. . . .
When we think how rare are truly religious men, how rare are the
defenders and champions of truth, when one sees ignorant persons who
imagine that the principle of [Islam] is hardness, severity, excess, and
barbarism, it is time to repeat these words: "Patience is lovable;
in God we place our trust."
Emir Abd el-Kader to the Imam Shamil

The Treatment of Prisoners

In the spring of 1883, at the announcement of the death of the Emir
Abd el-Kader, some journalists and political men exhumed the old
memory of a massacre of French prisoners with which his name had
been associated. Despite numerous reports and analyses that had subsequently exonerated him, the "massacre of the prisoners of the *deïra*,"
in 1846, remained an indelible blot on the memory of the Arab chief:
on the 24th of April, 1846, after several offers of exchange were ignored
and rejected by the French military authorities and the general government, the French prisoners were executed, presumably on the order of
the lieutenant Mustafa ben Thami. Abd el-Kader, who at the time was
more than six hundred kilometers from the *deïra*, did not learn of the
facts until several days later. He disapproved of his lieutenant's decision, but assumed the responsibility for it. Since the time of his release
in 1852, the Emir had nonetheless requested Alexandre Bellemare to
reestablish the truth regarding this affair which continued visibly to
weigh upon him: "You who remain among these French, make efforts,
either through your words or your pen, to efface the blood which, in
their opinion, exists between them and me."[1] In the chapter that he

---

1 Alexandre Bellemare, *Abd-el-Kader*, p. 324.

dedicates to the episode, the Emir's French biographer demonstrates with many details that the Emir, who was absent from the camp at the time of the execution, could not have ordered it. Aside from this material impossibility, the previous principles and acts of Abd el-Kader preclude that he could have been the author of such an order. Bellemare also emphasizes that the rumor blaming him had been knowingly spread by the French authorities and that "this blot which had been placed on the Emir's forehead as advised by political necessity"[2] should henceforth be effaced. The Emir had all the more suffered from this false accusation in that it was against the humanistic ethic to which he had held in the face of the scorched earth policy led by General Bugeaud beginning in 1841. Despite the chaotic situation which then reigned and the radical means employed by the French Africa Army, he had not given in to the cries of his men for vengeance, nor to the *lex talionis*, but on the contrary, had won fame by treating the French prisoners according to rules that broke with the customary cruelty.

Since the beginning of 1840, war once again raged in Algeria following the breaking of the Treaty of Tafna. The numerous imperfections and errors of formulation, whether deliberate or otherwise, which marred the Treaty of Tafna, sooner or later risked provoking its violation, with the logical consequence of a resumption of the war. In the end, it was a decision taken by Governor General Valée which furnished the occasion for breaking the peace. In the fall of 1839, Valée, accompanied by the Duke of Orléans, had organized an expedition which entailed crossing the pass named "The Iron Gates," situated within territory outside the limits foreseen by the treaty. This "promenade" the Emir deemed a *casus belli*. Pressed by the chiefs of the tribe to right this offense, the Emir wrote a letter to the Governor General, concluding with these words: "The break comes from you. Nevertheless, in order that you may not be able to accuse me of a felony, I warn you that I am at the point of renewing the war." War was declared on the 18th of November of 1839.

General Bugeaud had methodically prepared his return to the front from the House of Parliament in which he was the representative of Dordogne. The renewal of hostilities prompted him to a new policy, which radically broke with the spirit of Tafna which he had nonetheless promoted. On January 15, 1840, before the representatives,

2 Ibid., p. 336.

he announced, "The limited occupation is a chimera, and a dangerous chimera. Yet the Treaty of Tafna was based on this idea. Well then, it is a chimera!"[3] Bugeaud the deputy became a resolute partisan of an extreme colonization. From experience, the military man knew that such an option had a cost. He counted firstly on making the "Arabs" pay it by preventing them from "sowing, reaping, pasturing," in a word, from living. To the cries of outrage in the Assembly he replied in a tone tinged with cynicism: "Gentlemen, war is not made with philanthropy; who desires the end must desire the means." His new motto, "by the sword and by the plow," perfectly summarizes his state of mind at the time. A year later, Marshal Soult, head of the Cabinet and Minister of War, ratified his nomination to the head of the general government of Algeria.

When he had learned of the replacement of Marshal Valée by General Bugeaud, the Emir, according to Charles Henry Churchill, viewed it as a "happy omen,"[4] the possibility of renewing a peace treaty. The subsequent events would undeceive him. It was no longer the Bugeaud of the Treaty of Tafna who disembarked in Algiers on that day of February 22, 1841. The instructions to his supervisory minister were clear: "to pursue vigorously the war against Abd el-Kader and not to listen to any of his proposals."[5] Henceforth it was a matter of eliminating all the obstacles to domination. The new governor general enjoyed the trust of the King and the considerable means that the Cabinet placed at his disposal: an army of 85,000 men, at the head of which were placed the most able military staffs of the French army.[6] He established a military system of "acting columns"; more lightly equipped, they were able to move more quickly and overcome the difficulties of the terrain, leaving less time for the retreat of populations who refused to submit. The feeding of the soldiers was directly extorted from the civil popu-

3 S. Aouli, R. Redjala, and P. Zoummeroff, *Abd el-Kader*, p. 292.

4 Charles H. Churchill based himself on a letter of the Emir Abd el-Kader to General Bugeaud dated September 15, 1841. This letter was placed at the beginning of the work of Lieutenant-Colonel Scott, *A Journal of a Residence in the Esmailia of Abd-el-Kader and of Travels in Morocco and Algeria* (London: Whittaker, 1842).

5 Letter of General Bugeaud to his friend Esclaibes, dated January 14, 1841, cited in S. Aouli, R. Redjala, and P. Zoummeroff, *Abd el-Kader*, p. 294.

6 It will number 106,000 men in 1846, a third of the effective total of the French army of the time.

lace. The determination of the new governor-general was proclaimed bluntly: "I will enter into your mountains, I will burn your villages and your harvests, I will cut down your fruit trees."[7] The primary objective was to annihilate all hint of rebellion and to deprive the Emir of the support of the tribes. General Bugeaud also hoped to cause those under his administration to turn against their leader by having him bear the responsibility for their misfortune. The idea was to "pull the rug out from under the feet" of the enemy, and through terror placing the Muslim populations under the rod of the Africa Army. One of the first measures taken by General Bugeaud upon his arrival in Algeria was to impose upon natives "circulating in the pacified zone the obligatory and visible wearing of a hexagonal medal of white iron bearing the words 'submitted Arab' in French and Arabic."[8] And the goal was achieved, for what occurred was a complete collapse of support of the populace for the *jihad*.

This military strategy, which was followed until the Emir's surrender in December 1847, was accompanied by the methodical destruction of his State. His fortresses were taken, one after the other. The destruction of grain silos deprived his troops of necessary food reserves; the situation prevented the raising of extraordinary taxes so as to finance the battle. On October 16, 1841, the family village where the son of Muhyi ad-Din was born and raised was totally razed. This symbolical destruction was a further blow to the morale of the Emir and his followers. But the "indefatigable and tenacious enemy"[9] did not declare himself vanquished and scoured the entire country to rekindle religious fervor and exhort the defense of *Dar al-Islam*. He also turned towards England, Morocco, and the Ottoman sultan to ask for aid and assistance. But aside from arms from Morocco with English complicity, he was increasingly isolated and made several attempts to enter into peace negotiations. General Bugeaud then requested him to surrender and go in person "to implore the always great generosity of the king and of France."[10] That was the best way to assure that the Emir

---

7 Declaration of Governor General Bugeaud before the Chamber of Representatives, January 24, 1845.

8 S. Aouli, R. Redjala, and P. Zoummeroff, *Abd el-Kader*, p. 303.

9 Charles H. Churchill, *La Vie d'Abd el Kader*, p. 205.

10 SHAT, Fonds Série 1H88, Dossier 2, Province of Algiers, January 13, 1843.

would reject the proposal, which in any case did not seem to be taken seriously by the Head of the Cabinet: Marshal Soult was said not to believe "in the repentance of Abd el-Kader."[11]

If for the Muslims resistance was considered as a *jihad*, a war legitimized by religious motives for the defense of *Dar al-Islam*, in the enemy camp, and quite rapidly, the soldiers felt they were being drawn into a war of attrition that put fire and blood to the country: the cities, the villages, the encampments were set on fire, cultures were destroyed, the tribes were decimated little by little and reduced to a state of exhaustion. The private correspondence of the officers during the year of Bugeaud's government reveals the extent of the horrors perpetrated at the time.[12] Those of a Saint-Arnaud or of a Montagnac suffice to demonstrate the cynicism of most of the officers of the Africa Army.[13] "Behold the war in Africa!" wrote Saint-Arnaud. "We become fanatics in turn, and it degenerates into a war of extermination."[14] "Extermination": the term is encountered in the writings of many chroniclers of the time and it made Alexis de Tocqueville say: "I have brought back from Africa the distressing notion that at this time we are making war in a far more barbarous fashion than the Arabs themselves," which did not prevent even him from declaring: "In France, I have often heard

11 Ibid.

12 The most explicit testimonies are found in the correspondence of Marshall Saint-Arnaud (*Lettres du maréchal de Saint-Arnaud* [Paris: n.p, 1855]), in that of Lieutenant-Colonel Montagnac (*Lettres d'un soldat* [Paris: n.p, 1885]), and in the work of Count d'Hérisson (*La Chasse à l'homme: guerres d'Algérie* [Paris: n.p, 1891]). There exist numerous letters of French officers belonging to private archives, to this day unpublished, and which furnish details on the crimes perpetrated.

13 Some passages taken from the *Lettres* of Saint-Arnaud are sufficiently explicit so as to have no need for further commentary: "The country of the Beni-Menasser is superb. . . . We have burned everything, destroyed everything. Oh! War! War! So many women and children, hiding in the snows of the Atlas, dies of cold and misery there. . . . There are no more than five killed and forty wounded in the army" (April 7, 1842). "We ravage, we burn, we pillage, we destroy houses and trees. Battles: few or none" (June 5, 1942). The same tone appears in the *Lettres d'un soldat* of Lieutenant Colonel Montagnac: "Bring heads, heads! Block the shafts that have been pierced with the head of the first Bedouin that you meet. . . . I had him cut off his head and his right hand [speaking of a religious dignitary] and I arrived at camp with the head stuck at the end of a bayonet and his hand hanging from a ramrod. They were sent to General Baraguay d'Hilliers who was camping nearby, and he was delighted, as you can imagine."

14 Alexandre Bellemare, *Abd-el-Kader*, p. 284.

men whom I respect, but with whom I do not agree, say that it is bad to burn harvests, empty silos and in short seize unarmed men, women, and children. For me, these are distressing necessities, but those who wish to wage war on the Arabs will have to submit to them. . . . The power of Abd el-Kader will not be destroyed unless the position of the tribes who cleave to him becomes so unbearable that they abandon him."[15] This war was all the more barbarous in that it was made not on a government but on a people. Some observers, informed of the scorched earth policy had scathing reactions. Prosper Enfantin's critique even took on astonishing tones, beginning in April 1841, when the worst was still to come: "Algeria now disgusts me, or at least I am led to love only the Algeria of the Arabs and to blush at our French. I truly believe that if I were something of a warrior, I would go and join Abd el-Kader and offer him my blood to rout out these so-called civilizers."[16] Meanwhile, despite recurring criticisms in the capital against his methods,[17] the governor-general continued to cover-up and even encourage the abuses of his officers, as in this letter which he wrote to General Lamoricière in January, 1843: "I trust that after your successful raid, the weather, however bad, will allow you to push forward and fall upon this people whom you have so often put to flight, and that you will end by destroying them, if not by force at least through famine and other miseries."[18] Despite the care taken by Bugeaud to prevent his officers from opening themselves to the press, numerous articles circulated regarding the "barbarous" actions of his army. But the general seems to mock the reproaches leveled at him. Convinced of being in the right, he declared: "We have . . . destroyed much. Perhaps I shall be thought

---

15 *Sur l'Algérie*, pp. 111-112.

16 Cited in the introduction of M. Habart to Charles H. Churchill, *La Vie d'Abd el Kader*, p. 8.

17 If the "barbarous" methods of the general are blamed, the lack of durable and significant results is equally striking. Charles-André Julien wrote: "The results of the expedition were mediocre; the submissions imposed by terror were deemed unsure; the requisitions had prevented the harvests from being brought in normally. . . . In Algeria, people were very aroused against Bugeaud. . . . The casualness with which the Marshal acted, in defiance of the orders of the War Ministry, had provoked strong feelings in the Chamber. . . . Bugeaud had either to submit or resign." As we have seen, it is only in June of 1847 that Bugeaud would be removed in favor of the Duke of Aumale, only a few months prior to the surrender of the Emir Abd el-Kader.

18 Letter of General Buguead of January 24, 1843.

a barbarian; but I place myself above the reproaches of the press, when I have the conviction that I accomplish a useful work for my country."[19] His perseverance paid off, for he obtained, successively, in 1843, the Grand Cross of the Legion of Honor and the Marshal's baton that he had long awaited.[20] Moreover, Louis-Philippe was satisfied with the results of the year 1841. On December 27, in his Address of the Throne, he announced: "Our brave soldiers continue . . . in that land henceforth and forever French, the course of these noble efforts to which my sons have had the honor of being associated. . . . Following its glory, France will convey to Algeria its civilization."[21] However, the dissemination in the French press of some "barbarous" episodes and their repercussion in the public opinion, obliged the government to issue certain reservations concerning the methods employed by the Africa officers. For example, Colonel Pélissier, unable to reach the Oulad Riyah tribe, who had taken refuge in a rocky cave in the region of the Dahra, ordered blocking the entries and putting them to fire: several hundred men, women and children, as well as their flocks, died asphyxiated. The operation, concealed by General Bugeaud, aroused a heated debate in the Chamber of Peers, led by the Prince of Moskowa, later reported by the press. Marshal Soult, after the "smoke suffocations" of Dahra, expressed his regret, adding however, "In Europe such an act would be horrible and detestable. In Africa, that is what war is about."[22] His fatalism was shared by numerous French observers of the conquest. In Algeria, Father Suchet was one of the principal witnesses of the tragedy that unfolded at the time. As the vicar-general of Algeria, who had met the Emir in the spring of 1841, he furnishes in his testimonies details regarding this policy and the state of mind that prevailed in the French camp: "Many of the officers and the soldiers said aloud that it is not a

19 Cited in Charles-André Julien, *L'Histoire de l'Afrique du Nord*, p. 606.

20 At the beginning of June 1942, General Bugeaud wrote to one of his friends: "The war with Abd el-Kader nears its end. Hence, I may be made Marshal of France." A year later, not having received his Marshal's baton, he wrote to his wife: "I swear to you, moreover, that I have decided to ask for my definitive recall if within a month I am not the Marshal of France, but everything leads me to believe that I shall be" (cited in S. Aouli, R. Redjala, and P. Zoummeroff, *Abd el-Kader*, pp. 318, 333).

21 Paul Azan, *L'Emir Abd el Kader*, p. 175.

22 M.-C. Sahli, *Abd el-Kader, chevalier de la foi* (Algiers: n.p., 1953; 2nd ed. Paris: L'Algérien en Europe, n.d), p. 94.

war which is being undertaken in Africa, but perpetual assassinations, a veritable brigandism."[23]

At the heart of what had all the appearances of a hell, the Emir would rely upon his upbringing, his faith, his lofty sentiment of justice, in order to triumph over this dark aspect inherent in man, and which had here become unchained. He was inspired by the tradition, which for him encompassed "the Mosaic law, the Gospel, the Psalms, the Koran," for it is this which enabled the individual to perfect himself, in order to "hope to escape evil."[24] And it is courage[25] first of all which enables the unfolding of "generosity, bravery, energy, the spirit of sacrifice, endurance, clemency, firmness, the staying of anger, dignity, affection towards people"[26]—all of which are so many qualities necessary for taking up a double *jihad*. The Sufi Abd el-Kader obviously was not unaware that it is in these difficult moments that the *jihad al-akbar*, the "greater combat" against his own impulsions, acquires all its significance. The confrontation with the outer enemy, the "lesser combat," did not make him forget that the most dangerous enemy is firstly within oneself and that the true victory is not the one which one thinks.

According to Alexandre Bellemare, the young Emir, since the beginning of his career at the head of the tribes of the West, was distinguished for his gestures of clemency towards his prisoners. He noted that before his "elevation not a single soldier would fall into the hands of the Arabs to whom quarter was granted. Since 1833, the young sultan managed to take prisoners, to protect them from the barbarity of his soldiers, and to introduce among them this lessening of the miseries of war."[27] In the official correspondence, several letters point to releases without compensation carried out at the behest of the Emir.[28]

---

23 Abbé Suchet, *Lettres édifiantes et curieuses sur l'Algérie*, pp. 305-306.

24 Abd el-Kader, *Lettre aux Français*, p. 95.

25 For the Emir Abd el-Kader, there are four main virtues, which he expounds in a later treatise: knowledge, courage, temperance, and justice. However, they must be in balance among themselves. According to him, an excess of courage, for example, would lead to "fatal hastiness, boastfulness, arrogance, pride, conceitedness, irascibility" (*Lettre aux Français*, p. 76).

26 Ibid.

27 Alexandre Bellemare, *Abd-el-Kader*, pp. 324-325.

28 Following the ill treatment undergone by French prisoners transferred to Moroccan territory, the French consul in Tangiers sent a complaint to Sultan Abd ar-Rahman

Death by decapitation, humiliation, privation, as well as enforced apostasy were the trials most feared by the French military if taken prisoner. It was precisely on these points that Abd el-Kader would introduce a true reform. His attitude would give rise to numerous eloquent testimonies, above all from former prisoners, which give a clear insight into his ethic. In order to reassure one of his first prisoners[29] who had just entered his camp, the Emir was supposed to have said: "For as long as you remain with me you need not fear either ill treatment or insults."[30] And according to the author of this testimony, he kept his promise. To another one, who in a burst of pride declared to him that he would prefer to die than to abjure his religion, he replied: "Be at ease: for me your life is sacred. I like to hear you speak thus. . . . I honor courage in religion more than courage in combat."[31]

To a prisoner who had sacrificed himself to save his officer, the Emir delivered the medal of the Legion of Honor sent by the French government. Another fact drawn from the annals of the prisoners tells of "little Marie." Taken with her brothers and sisters, the little girl found herself prisoner in the *deïra*. Father Suchet recounts the exchange he had with her after her release: "Little Marie remained with Abd el-Kader, who had a father's affection for her: she slept in the tent of his wife, who cared for her as for her own child. . . . I asked her if anyone had spoken to her about becoming a Muslim. 'Yes, yes, often I was told: since you are with the Arabs, you must become a Muslim. No, no, I replied, never, never. You people don't have the mass.' Abd el-Kader himself never spoke to her about this."[32] If, as the case of little Marie attests, the prisoners could be the object of incitements to convert

in which, although qualifying the Emir as "a fierce enemy," he emphasized the generous liberation of all prisoners fallen into the Emir's hand and the fact that he "never alleged that his prisoners had embraced Islam and never constrained them to do so" (SHAT, Fonds Série H47, Dossier 2, Province of Oran, April 1837).

29 A. De France, an ensign on a beached vessel who was taken prisoner in 1837, published his testimony after his liberation under the pseudonym of Napoléon Maurice, *Les Prisonniers d'Abd el-Kader ou Cinq mois de captivité chez les Arabes* (Paris: Desessart, 1837), vol. 2.

30 Alexandre Bellemare, *Abd-el-Kader*, p. 326.

31 Charles H. Churchill, *La Vie d'Abd el Kader*, p. 224.

32 Abbé Suchet, *Lettres édifiantes et curieuses sur l'Algérie*, pp. 347-348.

to Islam, it seems however that the Emir was opposed to conversions that were not voluntary. This in any case is what the vicar of Algiers recounts: "Abd el-Kader has formally forbidden speaking to the Christian prisoners or others who are among the Arabs, of embracing Islam. He himself one day ordered that fifty blows with a stick be given to an Arab who had told a Christian to become a Muslim."[33] Like Monsignor Dupuch, the vicar probably had an opportune reason for praising the Emir on a matter that made him an objective ally of the Church. The reported attitude of the Arab chief remains plausible, nonetheless, for it is part of his wide spirit of tolerance. During this time Abd el-Kader initiated dialogue with Christian personalities and by means of this manifested an exceptional openness of mind. As an enlightened man, he preferred a Christian who dedicated time to prayer to a Muslim who had no respect for his religious principles. The adhesion to Islam of a non-Muslim had to be the fruit of a sincere and responsible choice and in no case constrained, as prescribed, moreover, by the religious law, which institutes the priority of the intention over the act and respect for the religion of the People of the Book. The Koranic verse, "There is no compulsion in religion. The right direction is henceforth distinct from error" (2:256) is often cited to invalidate forced conversions.

The first contact between Monsignor Dupuch and the Emir Abd el-Kader took place within the framework of negotiations involving exchanges of prisoners. The Bishop of Algeria had written a letter to the Emir, in the name of the family of the prisoner Massot, captured in the surroundings of Douéra a short while earlier. After having requested the release of the prisoner, he added: "Blessed be the merciful, for one day, they will be shown mercy!"[34] The response of the Emir was straightforward: "I have received your letter, I have understood it, it does not surprise me given what I had already heard concerning your sacred character. . . . Nonetheless, allow me to tell you that in view of the double responsibility you bear as servant of God and friend of men, your brothers, you should have asked me not for the freedom of one only, but rather for that of all the Christians who have been taken prisoner since the return of hostilities. Moreover, would you not be twice worthy of the mission of which you speak to me if you were not only content to procure such a kindness for two or three hundred

---

33 Ibid., p. 356.

34 Msg. Dupuch, *Abd el-Kader au château d'Amboise*, p. 40.

Christians, but would try to extend the favor to a corresponding number of Muslims who languish in your prisons? It is written: Do unto others that which you would have them do unto you."[35] The quote at the end of the extract does not refer to the Gospels, contrary to what is given by the translation, but to a *hadith* which says textually: "Only he is worthy to be a believer who loves for his brother that which he loves for himself."[36] According to the interpretation given by the Emir, the adversaries are assimilated to "brothers." This interpretation may seem daring, but we shall see elsewhere (in chap. 8, "The Man of Unity") that it fully corresponds to the spiritual evolution of Abd el-Kader. At the time, this letter, which the bishop describes as a "merciful provocation," left a deep impression in his mind.

In the spring of 1841, Father Suchet, sent on a mission by Monsignor Dupuch to recover other prisoners, set out in the company of an interpreter and a guide. On the way, he met with tribes fleeing before the French columns. His life was saved from the hands of these "unfortunate exasperated fugitives" only thanks to his function as a "marabout Rumi" (Christian priest) and to the crucifix hanging on his breast. After several days of long trekking, the small group arrived at the Emir's camp. The encounter was animated and enriching, and the mission a success. Monsignor Dupuch obtained from the Emir the releases he had requested, but also handwritten authorization that a Catholic priest might be sent to the French prisoners: "He will want for nothing with me . . . , wrote the Emir: I will make sure that he will be honored, respected among all of us, as befits his double character of a man consecrated to God and your representative; he will pray daily with the prisoners, he will console them, he will be able to correspond with their families and, in this way, obtain money, clothing, books for them, and in a word, all that they could desire that will soften the rigors of captivity; once and for all, however, upon arriving they will promise never to reveal in their letters either my encampments or the rest of my war." Again, the Emir was ahead of his times.[37] But the project did not

35 Ibid.

36 *Hadith* related by Abu Hamza Anas Ibn Malik, cited by Imams al-Bukhari and Muslim. The translation given clearly recalls a passage from the Gospel (Matt. 7:12; Luke 6:31) whose meaning, moreover, is quite close to the *hadith* more plausibly cited by the Emir Abd el-Kader.

37 It is no exaggeration that this proposal, in its break with practices current at the time and in the brutal context in which they arose, heralded international conventions

receive the approval of the governor-general. Without naming the one responsible for this failure, Monsignor Dupuch specified in one of his letters that "if this project did not succeed, it is fair to say that it was the fault neither of the Emir, who conceived it, nor of the one to whom his noble heart proposed it."

During the course of the year 1841, General Bugeaud had accepted exchanges of prisoners only exceptionally, and subsequently, he would forbid all fresh negotiations. Everything leads one to believe that he feared that such openings could be interpreted by the Emir as a change in his pitiless policy. The general was resolved to vanquish by force at all costs. Yet this did not prevent the Emir from continuing to free prisoners without compensation. In February 1842, Saint-Arnaud wrote, "Abd el-Kader has unconditionally returned all our prisoners, without an exchange. He told them: 'I have nothing more with which to feed you, I do not wish to slay you, I will return you'; noble treatment, for a barbarian."[38] The same cynicism was reserved for the emissaries of the Emir: sent to Oran and to Algeria to negotiate in the name of their master, they were thrown into prison, to join those whose freedom they had come to request.

However, Abd el-Kader was not an exception in his own camp: other personalities in his entourage matched him in their virtues. Affiliated to a Sufi brotherhood, most of his lieutenants acted, as did he, in conformity with the teaching which was dispensed there. Lieutenants Bou-Hamedi and Ben Arach are often mentioned by the chronicle, but it is Sidi Embarek ben 'Allal, whom Charles Henry Churchill designates as a "brilliant replica of the spirit of his master,"[39] who seems to have left a mark in the annals. Faithful to the end of the *jihad* to which he had sacrificed his goods and his family (after the taking of the *smala*, his family was taken prisoner and sent to the island of Sainte Marguerite. Marshal Bugeaud had tried to get Sidi Embarek to surrender by promising to return his family and children: in vain), he perished during the course of a battle in November 1843. A little more than two years earlier, with the blessing of the Emir, he had accompanied the

which would be adopted several decades later.

38 Letter dated February 14, 1842, in *Lettres du maréchal Saint-Arnaud*, vol. 1, p. 386.

39 Charles H. Churchill, *La Vie d'Abd el Kader*, p. 225.

return of the French prisoners of Sidi Khlifa[40] with a herd of goats. To explain his gesture, he wrote a letter to Monsignor Dupuch: "With these new prisoners, I send you twenty goats with their young to nourish with their milk the children who have no mothers; for I have not forgotten that you had bought two in order to feed the small children of our Arab women while they were prisoners in Algeria."[41] The Emir's family also contributed to softening the fate of the prisoners of war, in particular Lalla Zuhra, who had probably been one of their main supports on certain political matters, primarily on what concerned the fate of the captives. Captain Daumas writes regarding her: "She is a strong woman. She enjoys a certain influence on her son's mind, and he consults her often, it is said; more than once she has taken an interest in the fate of our prisoners and had it softened."[42] We also know that she participated in taking charge of the men and particularly of the women in captivity at the *deïra*: "Each morning, the prisoners present themselves to the Sultan's mother to receive a ration of biscuit, oil, butter, and some meat for their meal, which they are supposed to prepare for themselves. . . . When one of the unfortunates is ill, the widow of Muhyi ad-Din immediately sends them sugar, tea, coffee, and all that could be useful and beneficial for them."[43] In fact, women were among the victims of this war; canteen-keepers who accompanied the military columns, wives or daughters of isolated settlers, they constituted easy prey. "The repugnance of Abd el-Kader upon seeing women prisoners was extreme," wrote Charles H. Churchill. The thought that women were victims of war was a source of perpetual torment for him. One day, the cavalry of one of his *khalifas** brought him, as a brilliant catch, four young women. He turned away as a sign of disgust. "Lions attack animals who know how to defend themselves; jackals fall upon the others."[44] The reproach was directed to his men, but also to his adversaries. The situation in which the French military put the Arab

---

40 Charles H. Churchill wrote that after they recovered their freedom, former prisoners of Sidi Embarek contributed to "present him with pistols of honor" (*La Vie d'Abd el Kader*, p. 225).

41 Abbé Suchet, *Lettres édifiantes et curieses sur l'Algérie*, pp. 342-343.

42 G. Yver, *Correspondence du capitaine Daumas*, p. 302.

43 Msg. Dupuch, *Abd el-Kader au château d'Amboise*, p. 46.

44 Charles H. Churchill, *La Vie d'Abd el Kader*, p. 224.

women of the tribes which had not submitted was inspired by the policy of terror and humiliation willed by the governor-general, who had instructed his officers to take the greatest number of prisoners possible, and "above all women," for "that will make the natives despair and will produce outcries rendering the government of the khalifas more difficult."[45] Faced with this machiavellian strategy, the greatness of the Emir's soul inspired Charles H. Churchill to lines of enthusiasm mixed with bitterness: "The generous concern, the tender sympathy, shown by Abd el-Kader to his prisoners, are almost without parallel in the annals of war. The Christian generals on this point do not reach his ankles and may well blush at the degradation of their sentiments of humanity. To be sure, it cannot be denied that the prisoners taken by the Arabs were often exposed to insults of their barbaric vanquishers, when they fell into the midst of tribes exasperated by the sufferings inflicted upon them by the French. However, slowly but surely, the spirit breathed by the Sultan made its way. Barbarism withdrew before him, charity emerged, humanity triumphed."[46] The praise is lyrical, certainly partisan; nonetheless the English officer is not mistaken in comparing the practices of Abd el-Kader to the usual ones on the various fields of battle in Europe, for he knew them quite well. Mr. de Marandol, a former prisoner of the Emir, said nothing different: "Abd el-Kader acted towards me with a greatness that I would not have encountered in the most civilized countries of Europe."[47]

"Verily, God hath prescribed Mercy for Himself": this Koranic verse (6:12) throws light on the conduct of the Emir. The term "mercy" is present everywhere in the Koran, and the Islamic tradition affirms the merciful and universal nature of the mission of Muhammad,[48] who was the Emir's preeminent model. As with his co-religionists, he pre-

---

45 SHAT, Fonds Série 1H79, Dossier 2, Province d'Oran (December 11 to 18, 1841). Another testimony regarding the Arab prisoners of Lieutenant Colonel Montagnac is more explicit: "In a paragraph of your letter you ask me what we do with the women prisoners. Some we keep as hostages, others we exchange for horses, the rest are put up for auction like beasts of burden" (Letter dated March 31, 1842, in *Lettres d'un soldat*).

46 Charles H. Churchill, *La Vie d'Abd el Kader*, pp. 222-223.

47 Alexandre Bellemare, *Abd-el-Kader*, p. 328n.

48 "We sent thee not save as a mercy for the peoples" (Koran 21:107), regarding the mission of the Prophet. The Sufis use the idea of *'ayn ar-Rahma*, the "fountain of mercy", to designate the Prophet.

ceded his words and his acts with the formula "In the Name of God, the Clement, the Merciful." Acts performed under the authority of this Divine attribute necessarily bear the imprint of mercy. If mercy is an imperative towards all creatures, independently of their religious and cultural specificities, with all the more reason must it apply to the weakest—to prisoners, in the case at hand. "We have never made any distinction between the prisoners and our men as regards their food and shelter,"[49] affirms the Emir in the work of his biographer. If the son of the *muqaddam* himself honored the teaching he had received, as Commander of the Faithful he extended to his people the respect for the principle that governed him. The unleashing of the violence which began to become general and contaminated his camp obliged him to act promptly. The multiplication of the atrocities committed by his men upon the French prisoners made urgent the establishment of what Charles H. Churchill called a "decree concerning the treatment of prisoners," according to which "every Frenchman captured in combat or otherwise shall be considered a prisoner of war and be treated accordingly, until an occasion to exchange him presents itself."[50] In order to give it real efficacy, the Emir submitted it to an extraordinary council bringing together his lieutenants, religious dignitaries, and the chiefs of the tribes which had remained faithful, an assembly approved of by the majority. However, this had not been without difficulties, if one is to believe Monsignor Dupuch: "This measure . . . was almost the occasion of a general uprising in the Arab army."[51] Be that as it may, the regulation was adopted and communicated to all the territories administered by the Emir. One of its most explicit articles stipulates: "Every Arab having a Frenchman or a Christian in his possession is held responsible for the manner in which he is treated. Moreover, on pain of the most severe penalty, he is bound to conduct the prisoner without delay either to the nearest Khalifa or to the Sultan himself."[52] The summary executions by decapitation, mistreatments, etc., were henceforth proscribed, which caused one observer to give notice that "Abd el-Kader has neglected nothing to remove from war the cruelty which

49 Charles H. Churchill, *La Vie d'Abd el Kader*, p. 261.

50 Ibid., p. 229.

51 Msg. Dupuch, *Abd el-Kader au château d'Amboise*, p. 35.

52 Charles H. Churchill, *La Vie d'Abd el Kader*, p. 229.

the immemorial custom of decapitation had given it until then."[53] As in the case of the creation of the post of chaplain for prisoners, this regulation is of a remarkable modernity: a "moral revolution which had been motivated by religion and humanity,"[54] as Charles H. Churchill emphasizes quite properly. The rupture with practices contrary to Sufi teaching and human dignity are made precisely in the name of divine law and humanity, two notions often conflated in the writings of Abd el-Kader. The regulation was not long in producing results, which the vicar of Algeria celebrates: "There is but one voice among all the prisoners in singing the praises of Abd el-Kader; all congratulate themselves on the good treatment they have received, and what some of them have had to suffer were isolated, particular facts, which Abd el-Kader could not have known about; for he would certainly have punished their authors for them."[55] However it is probable, as can be gleaned from this passage, that the application of new measures was not always accomplished without difficulties or without infractions. Nonetheless, the most resistant persons to this clemency were found within the very midst of the French camp! The testimonies of former French prisoners had the effect of promoting the enemy and his emblematic chief. Fearing, as did other officers, that the decisions taken by the Emir would spread a current of sympathy through the ranks of the Africa army strong enough to affect the objectives of the war, Colonel de Géry declared: "We were obliged to conceal these things from our men as far as we could; if they had suspected them, they never would have fought as fiercely against Abd el-Kader."[56]

All the actions of the Emir were inspired by the Koran and the *Sunna*.* The Emir knew of the Prophet's clemency towards his enemies, as in this *hadith*: "Do no evil, and do not return evil for evil," and others of a similar nature, such as this one reported by the Imam at-Tirmidhi: "None of you would be so foolish as to say: 'When I am with people, if they do good I also do good, and if they do evil I also do

---

53 L.-A. Berbrugger, *Négociation entre Mgr l'évêque d'Alger et Abd el-Kader pour l'échange des prisonniers*, p. 35.

54 Charles H. Churchill, *La Vie d'Abd el Kader*, p. 227.

55 Abbé Suchet, *Lettres édifiantes et curieses sur l'Algérie*, p. 357.

56 Msg. Dupuch, *Abd el-Kader au château d'Amboise*, p. 27. Father Suchet confirms the fact in his work, *Lettres édifiantes et curieses sur l'Algérie*, p. 357.

evil.' Learn to be firm: if men do good, do the same, and if they do evil, avoid their misdeeds"; these served him as a juridical basis to justify his decisions. His conduct had the effect of revealing the contradictions of the "civilizing" conquest engaged in by his adversaries, and of exposing its limits: "A system of extermination, necessary perhaps until now, could not be prolonged without dishonor for France: it is time to think of victories which alone assure and legitimize the occupation of a country, a conquest of a kind more difficult than that of the land, the conquest of hearts and minds,"[57] wrote a French observer. For the Emir, a noble objective could be attained only by means of the same nature; the inhuman acts perpetrated in the name of "civilization" were merely an aberration. Concerning this point, it seems that it was the Emir Abd el-Kader who "conquered the hearts," as numerous former prisoners would attest.

At the end of the month of January, 1848, Captain Morisot, a former prisoner, requested from the Minister of War authorization to visit the Emir then imprisoned at Fort Lamalgue. The exchange with his former captor was not very lengthy, but it impressed the captain enough to write about it. Dated February 14, 1848, his letter summarizes the nature of the feelings which, years after the events, continued to tie former adversaries to Abd el-Kader: "You never cease being present in my thoughts: and indeed, how could I ever forget the good and generous man who surrounded me, I will say, not only with care, but with affection and charming thoughtfulness when I was in misfortune? . . . Did I not tell you during our meeting Friday, that that day was one which I count among the happiest of my life on this earth? And as you must know, happy days are rare in this world."[58]

The Anti-Christian Riots in the Summer of 1860

Syria had the unfortunate reputation of being the most turbulent province of the Ottoman Empire. The incessant and ancient quarrels between the Christian and Druze communities regularly gave rise to armed confrontations, and in the spring of 1845 they culminated in a

---

57 A. Cochut, "Compte rendu du livre du capitaine de Neveu sur les Khouans, ordre religieux chez les musulmans d'Algérie," *La Revue dex Deux Mondes du 15 mai 1846*, p. 611.

58 S. Aouli, R. Redjala, and P. Zoummeroff, *Abd el-Kader*, pp. 399-400.

major crisis. While the Ottoman Empire was breaking-up, the European powers were creating their network of influence in the region through their interventions in the various communities. The rivalry between England, the traditional ally of the Turkish and Druze nationalities, and France, who had taken the Christian communities under its protective wing, was not without consequences for the political equilibrium of this region. Following the Crimean War and the Treaty of Paris of 1856,[59] the intrusion of Europe increased in the political affairs of the Sublime Porte. In February 1856, Sultan Abd al-Majid, under the pressure of European allies, adopted the Hatti Humayun, a decree enforceable in the provinces of the Empire, which guaranteed the civil, military, and political equality of all the communities. Until then, the non-Muslim minorities of *Dar al-Islam* had the status of "wards" (*dhimmi*), as established by the *shari'a*. They had to pay a specific head tax (*al-jizya*), and were dispensed from having to pay the legal alms (*az-zakat*). While assuring them of a certain autonomy in the sphere of religious practice, this religious statute prohibited Christians and Jews from access to certain posts in the civil and military administration. Therefore, the application of the Hatti Humayun signified the end of the monopoly of Muslims in public functions, increasing their resentments against the Christian community, accused of being the principle beneficiary of the imperial decree. In the year 1859, the weak attempts at autonomy of the Christians in the face of their Druze neighbors had exacerbated tensions. Insurrection, fanned by the Turkish power, led to a general confrontation in the Lebanese mountains. Sadly, there were several thousand deaths on both sides, and numbers of Christian refugees fled to Damascus. This was the context during the summer of 1860, in which the dramatic events unfolded which made Abd el-Kader emerge from the shadows.

In 1860, the Emir entered his fifty-third year. Thirteen years had passed since he had laid down arms and definitively renounced playing a political role. Henceforth, his time was essentially dedicated to intellectual speculation and the quest of the Inexpressible, yet for all that he had not turned away from the world. He often received guests and accepted invitations. The diversity of the milieus he frequented—

---

59 The Crimean War (1854-1855), which opposed the Russian Empire and a coalition composed of Ottomans, France, and England, would in the end preserve the territorial integrity of the Ottoman Empire.

intellectuals, religious figures, politicians, Arabs and non-Arabs—enabled him to be in touch with the events and the currents of opinion of his time, which moreover he knew through regular reading of the Arabic press.

His status as a political exile obliged him to be discreet concerning his past role, but also concerning sensitive matters of the moment. According to a report of the French agent in charge of his surveillance, he was not in favor of the Hatti Humayun: "It has not been possible yet for me to know exactly what he thinks of the Hatti Humayun of last February 18; but I suppose that, in his heart, if he does not approve of the reforms that place Christians and even Jews on the same footing of civil, political, and religious equality with the Muslims, he understands that necessity must rule and, given his religious sentiments that I am aware of, I suppose he sighs at the fate in store for Islam in the more or less near future if it were to persist in wishing to be what it was at its origin."[60] The supposed reservation of the Emir Abd el-Kader referred less to the more egalitarian principle than to its possible use by the European powers. He may also have regretted that this political decision had been taken without recourse to the religious courts which had something to say regarding a decree which affected the civil and penal statutes of the populations. The Emir probably had a presentiment of the risks that a dramatic application of the political decree would entail, given that the religious statute which currently prevailed was several centuries old.

In the spring of 1860, attacks of Druzes against Christians took place at the very gates of Damascus. The Emir, through his numerous contacts, was well informed of the situation. Well before the outbreak of the riots, he had several times warned the French consul Mr. Lamusse of the imminence of a danger. Although the consul trusted the Emir's word, he did not succeed in convincing his superiors. It even seems that he had been considered "monomaniacal and a visionary."[61] However, after the repeated warnings of the Emir, and contrary to his superiors, he purchased weapons which he turned over to the Algerians of the city. In May, the Emir had written to the Druze shaykhs of the region of Hawran and of Mount Lebanon, reminding them of his friendship towards them and counseling peace: "These agitations

60 Cited in Bruno Étienne, *Abdelkader, isthme des isthmes*, p. 467.

61 Alexandre Bellemare, *Abd-el-Kader*, p. 432.

are unworthy of a community that is distinguished for its good sense and for the wisdom of its policies. We repeat, we are affected by all that reflects back on your reputation."[62] He also took the initiative with the Muslim religious dignitaries of the principal towns of the province requesting that they preach the return to calm. Finally, from the beginning of June, he met several times with the governor Ahmad Pasha and warned the Council of Damascus of the risks of conflagration, declaring in particular that "if the city is invaded, I will go and put myself with the cavalry in the midst of the Christian quarter, and there I will fight as long as I have breath; I will die, if necessary, for the honor of Islam, whose law forbids crimes of this nature."[63]

On July 8, crosses and miters were painted on the cobblestones and small shops belonging to Muslims. In retaliation, crucifixes were desecrated and Christians injured. The next day, the governor of the city, on the urgent demand of the Russian consul, decided to punish the Muslims guilty of these acts: this was the starting point of a drama that would last almost ten days. The Emir, who at the time was traveling to Ashrafia, returned to Damascus when he heard the news. In a letter to the guild of the textile workers of Kray, he gave his version of the facts: "Monday, July 9, at two in the afternoon, the war began, motivated by the punishment meted out by the governor of this city to some Muslims who had injured Christians. These Muslims enraged, fully armed, entered into the homes of Christians; they killed, burned, and pillaged at the same time."[64] The Christian quarters of Bab Thouma and Meidan were targeted; the consulates of France, Russia, the United States, and Greece were pillaged and sacked. A witness recounts: "The head of the French consulate, the vice-consul of Russia, and the vice-consul of Greece were searched for everywhere in order to be put to death; but all three, disguised as Arabs, were able to escape and reached the home of Abd el-Kader, where the American consul had just been brought. The Emir had also sent his cavalry to seek and bring back to his home the Lazarist priests and the Sisters of Charity."[65] Only the residence of the English consul, situated in the Muslim quarter, was

---

62 Charles H. Churchill, *La Vie d'Abd el Kader*, p. 312.

63 François Lenormant, *Les Derniers Événements de Syrie* (Paris, 1860), p. 64.

64 Cited in Baptistin Poujoulat, *La Vérité sur la Syrie et l'expédition française* (Paris: Gaume frères et J. Duprey, 1861), p. 447.

65 François Lenormant, *Les Derniers Événements de Syrie*, p. 139.

spared. The French observers saw in this a proof of England's complicity with the rioters. The Emir continues his narration: "The Turkish soldiers ran to their aid, with the apparent aim of quieting the revolt, but joining them in killing, stealing, and pillaging. Some old Muslims made efforts to halt this affair, but the leaders of the Turkish soldiers did not want peace, and on the contrary pressed their soldiers against the unfortunate Christians; these soldiers were supported by hordes of pillagers of all sects. Seeing such a state of things, I ran quickly to gather under my protection all these unfortunate Christians; I took with me my Algerians, and we were able to bring back alive men, women, and children." It seemed to be the case that the Turkish soldiers were complicit with the pillagers from the beginning of the riots, and several witnesses denounced the shameful attitude of the Turkish governor of the city who, by taking refuge in the citadel and fleeing his responsibilities, had encouraged the band of assassins. However, the testimonies differ. One survivor recounted that "the governor, seeing that the troops under his command were absolutely insufficient to quell the disturbances, recruited a mass of *bachi-bozouks* (ragtag mercenaries), without paying much attention to what sort of men he was arming. This was a serious error, and it had dreadful consequences."[66] If the governor of the city was accused of evils, it seems that the situation on the ground gave him a number of extenuating circumstances in the face of his so-called "desertion." It appears that the Trukish officers had refused to obey his order to fire upon the Muslim rioters. The governor then resigned himself to opening the citadel to the rioters. The witness continued: "Nevertheless I can say this to do justice to Ahmad Pasha, that if he allowed so many evil men to perish through cowardly and stupid inaction, he nonetheless did everything in his power to save those whom he sheltered in the citadel."[67] In his *Tuhfat*, the son of the Emir specifies that the governor had not refused the arms and munitions his father had requested. The Emir noted the intervention of several Muslim dignitaries to stop the rioters. In the Meidan quarter, the crisis was checked thanks to the intervention of notable Muslims.[68]

66 Richard Edwards, *La Syrie (1860-1862)* (Paris: Amyot-Librairie-Éditeur, 1862), p. 175.

67 Ibid., p. 174.

68 A witness recounts: "Some city notables tried to appease the people, but it was no use. It is to one of them that I owe my life. He led me to his home, but since his home was being attacked, he had to shelter me at the citadel" (Ibid., p. 176).

Some offered the protection and shelter of their homes; another, Salih Rzorbatsy-Mahaini-Zadé, was distinguished for defying the rioters; and a Druze shaykh from Hawran, Assad-Amer, sent a troop of armed cavalry to lend a strong hand to the Emir.[69] If on July 9, according to several witnesses, the rioters were composed exclusively of Muslims, the next day they were joined by groups of Druzes who had rushed in from the surroundings of Damascus, and also by members of other communities, notably the Bedouins and the Metwalis of the Bekaa as well as members of the Jewish community. Although everything led one to believe that the events amounted to a generalized attack against the Christians, accused of collusion with the European powers,[70] the situation in reality was more complex, and in any case was far from being a battle of "the crescent against the cross" as presented by the manichean accounts of most European newspapers. A witness would say that "the mass of the Muslim population of Damascus took no active part in the massacre."[71] Another survivor wrote, "I must render justice to a large part of the Turkish population: it came spontaneously to the aid of the Christians."[72]

The cowardice of the Turkish authorities of the city and the entry of the Druzes into the ranks of the rioters precipitated the massacres. "Wednesday, on the pretext that two Muslims had been found dead, which was not true, the war began. Although Damascus has a governor, yet it is as though it has none," recounted Abd el-Kader, who however succeeded in obtaining arms from him for his men. Surrounded by his companions in exile, he would henceforth play a key part in what was transformed into a civil war.

His son al-Hashimi, who had seconded him in his action, recounts that "the Emir himself went to the Christian quarter. He gathered all his family into one house, and placed at the disposal of his wards the entire

69 Baptistin Poujoulat, *La Verité sur la Syrie*, letter 38.

70 Charles H. Churchill, an expert in Syrian communities, to which he dedicated several studies, confirmed the precarious position of the Christian communities, whose members were often accused of being "the key of the French." The Turks viewed them as being ever ready to welcome and aid a descent of French invaders, to resupply them, and to introduce them by one way or another into the secret of the possibilities and resources of the country" (*La Vie d'Abd el Kader*, p. 309).

71 Cited in Bruno Étienne, *Abdelkader, isthme des isthmes*, p. 295.

72 Cited in Richard Edwards, *La Syrie*, p. 179.

quarter he inhabited, and at the same time taking charge of their subsistence. He spent his days and nights at the threshold of his door on a carpet. His eldest children, Muhammad, Muhyi ad-Din, and Hashim, by his command put at the head of the Algerians, went seeking Christians and gave shelter to their wives, children and belongings"[73]—an action in all respects like that of his own father, Sidi Muhyi ad-Din, performed previously when he offered shelter to the oppressed of the province of Oran. When the rioters demanded that the Emir give them the "Christians," the son of the *zawiya*, replied: "The Christians you shall not have, they are my guests";[74] thus "his home became the most secure of shelters."[75] Yet the Emir was not content with staying home to watch over those who had found refuge there. "He patrolled the burning streets. His men went from house to house, entering and crying out: "Christians! Come out! Do not fear us, we are the men of Abd el-Kader who have come here to save you! Come out, come out!"[76] More than once, he risked his life and that of his family and companions for what he deemed to be a "sacred duty."[77] A French physician, who had to abandon the Greek embassy where he had taken refuge when the Turkish soldiers ceased protecting it, recounts: "After the desertion of those traitors, we were in consternation, all of us quite convinced that our last hour had arrived. . . . In that expectation of death, in those indescribable moments of anguish, heaven, however, sent us a savior! Abd el-Kader appeared, surrounded by his Algerians, around forty of them. He was on horseback and without arms: his handsome figure calm and imposing made a strange contrast with the noise and disorder that reigned everywhere."[78] During the ten days or so that the riots lasted, the Emir did not slacken his vigilance. The number of refugees grew, and he led them to the Turkish fortress, escorted by Algerian detachments. "For my part," he wrote, "I sigh over this unfortunate affair that has fallen on the poor Christians; the sites of their homes are

---

73 Marie d'Aire, *Abd-el-Kader*, p. 245.

74 Alexandre Bellemare, *Abd-el-Kader*, p. 445.

75 François Lenormant, *Les Derniers* Événements *de Syrie*, p. 141.

76 Charles H. Churchill, *La Vie d'Abd el Kader*, p. 313.

77 The Emir, cited in the September 23, 1860 edition of the newspaper *La Patrie* of (in S. Aouli, R. Redjala, and P. Zoummeroff, *Abd el-Kader*, p. 463).

78 Testimony which appeared in the August 2, 1869 edition of the newspaper *Le Siècle*.

unrecognizable, they are all in ashes; the number of their dead is not known, but is estimated to be more than 3,000 victims.[79] At least, all the Europeans and Christians that I could gather are sheltered at my home; I have offered all that they need and I pray to God to save these poor Christians from the hands of these maniacs."

Around July 18, the riots diminished in intensity, and order was progressively reestablished. Starting from that moment the dispatches multiplied in the articles of the principal French newspapers, dithyrambic articles making Abd el-Kader the "hero of those sinister days."[80] The progressive arrival of testimonies from consular agents, interpreters, ecclesiastics, religious, or simple travelers, fed this press campaign in honor of the Algerian exile.

However, the Syrian province would long harbor the legacy of the drama. The Christian families who lost everything during the violence resigned themselves to exile, out of fear of another outbreak. Several weeks after the events, a witness wrote that "there is no security in Damascus, and without the presence of Abd el-Kader and his Algerians the few Christians who remain there, still insulted by the Muslims, would continue to be assassinated!"[81]

But the self-sacrifice of the Emir had left its mark on minds: "Without him and the Algerians, not a single Christian male would remain in Damascus." During the following weeks, the men of Abd el-Kader were once again put in charge of accompanying groups of Damascene Christians who had decided to leave the city: "In Beirut, a caravan of Christian emigrants from Damascus is anxiously awaited; it is escorted only by some of Abd el-Kader's Algerians. It is feared that the Druzes, whose rage has been aroused since the arrival of French soldiers in Syria, could attack this caravan, comprised mostly of women and children, and that some appalling massacre might be renewed."[82] The English biographer of the Emir, with his customary lyricism, wrote that

---

79 One witness is more circumspect: "I cannot specify the number of dead. I heard around me that it was from two to three thousand victims. I imagine that is an exaggeration. Ten bodies in the same place look like fifty in the eyes of a horrified man. For my part, I estimate and hope that the number of victims has not exceeded a thousand" (cited in Richard Edwards, *La Syrie*, p. 177). European observers who spoke to the press, estimated the number between 8,000 and 10,000 dead.

80 François Lenormant, *Les Derniers* Événements *de Syrie*, p. 141.

81 Baptistin Poujoulat, *La Verité sur la Syrie*, letter 36.

82 Ibid., letter 4.

"a descendent of the Prophet had sheltered and protected the Bride of Christ."[83] And Bellemare writes: "The passing of this descendent of the Prophet through the bloody streets of Damascus, surrounded by priests, religious, children, whom he had just snatched from death, must surely have been a great and magnificent spectacle."[84] This general gratitude once again placed Abd el-Kader at the head of the international political scene.[85]

At the beginning of August 1860, the *Journal officiel* published the decree announcing the elevation of the Emir to the "dignity of the Grand Cross of the Imperial Order of the Legion of Honor." The tribute was followed by other countries: "Letters, gifts, decorations, came to him from all sides . . . from Russia, the Grand Cross of the White Eagle, from Greece, the Grand Cross of the Savior, from Turkey, the Medjidie of the First Class. England sent him a double-barreled shotgun magnificently inlaid with gold, from America, a pair of pistols also gold-inlaid, the Order of French Masons in France sent him a magnificent star."[86] Abd el-Kader also received the Order of Pius IX, thus becoming, it seems, the sole Muslim distinguished by the Supreme Pontiff.[87]

"Providence," "Savior," "Good Samaritan," are so many qualifications that fed the new hagiography of Abd el-Kader, which recall the comparisons made during the French conquest. "Yes, Abd el-Kader has breathed the harsh and hot wind of the Sinai; the rays that enveloped Christ have brushed his forehead,"[88] one can read in an article of 1861. These tributes contrast with the anti-Muslim sentiments that

---

83 Charles H. Churchill, *La Vie d'Abd el Kader*, p. 316.

84 Alexandre Bellemare, *Abd-el-Kader*, p. 442.

85 Bruno Étienne cites the testimony of a discordant voice in the chorus of praise, that of a voyager who arrived there five months after the events and who tempered the general enthusiasm by expressing reservations regarding the spontaneity of the Emir's action: "Abd el-Kader remained below his task, he did not fulfill all the hopes that one had the right to place in him at the hour of peril. He did what was good passively and just enough so as not to incur blame, but not enough, given his lofty position and the moral influence which he exercised on the population of Damascus" (*Abdelkader, isthme des isthmes*, p. 293).

86 Charles H. Churchill, *La Vie d'Abd el Kader*, p. 317.

87 Our researches in the Vatican archives trying to find a possible letter of the Pope to the Emir have remained unfruitful until this day.

88 Ernest Laharanne, "La nouvelle question d'Orient," 1861, cited in Charles H. Churchill, *La Vie d'Abd el Kader*, p. 347.

developed in certain French Catholic circles in which the recent events were interpreted as a resurgence of the Crusades. *L'Ami de la Religion* ["The Friend of Religion"] in an impassioned style wrote: "Well then, crusade against crusade! flag against flag! To the crusade of fanaticism and barbarity we oppose the crusade of Christianity and civilization: to the green flag we oppose the cross."[89] Whenever the declaration was accompanied by a tribute to the Emir, it was because the eminent representative of the derided religion was supposedly penetrated with Christian ideas. Already in 1848, regarding the magnanimity of the Emir, a French author wrote: "Without being aware of it and in spite of himself, Abd-el-Kader daily acquires some of the customs of his enemies. . . : generosity, humanity, clemency, fidelity, these virtues, almost unknown among the Arabs and forbidden by the Koran with regard to Christians."[90] Others, more realistic, saw in the recent events the expression of Abd el-Kader's friendship with "Christian France."[91] The ultramontane publicist, Baptistin Poujoulat, who met him shortly after the summer of 1860, wrote straightforwardly: "Abd el-Kader has the nature of the elect. The divine rays of the Gospel would magnificently enlighten him. What joy for the Christian world if it were to learn one day that Abd el-Kader had entered into religious truth!"[92] This wish to see the Emir join the Christian community seems to have been quite widespread among the contemporary Catholic chroniclers. During the same time there were published translations of letters exchanged between the Emir Abd el-Kader and Cardinals Monsignor Morlot and Monsignor Donnet, who knew him during his captivity. In this extract of the tribute he pays to the Emir, the Archbishop of Bordeaux does not conceal his wish to see him converted: "Your name is on all tongues; there are no Christian lips who do not ask God to cause you to enter into the Catholic family, of which you are already one its bravest soldiers."[93]

---

89 *L'Ami de la Religion*, p. 305.

90 In A. de Lacroix, *Histoire privée et politique d'Abd el-Kader* (Paris: Librairie littéraire et politique, 1845, 1848).

91 *La Patrie* of September 23, 1860, in S. Aouli, R. Redjala, and P. Zoummeroff, *Abd el-Kader*, p. 463.

92 Baptistin Poujoulat, *La Verité sur la Syrie*, letter 38.

93 "Discours de son éminence le cardinal Donnet, archevêque de Bordeaux, sur Abd-el-Kader et les massacres de Syrie," *Revue d'Aquitaine, journal historique*, n° 5, vol. 5,

Portrait of the Emir Abd el-Kader, age 29, based on a sketch done by
Léon Roches in 1836

Engraving of Abd el-Kader in
combat during the 1840s

Engraving of Abd el-Kader depicted as
Saladin, from the 1840s

EL-HADJI-ABD-EL-KADER.

Abd el-Kader on horseback, by Henri Félix Emmanuel Philippoteaux, 1846

Portrait of Louis Napoleon announcing the liberation of Abd el-Kader
on October 16, 1852, by Ange Tissier, 1861

Portrait of Abd el-Kader with prayer beads in the Château d'Amboise after his
liberation, by Ange Tissier, 1853

Photo of Abd el-Kader at his home in Damascus, attributed to
Gustave Le Gray, c. 1860

Engraving of Abd el-Kader saving the Christians of Damascus, 1861

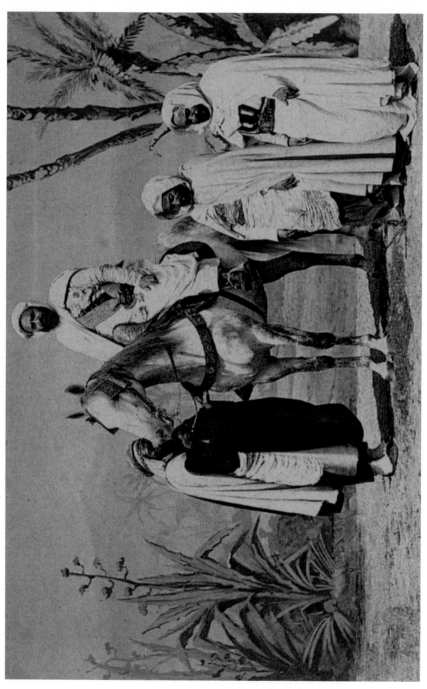

Abd el-Kader with his most faithful companions,
photo by Louis-Jean Delton, 1865

The Château d'Amboise around the end of the 19th century

Photo of Abd el-Kader (center) with Ismail Pasha, the Khedive of Egypt, and Ferdinand de Lesseps at the inauguration of the Suez Canal, Port Said, Egypt, 1869. This is the last known photo of Abd el-Kader.

Portrait of Abd el-Kader in Istanbul, by Stanislaw Chlebowski, 1866

Full length portrait of Abd el-Kader, Simon Agopian, 1906

Abd el-Kader, photo by Étienne Carjat, 1865

Just as he captivated the Christian milieus, Abd el-Kader aroused the interest of numerous intellectual fraternities in France, who praised him for rallying to the cause of civilization. In September 1860, he was contacted for the first time by a Masonic lodge affiliated to the Grand Orient of France. The Saint Simonians,[94] particularly active under the Second Empire, made him a cornerstone of their project to connect East and West. This enthusiasm was not without ulterior motives: the recovery of Abd el-Kader's prestige, his being used politically in the context of a battle of influence between the European powers within a dissolving Ottoman Empire, also explain these advances.

If the Emir did not conceal his sadness faced with the snubs to the governments of *Dar al-Islam* and the decadence that existed at the time in the Muslim societies, he did not, however, blame Islam for it. How would that have been possible on the part of a man who, precisely, had made the Muhammadan Way his reason for being in the world and of Muhammad his model of life? And yet this was the thesis which circulated in the European press. The origin of this rumor was a letter attributed to the "hero," published in its Arabic language journal, *Birgis Baris*, "The Eagle of Paris," financed by France. Its content has eschatological accentuations which in fact recall the style of the Emir. However, there is a passage that can only with difficulty be attributed to him: "I weep, O my God! at the destruction of Islam."[95] Was this a

1861, p. 141.

94 Translator's note: Saint-Simonianism was a French political and social movement of the first half of the nineteenth century, inspired by the ideas of Claude Henri de Rouvroy, Count of Saint-Simon (1760-1825). Saint-Simon envisaged a society transformed and regenerated by industrialization and scientific discovery, thereby becoming "productive"; hence the performance of "useful work" would be the basis of his idea of "equality," thus leaving behind what he deemed to be outmoded medieval theocratic notions of temporal and spiritual power. In his essay, *De la réorganisation de la société européenne* ("On the reorganization of European society"), he foresees a European unity sharing the same laws and institutions. After his death, his followers divided into two groups: a "charismatic" faction, led by Barthélemy Prosper Enfantin, in search of Messianic revelations in the Middle East. Their community at Ménilmontant, on the outskirts of Paris, was eventually banned by the authorities. The other and "practical" group comprised members involved in the French economy and founded a number of important concerns, such as the Crédit Mobilier bank, and the Suez Canal, the latter a project which Enfantin had unsuccessfully first promoted in 1833, but was successfully undertaken by Ferdinand de Lesseps.

95 Philippe d'Estailleur-Chanteraine, *Abd el-Kader, l'Europe et l'Islam au xix* siecle* (Paris: J.-B. Janin, 1947), p. 270.

clumsy translation of the Arabic or a deliberate manipulation? Be that as it may, the alleged religious defeatism of Abd el-Kader, who supposedly felt "out of his element in Mahometism,"[96] would be rather widely taken up in the French press. In his first report, the agent Georges Bullad wrote that he had often heard him declare: "The religion of Islam is dying for lack of Muslims, true Muslims." Yet the Emir said nothing different to the Imam Shamil or to Monsignor Pavy; thus, to the latter he wrote: "But those who belong to the religion of Muhammad have gone astray. That is why God has let them go astray. The reward has been of the same nature as the fault."[97] In a letter to Napoleon III, thanking him for having received the Legion of Honor, he declared in a preremptory manner: "Those who have committed blameworthy acts are in Islam in name only and do not know how to discern virtue from crime."[98]

At the end of the crisis, and in spite of his fame, Abd el-Kader was left in an uncomfortable situation. He was not unaware that a war in Greater Syria (sham*) between Europeans and Muslims would oblige him to choose one of the two camps, and that neither choice would be viable! The worsening of the situation would entail a massive expedition of a European army to Syria, which would provoke a call to a *jihad* and would place the Emir Abd el-Kader in an untenable position. Georges Bullad understood this perfectly: "One fact which I even had occasion to witness, concerning which there is no doubt whatever, is that Abd el-Kader dreaded receiving the order to return to France, should war break out."[99] The Emir therefore greatly feared an aggravation of the situation whose foreseeable end would be the transformation of the ancient Ottoman province into a European colony: in that case, the Levant would be exposed to the same peril as the ancient regency of Algeria. He was aware that the massacre of innocent Christians could not but arouse the imperialist dreams of the European countries. It was an argument that he had already used when facing the

---

96 See the introduction by J. Noulens to the discourse of the Archbishop of Bordeaux in "Discours de son éminence le cardinal Donnet," p. 141.

97 Letter dated from the month of *Muharram* 1279—July 1862—the original of which is in the Historical Archives of the Archbishop of Algiers.

98 Letter in manuscript addressed to Napoleon III, Paris, ministère de Affaires étrangères, Correspondance politique des consuls, Turquie, Damas, vol. 6, fol. 70.

99 Cited in S. Aouli, R. Redjala, and P. Zoummeroff, *Abd el-Kader*, p. 474.

rioters: "I warn you that France will avenge the Christian blood that you have unjustly and cowardly spilled. France will come here with soldiers; she will strike you, she will occupy Syria, and the least result of your crazy behavior will be to see a Christian bishop in your grand mosque instead of a Muslim leader."[100] But to those who exhorted him rejoin their ranks against the Christians, as he had done in the past, the Emir retorted: "If I have killed Christians . . . it was in accordance with our law, it was a question of Christians who had declared war on me, and had taken arms against our faith."[101] Nothing authorized taking arms against innocent people, and those who did so were "assassins," not "soldiers": "Is this a day of battle, for you to have the right to kill men? To what depths have you fallen? Has God not said: 'He who slayeth a man that hath neither committed murder nor hath caused disturbances in the land shall be deemed as one who hath murdered all mankind'?"[102] By this saying drawn from the Koran, the Emir expressed his faith in a universal ethic. The sacredness of life puts the question of religious affiliation in second place: the divine law becomes a privileged means of preserving the life and dignity of individuals above and beyond their religious affiliation or ethnicity. He broadens brotherhood to include all humanity, the worship rendered to God is then conflated with service to humanity. To Monsignor Pavy, then bishop of Algiers, who had sent heartfelt thanks for his action, he wrote: "The good we did towards Christians we had to do out of fidelity to the Muslim faith and to respect the rights of humanity. For all creatures belong to God's family, and the most beloved of God are those who are the most useful to His family."[103] The "rights of humanity" are aligned with the religious law. The Emir notably made use of the same terms in other letters, and particularly in the one addressed to the hero of the Caucasian Indepen-

---

100 Baptistin Poujoulat, *La Verité sur la Syrie*, pp. 38-46.

101 Charles H. Churchill, *La Vie d'Abd el Kader*, p. 313.

102 Alexandre Bellemare, *Abd el-Kader*, p. 444. The verse of the Koran (5:32) which is cited by memory by the biographer of the Emir is the following: "For that cause we decreed for the Children of Israel that whosoever killeth a human being for other than manslaughter or corruption in the earth, it shall be as if he had killed all mankind, and whoso saveth the life of one, it shall be as if he had saved the life of all mankind."

103 The Arabic text specifies *al-huquq al-insaniyya*, a rarely employed notion during this time and which explicitly refers to the modern notion of the "rights of man." Letter dated the month of *Muharram* 1279 (July 1862). The original is in the Historical Archives of the Archbishop of Algiers.

dence, the Imam Shamil. Shamil emphasizes the full conformity of the Emir's action with the Muhammadan model: "In truth, you have put into practice the teaching of the great Apostle sent by God Most High, as evidence of the compassion for His humble creatures, and you have erected a barrier against those who would reject his great example."[104]

According to the words of the Emir, the Imam Shamil (1799-1871), born in Daghestan, in the Caucasus, "followed the same path" as the Emir himself. Member of a Sufi *tariqa*, he was chosen in the mid-1830s to lead a *jihad* against the armies of the Czar. After a war of almost twenty-five years, he surrendered in September 1859. He was then exiled to the Caucasus in the region of Moscow, where he was held in captivity. It was during this time that he wrote to the Emir: his letter is at once a tribute to the Algerian exile for his gesture in favor of the Christians of Damascus and, it seems, a means of drawing attention to his situation as a captive. During his journey to France in 1865, the Emir brought up the situation of the Chechen captive to Napoleon III and expressed the wish to go to Saint Petersburg to plead his cause. His request was refused. In 1869, the Imam Shamil finally received authorization to go to Mecca. It was on the way to the Hijaz, in Egypt, that the two men met for the first, and it would appear, only time. The Imam Shamil died in the month of February, 1871, in Medina. The closeness of the two figures was such that one Russian historian wrote that "Shamil was the Abd el-Kader of the Caucasian independence."[105]

During that year of 1860, several events stood out in the French annals: the victory in Italy,[106] the attachment of Savoy and of the county of Nice to France, the voyage of the imperial family to Algeria, and lastly the riots of Damascus. There was no need to arouse patriotic sen-

---

104 On Imam Shamil, see M. Canard, "Shamil," *Annales de l'Institut d'études orientales*, vol. 14, 1956, p. 318.

105 Ibid.

106 General Lomoricière, the same one who had signed the surrender treaty with the Emir Abd el-Kader in 1847, and who had refused to adhere to it as Minister of War, underwent a terrible trial in 1860. Leading the Papal Zouaves, he was severely defeated at Rome. To the humiliation of the defeat, he had to suffer the ridicule of the French press, which called him a traitor to his country just when the Emir was being celebrated as a French patriot! [Translator's note: The Papal or Pontifical Zouaves, originally formed of Algerians, were light-infantry corps in the French army, recruited largely from French soldiers, but also Irish. At Rome in 1860 and under General Lamoricière, a former commander in Algeria, they unsuccessfully defended the temporal sovereignty of the Pope against the Italian Reunification or *Risorgimento*.]

timents: the need for a military intervention in Syria, towards which public opinion was favorable, quickly became a matter of national honor. After intense negotiations, the European countries, in consultation with Turkey, decided to send a military and diplomatic mission to the region. The arrest and execution of the governor of Damascus and his principal officers, the imprisonment of hundreds of rioters, and the gestures in favor of the victims apparently were not enough to reassure the Syrian population and the European chanceries. Several months after the riots, the presence of Abd el-Kader in Damascus continued to be a guarantee of security for the Christians. The pursuit of a solution that would both reassure the Christians and manage Muslim sensibilities had led certain observers to envisage that the Emir might play a political role in Syria. The idea of employing him to serve the interests of France goes back to the beginning of his settling in Damascus. A report of Georges Bullad, dating from 1857, already raises the question: "Perhaps the day will come when it will be very advantageous for France to have, in the midst of Syria, a man such as Abd el-Kader who, either as instrument or as ally, can bring a certain influence to bear on the destiny of the Ottoman Empire."[107] The Emir's popularity, which had spread to all the Christian communities of the Levant, had not in fact damaged "at all his prestige among the Muslims."[108] A French observer wrote: "Perhaps only our former enemy would be able to gather under his authority all the Arab tribes of Syria and at the same time govern Muslims and Christians. For the Muslims, he is one of the glories and one of the most valiant champions of Islam in our century; for the Christians, his noble conduct in Damascus is a gauge of what his government would be."[109] A pamphlet which appeared at the end of the year 1869 justified this possibility, affirming that "among the Arabs, where his fame has spread, Abd el-Kader . . . will have all the elements capable of satisfying his ambition, his generosity and his gallantry, and . . . in the affairs of Syria, he has taught Europe the true interpretation of the maxims of the Koran and how a true, sincere believer should apply them."[110] He who had once been dreaded in certain circles of power

---

107 Cited in S. Aouli, R. Redjala, and P. Zoummeroff, *Abd el-Kader*, p. 466.

108 F. Charles-Roux, "Abdelkader et Ferdinand de Lesseps," *Revue de la Méditerranée*, n⁰ˢ 70, 71, and 72, 1955-1956, p. 9.

109 François Lenormant, *Les Derniers* Événements *de Syrie*, p. 161.

110 The pamphlet, entitled *Abd el Kader, empereur d'Arabie*, was published in 1860. Cited in Paul Azan, *L'Émir Abd el Kader*, p. 274.

in Paris was henceforth wooed for the influence he retained among his coreligionists! The prohibition of traveling outside of Syria that had been given him since his arrival in Damascus was withdrawn. Baptistin Poujoulat sounded out the Emir on the possibility that he might take on the function of "governor of Syria," as certain French and English newspapers had suggested.[111] The Emir was not unaware of these rumors which, according to him, explained the "vexations of Turkey" regarding him. Indeed, after the end of the riots, Fu'ad Pasha, the emissary of the government of the Ottoman Empire, in order to reestablish authority and to judge those responsible, required the Algerians of the city to give up their weapons. This decision aggravated the relation between the emissary of the Sultan, who enjoyed the support of the English, and the Emir Abd el-Kader, who remained France's trump card in the region. The Emir replied without any possible equivocation: "My political career is finished. I no longer desire anything else, I have no ambition for the honors and the glory of this world. Henceforth, I wish to live in prayer to God Most High."[112] He whom France henceforth considered its "most faithful and devoted friend"[113] would systematically refuse the repeated proposals to put himself at the head of a national Arab entity placed under the tutelage of the European countries. In 1865, during a visit to Paris, he received the Legion of Honor, awarded five years previously. His friends and the Arabophile milieu then mounted a press campaign in his favor, during which Émile de Girardin, who had supported him during his captivity, and the Saint Simonians stood out. These last, represented by Ismaïl Urbain, played a not negligible role in the Algerian and Levantine policies of Napoleon III. It seems that the Emir was proposed several times as the commander

111 In 1861, the French publicist Ernest Laharanne concluded in "La nouvelle question d'Orient": "Abd el-Kader—Europe owes it to him—will be the Emperor of Arabia" (cited in Charles H. Churchill, *La Vie d'Abd el-Kader*, p. 347). Concerning this question see Charles. R. Ageron, "Abd el-Kader, souverain de un royaume arabe d'Orient," *Revue de l'Occident musulman et de la Méditerranée*, numéro spécial, 1970, pp. 15-30.

112 Baptistin Poujoulat, *La Verité sur la Syrie*, letter 39.

113 Certain verified tributes were then composed to signify the adoption of the Emir Abd el-Kader by the French nation. An example among others: "Brave Emir, our friend, our brother, thou whom history will inscribe among the benefactors, under other skies receivest light, but thy great heart is that of a Frenchman. Ah, henceforth is France thy country" (Alexis Dalès, *Notice biographique sur l'émir Abd el-Kader, sauveur de 13000 chrétiens en Syrie. Sa prochaine arrivée à Paris* (Paris: chez Roger éditeur, 1865).

of an "Arab kingdom" in Syria. But this idea had its detractors not only in London and Constantinople, but also in France, where the powerful "colonist" milieu, gathered around the newspaper *L'Opinion nationale*, looked with a jaundiced eye at the return to the political scene of the former enemy, who in their eyes remained a threat against the interests of the colonization. In any case, Abd el-Kader would not deviate from the course that he had taken in his life since his surrender in December 1847: from then on he had considered himself to be dead to temporal power and had dedicated himself to the Way of the "poor in God."

His inward quest, which had become permanent, henceforth permeated all aspects of his existence. Thus, the Sufi Abd el-Kader lived under the influence of intense spiritual phenomena; the experiences of unveiling and the inspirations, to which we shall return later, had direct consequences on his thought and his actions. To a journalist who had asked what were the reasons that caused him to intervene in the events of the summer of 1860, he replied: "God ordered me to."[114] In a letter to Alexandre Bellemare, he evokes this superior and inspiring influence: "I have received your letter in which you congratulate me for what I did in Damascus in favor of the Christians. You are mistaken in congratulating me: I do not deserve it, for in the midst of these events I was merely an instrument. Send your praises to Him who directed me, to your Sultan and mine. When I advanced through the streets of Damascus, I was seeing Him walking before me. He would tell me: 'do this,' and I did it; 'go this way,' and I went, 'save this man,' and I saved him. Thus, I did naught but obey, and obedience does not justify the praises you bestow upon me; they all belong to Him who commanded."[115] At the center of his spiritual meditations, Abd el-Kader places the theme of the "Sole Agent," regarding which he writes: "The masters of contemplation contemplate God manifesting Himself as Agent, Shaper, and Creator in all the atoms of the universe" (*Mawqif* 275). He was clearly already one of these "masters of contemplation," and the Sultan to whom he refers in his letter to Bellemare is none other than God Himself.

114 Abd el-Kader, cited in the September 23, 1860 edition of the newspaper *La Patrie*, in S. Aouli, R. Redjala, and P. Zoummeroff, *Abd el-Kader*, p. 463.

115 Alexandre Bellemare, *Abd el-Kader*, p. 450.

CHAPTER 6

A Man of His Time

I have not made the events:
it is the events that have made me what I have been.
Abd el-Kader

Tell him who considers his contemporaries as nothing
and gives preeminence to the ancients, that the ancient was modern
in his time and this modern will one day become ancient.
Reminder to the Intelligent, Warning to the Indifferent

A Man of *Ijtihad**

Junayd, the eminent Sufi master of the tenth century, upon whom the
Emir Abd el-Kader had meditated, counseled one of his companions
in the Way to learn how to "know his contemporaries and understand
those of his time and of his age."[1] In the same letter he wrote: "I note
that the entire concern of most creatures is for this lower world, and
that they seek the fragile goods that are within their immediate reach.
. . . The seeking of perishable realities has blinded minds and hearts,
occupied with the sole desire for the most vain of these. . . . Men are
totally fascinated by the present life, and the things of the future life
have become inaccessible to their clouded mind."[2] The Iraqi master,
who moreover was extremely lucid regarding the state of decadence of
his society, in this way recalled that it is necessary to decipher a divine
Wisdom (*hikma*) behind the often deceptive appearances. To discover
it, the aspirant must be integrated in the society and share the preoccupations of his contemporaries. This was the standpoint of the Emir
Abd el-Kader. As a man of *jihad*, he was also a man of *ijtihad*, of the
effort of reflection and adaptation in the face of the challenges encountered in the contingent world. In the sphere of religion, he had a rational and judicious approach towards tradition. By clarifying it through
a living reflection, nourished by the observation of the realities of his

---

1 Junayd, *Enseignement spirituel*, trans. R. Deladrière (Paris: Sindbad, 1983), p. 51.

2 Ibid.

time, he prevented it from being transformed into a collection of rigid and stale precepts. The divine Will, which is present permanently in Its creation, "creates something new each day," says the Koran (55:29), and forbids all inertia. During his exile in Turkey and then in Syria, the Emir asserted the need for the religious law to adapt to the present requirements of the community in which it was to be applied. Already during the *jihad*, and in the most eloquent way possible during his captivity and stays in France, he himself offered the example of such adaptation. Confronted with cultural and religious realities that clashed radically with those of his society, he was able to sacrifice certain cultural customs in the name of usages which he deemed superior. This suppleness and openness of mind were also that of a mind resolutely turned towards modernity, interested in the technical progress issuing from Europe, and lending his support to the leading projects of his age.

During the course of the first centuries of the Muslim expansion, the development of *ijtihad* had facilitated the diffusion and establishment of Islam in heterogeneous societies. The Muslim assimilated a culture, a language, and he set aside only those habits which manifestly failed to comply with the divine Law. Facts and customs which were not explicitly dealt with in the religious corpus, as well as the different aspects of law, were subjected to *ijtihad*. The effort of reflection and interpretation were not limited to the domains of jurisprudence, but extended to all spheres of society. Thus, Muslim civilization experienced its full expansion in the flowering of an exceptional intellectual, political, and spiritual diversity. The end of *ijtihad*, the beginning of an intellectual decadence of the Muslim world, has generally been fixed around the tenth century, and was due in great part to the effort of interpretation becoming confined to the juridical sphere alone, thereby provoking a rise in the power of the doctors of the Law. This phenomenon soon gave rise to a way of thinking that was overly homogeneous, preventing any renewal of religious interpretation, all innovation being deemed heretical (*bid'a*). Already Ibn Khaldun (fourteenth century) and Sha'rani (sixteenth century) observed that the hegemony of juridicism in all the spheres of Islamic culture had provoked a pathological hardening both of that culture and of the *shari'a* itself, leading to a kind of pharisaism. This sclerosis of Islamic culture became aggravated as time went on. During the Ottoman period, increased control of the religious sphere by the political further impeded the revivification of the religious and profane sciences called for by reformist groups. In the nineteenth century, in a general way, self-absorption and the rejection of new ideas became a norm in the juridical milieus, depriving Muslim society of all reflection on the challenges of the century.

Apparently, the Emir very early distanced himself from the old juridicism. Further affirmed during his exile in Damascus, this sensibility was already clearly expressed in *Reminder to the Intelligent, Warning to the Indifferent*, written in 1855 in Bursa, where he affirms the necessity of adapting religious prescriptions to the times and to the cultural surroundings. With the exception of the immutable principles of Islam—the affirmation of the Divine Unity and the acts of Worship—everything can be the object of a reinterpretation and adaptation: in his *Lettre aux Français*, he writes that it is possible to "judge the wisdom of a given measure of abrogation and its usefulness by taking into consideration the extent to which the religious law serves the interests of God's servants. . . . It is possible for these temporal interests to change, and this change similarly affects the law in question. . . . The religious laws dictated by the prophets vary in accordance with the juridical considerations which inspired them, for men's interests change during the course of centuries, so that every judgment is just only in relation to the interests of the people of the age in which it was promulgated, that is to say, taking into account the true needs of man, the sole object of the prophetic message."[3] Nourished by the experience of temporal and religious power, the thought of Abd el-Kader takes up the main themes and the arguments of the reformers of religious thought. On the one hand, the *shari'a* was established by the Koran and the *Sunna* of the Prophet, and on the other by the effort of reflection and interpretation. *Ijtihad* is precisely the tool serving to harmonize the traditional religious precepts with the needs of the time, even abrogating those which the evolution of society had rendered obsolete. In its essence, the objective of the divine Law is not to subjugate man, but to serve him by progressively leading him towards a full expansion of his natural and spiritual faculties. *Reminder to the Intelligent, Warning to the Indifferent*, as we have already emphasized, is a tribute to discursive reason. Abd el-Kader places the effort of reflection and of the critical mind at the heart of the revivification of religious thought, and condemns "the unthinking adoption of established opinions." Those who are content with blind imitation cannot arrive at the truth ow-

---

3 *Lettre aux Français*, p. 114.

ing to "beliefs anchored in their souls, and upon which their minds are fixated. . . . Those who call people to imitation pure and simple by excluding the participation of the mind are ignorant."[4] Implicitly, the Emir has in view the traditionalist ulemas who exhort people to reject all that is able to call into question a Law conceived as intangible. "The harm that can be dealt to laws of religious origin is, alas, further provoked by those who wish to assure their triumph by means which are appropriate only for those whom they are combating."[5] Thus, Abd el-Kader clearly positions himself as a *mujtahid*, an adept of *ijtihad*. But if religion needs reason in order not to desiccate, at same time he warns the French, to whom the text is directed, that reason without the "lights of divine aid" also leads to an impasse. As a proponent of the *via media*,[6] he calls for a balanced attitude: "Beware of becoming party to one or the other of these two groups, but take what is good from the one and from the other."[7]

A Peaceful Immersion

Since the mid 1830s, when the first negotiations with France took place, the young Commander of the Faithful had probably foreseen that his fight went beyond the strict framework of a military confrontation. What he had first deemed a threat, came to resemble during the following years a religious and cultural challenge, decisive for the future of his country and, in a more general way, for *Dar al-Islam*. His eschatological interpretation of the "Christian" conquest, according to some of his letters, precipitated his surrender. At the request of Émile Ollivier, the commisioner-general of Bouches-du-Rhône, the Emir wrote a letter to the provisional government. His comments are in the spirit of those recounted by the English biographer: "I have defended my religion and my country as much as I could. . . . When I was defeated, when it was no longer possible for me to doubt that God did not wish to give me His support against you, I decided to retire from the world."[8]

4 Ibid.

5 Ibid.

6 In his balanced position, the Emir Abd el-Kader belongs to those referred to in the following verse: "Thus We have appointed you a middle nation" (Koran 2:143).

7 *Lettre aux Français*, p. 96.

8 Cited in Alexandre Bellemare, *Abd el-Kader*, p. 356.

To his last companions in arms, he recalled that there is a divine Wisdom in the victory of their adversary.[9] There is no need to see in this any fatalism; his commitment in battle excludes this interpretation. His words attest rather to his trust (*tawakkul*) in a superior will which also guided him during his constrained stay in France. It is probable that it was in captivity, on non-Muslim ground, that Abd el-Kader began a deep reflection on his tradition. His view of the religion was in any case clearly transformed. His writings are rather discreet on this matter, but the testimonies and the chronicles of the time are eloquent.

In January 1848, while he was in captivity at Toulon, Abd el-Kader wrote to the provisional government: "You are educated men, and you must understand that I cannot live in a country where everything differs from ours: language, customs, food, clothing."[10] Four years later, in a letter to the mayor of Amboise, Mr. Trouvé, he expresses his desire to participate in the voting that would reestablish the imperial regime: "Our children have seen the light of day in France; your daughters have breast fed them;[11] our companions have died in your country and lie amongst you, and your Sultan, the just among the just, has numbered me among his children, among his soldiers, by giving me a sword with his own hands."[12] What has taken place between these two dates? The first letter is that of an injured man, the victim of a betrayal, the second is signed by a man who has had his freedom restored, who expresses his gratitude towards the president of the Second Republic on the verge of being crowned Emperor of the French. But that was not the sole reason for the change. From the year 1848 until his departure for the East in 1852, from the depths of his successive prisons, the Emir would learn to know and accurately assess the real worth of his former adversaries.

The seclusion of the "illustrious captive" had not only been a time of spiritual retreat but also one of observation and reflection on the French. This may seem strange on the part of a man most often con-

---

9 Charles H. Churchill, *La Vie d'Abd el Kader*, p. 271.

10 Letter addressed to the provisional government, dated 9 *rabi' al-awwal* 1264 (March 1848), cited in Alexandre Bellemare, *Abd el-Kader*, p. 357.

11 Certain children who suffered from rickets and who risked succumbing to malnutrition were suckled by wet nurses from Amboise.

12 Published in *Le Moniteur universal*, December 2, 1852, cited in Alexandre Bellemare, *Abd el-Kader*, pp. 404-405.

fined to his quarters in a castle with his family; in fact it was rather this Algerian microsociety, kept under such close observation, that offered an excellent opportunity to study the military authority with time on its hands.[13] Nonetheless it was indeed in these unusual circumstances that the Emir familiarized himself with the mentality and customs of his "hosts." Aside from officers and soldiers whom he frequented daily, he received very diverse visitors, furnishing him with a faithful cross-section of the French population: ecclesiastics, tradesmen and workers, politicians and journalists, artists and teachers, or again, a succession of ordinary citizens of Toulon, Pau, and Amboise.

The presence of the Algerian prisoner in France had coincided with one of the most turbulent chapters in the history of the country. His captivity passed through five governments and three successive regimes: first under the monarchy of July and the Guizot government, then under the Second Republic and the Presidency of Louis Napoleon Bonaparte, and finally under the Second Empire. The Emir's jailer, the cultivated and very discreet artillery officer Estève Boissonet, informed him of the main events. As Alexandre Bellemare relates: "Daily spending several hours with him, Boissonet would explain our [French] customs, our habits, the marvels of the sciences and industry, our history, the main events of the first revolution, the history of Napoleon I in particular. . . . In addition to the accounts of these events there would often be scientific, literary, philosophical, or religious discussions."[14] Thanks to the accounts in the French press and to the news brought by visitors regarding the discussions in the two Houses of Parliament, the Emir closely followed the political debates and readily gave his opinion to those who asked him. The days of February 1848, which ended with the abdication of Louis-Philippe, inspired a bitter comment from him: "Behold a Sultan who is proclaimed powerful, who had made alliances with many other sovereigns, who has a numerous family . . . yet three days sufficed to overthrow him! And you do not wish me to

---

13 At Amboise, the French military authorities had tried to make the Algerian captives more "aware" of French customs, requesting for this purpose that an institution be placed in Algeria, directed by Luce Alix. The experiment lasted less than one year, and did not seem to have produced unanimity among the Algerian prisoners. See J. L. Sureau and Alexis Feulvarc'h, "Abd el-Kader au château d'Amboise," in "Mémoires et images d'Abd el-Kader," Société des amis du château de Pau, numéro spécial, Pau, 2007, p. 94.

14 Alexandre Bellemare, Abd el-Kader, pp. 377-378.

be convinced that there is no strength or truth than that of God!"[15] The constitution of the provisional government evoked a radical criticism: "There is only one God for the entire world. Is that not the proof that on this earth as well there should be only one master for each people, one sole impetus?" And the Republic, which deprives him of his liberty, attracts a sarcasm: "Liberty, Equality, Fraternity, these are mere words as far as the government is concerned."[16]

Nonetheless, thanks to this immersion in French society, Abd el-Kader's perception of the French in particular and of Europeans in general evolved. In this environment which in every sphere was a break with what he had known before, he was also led to consider his own tradition in a new light. Uncertainty, especially, led the captives to question themselves concerning their future. In Toulon, the death of a little girl, then of a companion, followed by those of five children in Pau, reawakened in the Muslims the fear of dying and being buried far from the land of their ancestors. In following the Emir in his exile, most expected to end their days in Mecca, but almost a third of them would ultimately be buried in France. Aside from his own pain at losing a wife and several children, the Emir was affected by the unexpected character of the situation, and was constrained to reflect on its theological implications.

But it was the French customs and culture which opened a new perspective on his tradition. When a devout person offered him holy images, an apparently harmless episode, it was the statute concerning figurative representation in Islam that was questioned. While the *shari'a* does not formally condemn it, it does however warn against the use that can be made of it. In the imagination of the Muslim, human or animal representations most often reflect the worship of idols, and for this reason appear as a form of denial of monotheism. The mitigated position of the religious law on the matter has given rise to strict interpretations on the part of jurists (*fuqaha'*) arousing a defiance towards all forms of figurative representation. According to testimonies, however, not only did the Emir have in his possession painted portraits and photographs, he also agreed to having his portrait painted. Since January 1848, the Parisian painter E.H. Pingret had requested an official authorization to go to Toulon to paint the Emir, in hopes, he

---

15 Ibid., p. 354.

16 M. Perras and E. Boislandry Dubern, "Abd-el-Kader en exil," p. 355.

wrote, of being "the first artist from Paris who will obtain this sacrifice or this favor from Abd el-Kader."[17] This "favor" ultimately was given to the official court painter, Horace Vernet,[18] to the surprise of Eugène Daumas, who was aware of the reticence of Muslims regarding the art of portraiture: "I thought that in your religion it is a sin." "Statues in gold, silver, and copper," explained Abd el-Kader, "are totally forbidden because they pertain to the class of idols, but the representation of figures with colors on canvas or paper is tolerated."[19] The Emir chose to interpret the Law flexibly, not oriented towards strictness, an approach that also demonstrates a rational mind devoid of superstitious beliefs. In Amboise, he sat as the model for several paintings and drawings. One of the rare portraits of the Emir during his captivity at Pau is due to Charles Eynard. It seems, however, according to several recovered documents and testimonies, that it was done partly in person and partly from memory, and that Abd el-Kader had not been requested to authorize it. Earlier, we saw that the scene representing his liberation by the Prince-President was entrusted to Ange Tissier. Another series of three portraits, from three different angles, was done by Maxime David, a painter of miniatures, who came to the castle the day before the departure of the Algerians for Bursa. A journalist did not fail to point out the "religious sacrifice" to which the subject had consented: "Despite his Muslim strictness which forbids every kind of painting and image, the Emir wished Mr. David to multiply his children as he had multiplied their father, and the painter undertook this sacred task, animating on ivory the entire young family of the great man."[20] Aside from these representations on canvas and paper, the Emir was portrayed by the sculptor Jean-Baptiste Carpeaux. Still young at the time, the future author of *La Danse* had made a preparatory study for a bas-relief in the rooms of the Algerian embassy in Paris. The chronicle mentions that the Emir praised the young artist for his talent, and deemed the detail of the head to be a close likeness.[21] He also took

17 E.H. Pingret, letter of January 16, 1848.

18 The project would be abandoned following the abdication of King Louis-Philippe.

19 M. Perras and E. Boislandry Dubern, "Abd-el-Kader en exil," p. 353.

20 Le Musée des Familles, "Chronique du mois: Le Salon de 1853," vol. 20, 1853, p. 283.

21 Jean-Baptiste Carpeaux, preparatory design for the bas-reliefs, *La Soumission d'Abd el-Kader*, Orsay Museum. The Emir would never see the final sculpture. Carpeaux

pleasure in posing before the *camera obscura*, the typical invention of his century, and the abundance of his photographic portraits attests to this. The first portrait probably goes back to the summer of 1851,[22] and henceforth, every voyage in France was the occasion of a new one. In Constantinople, Abd el-Kader agreed to be photographed by the 'Abd Allah brothers and at the same period his portrait by the Polish painter Stanislaw Chlebowski was done there. In Damascus he received the English photographer Francis Bedford, who left an *intimiste* portrait of him in Syrian costume. There also exist a number of photographs taken on the occasion of the inauguration of the Suez Canal, at the end of 1869. Photography at this time was still in its infancy. Numerous superstitions were propagated concerning it, in Europe as well as in the countries of the Levant, where it even had been banned by the traditionalist ulemas. The new handmaiden "of the arts and letters," as Charles Baudelaire—who did not care much for it—qualified it, provoked a veritable revolution in the representation and imitation of reality. The craziest superstitions circulated around these "catchers of the spectrum." Theophile Gautier, to cite but one talented observer, was haunted by the irrational fear that part of his soul would be spirited away by a camera shot. Abd el-Kader himself was initially captivated by this prodigy of modern times, and saw in it, above and beyond the technical prowess, another allegory of the mirror, so dear to the Sufis. The issue of pictorial representation is not formalized in Islam. Depending upon whether one is for or against it will indicate the degree of liberty granted to conscience. For the Emir, it was a matter of having the intention prevail over the act, in accordance with the tradition of the Prophet, who in a well-known *hadith* declared: "The worth of the action depends on the intention which motivates it."[23] In the case of images, the Emir had no intention other than an aesthetic one, and in no wise devotional, as some of his more obtuse antagonists supposed.

---

made a vigorous composition representing the Emir on his knees clasping the hand of his liberator, which certainly was not in the spirit that Abd el-Kader would have expected!

22 Gustave Le Gray had combed the shores of the Loire for a project concerning the national patrimony ordered by the Commission for Historical Monuments. It is probably at this time that he passed by Amboise castle.

23 This *hadith* is mentioned several times by the traditionists, notably by the Imam al-Bukhari, who deemed it a fundamental theological principle.

As with images, music, theater, and cultural diversion were condemned by the strict ulemas, who saw in them frivolous practices distracting from religious observations. On these matters, the Emir gave fresh proof of his originality. In Pau, we learn from a military report that he attended concerts improvised by an officer of the castle and that he seemed "to very much enjoy and find too short" the melodies of Schubert played on the piano. After his liberation, he would be seen, with a naturalness that was disconcerting to a number of chroniclers of the time, going to the music Academy or to the Opera in Paris, in order to hear a varied program of lyrical works. On the occasion of a concert in a Parisian theater, the November, 1865 edition of *Le Journal illustré* reported that "numerous personalities, including the Emir Abd el-Kader, had wished to attend the performances of Adolph Sax to hear the new instruments, the praise of which had reached their ears. The instruments are called sahorns, saxotrobas, trumpets, trombones, etc." Several newspapers reproduced a full page photogravure of this concert, which included the Emir Abd el-Kader seated in the first row, conversing with the Belgian inventor of the saxophone! If the Emir was little given to public entertainments, he did not forbid those near him from going to shows in order to be distracted from the rigors of captivity. *Le Mémorial de Pyrénées*, in several articles during the course of spring 1848, recounted that the children and brothers of the Emir went to the circus which was in Pau. He also accepted the invitation of Princess Mathilde to her worldly salon at the rue de Courcelles, where the brothers Goncourt, Dumas, Théophile Gautier, or Gustave Flaubert were habitués. The visit to Amboise castle by a jurist from Constantinople, Sidi Shadhili al-Qusantini, who convinced him to play chess, somewhat set aside the habits of the Emir by taking him away from his "ascetic practices." In the enthusiastic pages he later dedicates to this millennial game, he wrote: "The game of chess is at once a philosophical allegory and a scientific invention. It provokes thought, increases strength of mind, distracts from sadness, reveals characters, gives an image of war, and shows to what extent victory against an adversary and triumph against the enemy are agreeable, and to what extent defeat and giving up are bitter."[24] It may be supposed that this slackening of his austerity and the setting aside of received traditional teaching did not take place without inner resistance. It is not too much to say

24 *Lettre aux Français*, p. 155.

that Abd el-Kader had been confronted with a real shock, both cultural and religious. As a visionary, he quickly understood the impasse to which he would be led if he remained closed to these newly discovered realities. Hence he faced them with discernment, refusing to reject something simply because it was foreign to his society of birth.

Abd el-Kader's behavior with women is perhaps what is most revealing of his religious and intellectual suppleness. The place and status of women in Islam have aroused some of the most intense debates between the defenders of a flexible interpretation of the religious law and the rigorists. While he often has recourse to the allegory of femininity in his spiritual texts, as in *Mawqif* 249, the Emir himself wrote little on the juridical and theoretical aspect of the question, outside of a very short volume, *La Femme arabe*,[25] in which he sets forth in a classical manner the questions of marriage and divorce. His gestures and his acts, however, show that he was able to shed the inherited reservations of his ancestors in this sphere in order to open himself and adapt to the culture of his "hosts" and fashion a new type of relationship. While remaining faithful to his tradition, he was able to show himself respectful towards women without falling into paternalism, of showing modesty without being prudish. During his period of combat, he sent appeals to the queens of France, England, and Spain to put an end to the violence in Algeria. He had appealed to Queen Amelia to try to convince Louis-Philippe not to cede to the pressing appeals of his generals to resume the war; and during his captivity, it is to the women that he directed himself, persuaded that the French women would better understand the misfortune in which he and his followers were plunged. Émile Ollivier reports a scene on the occasion of a reception given in honor of the Emir: "Two charming ladies came to see him; he told them that he had always known that he had on his side part of the population—the women."[26] In Pau, he maintained friendly and ongoing relations with the Countess de Barbotan, a leading figure, along with Charles Eynard, of the "Abdelkaderian" committee formed in order to obtain the freedom of the "illustrious captive." The number of letters exchanged with her gives an idea of the strength of the bond that united them, revealing as well an Emir able to express his feelings

25 *La Femme arabe*, cited in Bruno Étienne, *Abdelkader, isthme des isthmes*, p. 476. This essay was partly put into the *Tuhfat* of the Emir's son, Muhammad Sa'id

26 *Journal*, vol. 1, pp. 131-132.

easily, as in these verses he wrote with which he embellished his letters: "My heart is suffering since I no longer see de Barbotan. My tears do not cease to flow, how could it be otherwise; I feel the absence of my friends!"[27] Olympe Audouard, at heart a Saint-Simonian and one of the pioneers of feminism, was struck by his courtesy and his ease in the company of women when she met him in Egypt: "It is mistakenly thought that the Arab is incapable of gallantry or even politeness towards women. I can assure you that the Emir was exquisitely polite towards me and of an altogether knightly gallantry. When we arrived in an Arab village and an Arab, as is the oriental custom, served him before me, he quickly passed me his cup, or made a sign that I should be served first which, by the way, did not at all unsettle these good Arabs."[28] To Colonel Daumas, who wished to invite him for dinner at his home but feared upsetting him by putting him in the presence of his wife, Abd el-Kader partly explained his point of view: "In the Muslim religion, the woman can perfectly well take part in gatherings. If we Arabs have them veil themselves, it is only—beneath our ardent sky—so as not to enable bad thoughts to arise. Bad thoughts, as you know, often lead to bad actions."[29] In putting forth a pragmatic argument, that of protecting women and preserving morals, the Emir Abd el-Kader does not absolutize the wearing of the veil, an approach which also demonstrates undeniable pedagogical qualities towards the legitimate questions of his French interlocutors. It is this same trait of his personality which led him to answer a young French woman who asked with a certain levity for the reasons for his polygamy: "If I had known French women, I would only have married one of them."[30] This certainly was said with a sense of humor, but the reply also resulted from the flexibility of his thought and his attitudes. Although he was not unaware that he could ruffle certain sensitivities amongst his intimates, he also knew that his gesture did not contravene the fundamental principles which the tradition had bequeathed him. He had not

27 Some of these letters were reproduced by A. Temimi, "Lettres inédites de l'émir Abd el-Kader," p. 166.

28 Olympe Audouard, Les Mystères de l'Égypte dévoilés (Paris: E. Dentu, 1865), p. 31.

29 Notes of Colonel Daumas to Toulon, in M. Perras and E. Boislandry Dubern, "Abd-el-Kader en exil," p. 352.

30 Gustave Bascle de Lagrèze, Le Château de Pau et le Béarn. Souvenirs historiques (Paris: Hachette, 1862, 4th edition), pp. 372-373.

the slightest intention of calling it into question, but to make a supple and intelligent interpretation, adapted to the times. "God wishes for you ease and not constraint," says a verse of the Koran (2:185). In this may be seen a summary of his vision. By giving priority to the rules of propriety of his hosts, he risked setting aside his own in order to arrive at a balance between the two while respecting his religious duties. On Saturday, October 30, 1852, on the occasion of his meeting with Louis Napoleon Bonaparte at the presidential palace in Saint-Cloud, the Emir alluded to the specific customs of both sides in these terms: "I beg you not to judge me in accordance with your customs that I am unacquainted with, for I am a foreigner, but in accordance with mine. Perhaps, from the standpoint of French customs, I may commit a fault; from our point of view, that is not the case; I ask to be judged according to mine."[31]

Of a non-conformist, audacious, and open mind, the Emir nourished his faith and his practice upon contact with reality, welcoming its complexity and its movement. Thus he rejoined the original conception of the *shari'a*, which implied a fruitful dynamism, always in search of a renewed and inspired equilibrium in life so as to better apply it. As a "son of the moment," according to Sufi terminology, he knew how to come to a compromise with his epoch and to decipher in it God's plan. Thus, in seeking to be in harmony with the contemporary world, the Emir sought to be in harmony with the divine Will.

A Divine Age

"Disparage not the age (*dahr*) for the age is God."[32] This holy tradition (*hadith qudsi*) goes beyond acknowledging God's omnipresence in History. It suggests that the time (or the "age") is an attribute of God and as such must be apprehended with respect and consideration. The aspirant must therefore try to decipher the divine Will in the historical events. Abd el-Kader's unconditional trust in God's plans finds expression in an enthusiastic confidence in the future of humanity: because it is inspired by God, History necessarily has a meaning.

---

31 Alexandre Bellemare, *Abd el-Kader*, p. 396.

32 There exist several versions of this *hadith qudsi* reported by Abu Hurayra and authenticated by the Imam Muslim. Here is another: "Allah said, 'The offspring of Adam inveigh against the *Dahr* (the vicissitudes of the age), but I am the *Dahr*; in My Hands are the night and the day!"

If modernity in the Europe of the nineteenth century seemed like a rupture with the past and with inherited traditions, it was otherwise for the Emir, who remained attached to tradition. However, determined to live according to the rhythm of his time, he refused the entrenchment of archaic customs for the sole reason that they are ancestral. Although a man of tradition, he was not a worshipper of the past: "The ancients have left much to do for the moderns," he wrote; their heirs have the duty to make fruitful the inheritance which has been transmitted to them. Modernity and the upheavals that it entails, in techniques as well as in mentalities, are not a scourge or a divine punishment, but a challenge to be met. Whereas the dogmatism of the Muslim jurists leads them to reject Western rationalism without discernment, the Emir, being a worthy inheritor of the Muslim humanists and of the "great human heritage" of the ninth century Arab philosopher al-Kindi, entrusts reason with the correct appreciation of the sciences, ideas, and techniques of Europe; a Europe which he admires for its sense of creativity, its spirit of organization, and the richness of intellectual debate that it nourishes.

Abd el-Kader sees in the diversity of the sciences as well as in their objects a means of apprehending both the divine Unity and the phenomenal realities which manifest it. Religious and profane sciences are complementary: "The Prophets did not come to argue with the philosophers nor to do away with the sciences of medicine, astronomy, or geometry. They did not come to dispute with one who says: 'Bodies are composed of four elements,' nor with one who asserts: 'The Earth is spherical in form.' Cases of this sort do not in the least contradict what the prophets have brought. He who asserts: 'Such scientific knowledge contradicts religion,' or 'Religion is opposed to such scientific knowledge,' sins against religion."[33] Neither knowledge is superior over the other, both are illumined by reason (*'aql*) and are instruments glorifying the Creator. An immense task is therefore reserved for scholars: "The productions of thought cannot be limited; the free use of the mind is in fact a properly infinite exercise. It is therefore not impossible, nor is it extraordinary that God has reserved certain benefits which He did not grant to some of the Ancients, to certain Moderns today."[34] Hence it is necessary, according to the author, to encourage

33 *Lettre aux Français*, pp. 121-122.

34 Ibid., p. 143.

scholars to add their stone to the edifice of science and warn those who would be tempted to be satisfied exclusively with what "their predecessors did before them, which is a great danger as well as the sign of a weak mind."[35] The sciences are threatened with sclerosis owing to the inertia of those who, under the cover of preserving principles, are in reality opposed to progress. Aside from the fear that the profane sciences would be exploited by narrow religious minds, *Reminder to the Intelligent* affirms the urgency, for the Islamic societies of the middle of the nineteenth century, to join modernity by the emancipation of knowledge, the preeminent instrument of technical progress.

The intellectual openness demonstrated by Abd el-Kader is all the more remarkable in that *Dar al-Islam* was then at a phase of an introverted assertion of its identity and culture due in part to the multifarious crises which shook it and to the growing hegemony of the European powers. As a thinker, he was very aware that the West owed its supremacy above all to the power of reason focused on the technical mastery of the world. Is it necessary to recall that his first contact with modernity was military confrontation? It was on the occasion of a *jihad* against one of the greatest European powers of the time that he discovered how much his own society was far behind the times technically and politically. It was therefore vital that Islam open itself to Europe. But he who was the Commander of the Faithful and the founder of a State was convinced that a reform of *Dar al-Islam* would not be efficacious unless the Muslims themselves controlled their own political future. He criticized the arbitrariness of the Ottoman administration, whose authoritarian policy against its subjects made it unpopular. Thus around him gravitated figures of emerging nationalist and modernist movements prefiguring the Arab renaissance (*nahda*), who saw in him a precursor. After the Crimean War, and the events of July, 1860, the Emir even suggested the idea of a common destiny for Turkey and Europe.

A Curious Mind

During the *jihad*, the young Emir had very quickly understood that if he wished to have a chance of resisting the technological power and the organizational genius of his adversaries, he would have to adapt. Devoid of experience, he showed an exceptional curiosity and practi-

35 Ibid., p. 144.

cality: "See with what promptness he was able to appropriate the useful arts, the science and the industry of his enemy," writes Monsignor Dupuch.[36] He discovered the "marvels of civilization" and other techniques invented by his adversaries shortly after the end of his captivity in France in December, 1852. The visit to the Museum of Artillery captivated the man of war, but it was the Government Printing Office which most impressed him: "Yesterday I saw the house of canons with which ramparts are toppled; today I saw the machine with which kings are toppled." It was during the time of the *jihad* that Abd el-Kader, who received reports from the French newspapers, had gauged the influence of the press on the political life. He had been able to witness its ability to inflict damage as an instrument against power in playing an intermediary role between government and peoples. As extraordinary as the technology of printing was, it nonetheless was no more than a tool capable of the best as well as of the worst: "What it produces resembles a drop of water that falls from the sky: if it falls on the half-open seashell it produces a pearl; if it falls into the mouth of a viper it produces poison."[37] But in an altogether general way, the Emir, who wanted to "make his people happy," considered modern technology as a means in the service of the common good, a tool inspired by God whose aim it is to lighten mankind's living conditions.

Towards the middle of the nineteenth century, the triumph of capitalism crowned the economic revolution that had begun in the previous century in England. Industrial development and progress swept the European powers, with England and France at their head, into an intoxicating enthusiasm. Technical inventions by human genius henceforth had their international expositions. In Paris, on the Champs-Elysées, there took place in 1855 the first Universal Exposition. Its success was immense: close to 24,000 exhibitors, some thirty countries represented, and more than five million visitors.

Abd el-Kader visited the Exposition several times. Among the numerous machines exhibited, those which most attracted his attention were those that related to ironwork in general, the weaving machines, and the sewing machines. The year before the Universal Exposition, when he was still in Bursa, the Emir sent a herd of angora goats to France. The wool taken from the animal was reputed to be "fine and

---

36 Msg. Dupuch, *Abd el-Kader au château d'Amboise*, p. 83.

37 Alexandre Bellemare, *Abd el-Kader*, p. 400.

silk-like" and particularly fit for machine spinning. Observing the technical prowess of machines "which multiplied man's work a hundredfold with admirable perfection," he was said to have exclaimed: "This place is the palace of intelligence animated by the breath of God."[38]

Enthused by this first Exposition, he returned to Europe in 1865 and went to the industrial Exposition at the Crystal Palace in England and, two years later in Paris, to the second Universal Exposition organized in France. Above and beyond the promotion of industrial society, the promoters of these cosmopolitan expositions wished them to be "celebrations of peace" to assure "the happiness of humanity." Carried by his unquenchable faith in the destiny and the unity of the great human family, Abd el-Kader certainly shared this somewhat idealistic vision. In the *Reminder to the Intelligent*, which he sent to the director of the Asiatic Society the year of the first Parisian Exposition, he describes Napoleon III as he "who does not deny God the right to one day reunite the world into a harmonious community";[39] and the entire letter is the expression of a conviction that men are destined to be united by universal values.

The Projects of the Century

The digging of the Suez Canal, which he supported from the outset, offered Abd el-Kader the perfect occasion to express his confidence in the irenic virtues of progress. Like the Saint-Simonians of Egypt, who initiated that pharaonic project, he saw in the canal, the aim of which was to join the Red Sea and the Mediterranean, the possibility of connecting the continents and its peoples. In the minds of the followers of Father Enfantin, the technical challenge was supposed to be subordinated to a superior ideal: the union between West and East, which would give birth to a new civilization, a utopia in which Ferdinand de Lesseps, student of the Saint-Simonians, also believed and which he would transform into a reality. Ferdinand de Lesseps belonged to a dynasty of diplomats. He earned his spurs in the beylicate of Tunis, in Algeria, and from 1832 in Egypt, where he was first vice-consul and later consul in Alexandria and Cairo. It was during this time that his project to dig the canal was born. The foundations for it would not be

38 Ibid., p. 415.

39 *Lettre aux Français*, p. 168.

launched until twenty years later, and he who would later be surnamed the "Great Frenchman" was initially the victim of the mockery of his contemporaries. But relationships woven during the course of a rich diplomatic career, his persuasive ability, and an unquenchable faith in his project, gained him initial support.

Ferdinand de Lesseps very soon understood that although support in Europe was indispensable, he could not neglect those which came from the Levant. After the successors of the viceroy of Egypt, Muhammad Ali, with whom he had long maintained relations, it was the stamp of approval of the Emir Abd el-Kader which he sought. The two men already knew each other. In his *Mémoires*, Ferdinand de Lesseps recounts that in 1848 he had visited the Emir in Pau, at the castle of Henry IV, and that he had already been "struck by his noble and calm resignation."[40] The events of July 1860, gave him the opportunity to renew contact with the famous Algerian exile. At the onset of 1861, de Lesseps went to Damascus to meet him. He recounts the extraordinary welcome given him: "When my caravan was pointed out to him, he hurried to meet me, had me sit next to him in his carriage, and that is how we crossed the city of Damascus, whose inhabitants, standing in rows before their homes, bowed to the ground to the Emir and his guests. For days we were welcomed everywhere as friends."[41] The Emir's popularity had doubtless made the Frenchman decide to make him a chief ally in his enterprise; a momentous choice, for the hero would put all the prestige he enjoyed among the populations of the Levant to promote the project of his friend de Lesseps, in whom he had faith; and he did so all the way to the heart of Islam: "In the holy place of Islam, in the midst of the annual event of the Muhammadan pilgrims, Abd el-Kader continued his propaganda in favor of the Suez canal."[42] The radiation of the Emir and his enthusiasm for the project were obviously exploited by the Canal Company. He was received with all honors at its Parisian headquarters during his stay in France in January 1865, and the press campaign launched around the project presented him as a privileged partner and crucial to its success.[43]

40 "Abd-el-Kader," *La Nouvelle Revue*, Paris, May-June 1883, p. 735.

41 F. Charles-Roux, "Abdelkader et Ferdinand de Lesseps," p. 6.

42 Ibid., p. 21.

43 Ferdinand de Lesseps had suggested that the Emir be among the first to benefit

But while the Emir, as Ferdinand de Lesseps often would remind him, had been one of these "believers from the very beginning," without whom the mad enterprise would not have been able to begin, it probably did not have the same significance for the shareholders of the Company. The Sufi Abd el-Kader, who was entering a decisive phase of his spiritual path, never lost sight of the metaphysical dimension which encompasses all phenomenal reality.

His correspondence with Ferdinand de Lesseps and the speeches given during his visits to the construction site of the isthmus clarify the reasons for his faith in the project of building the Canal. There are constant religious and spiritual references in them. In Damiette, he expresses a profound intuition to the French engineers and technicians regarding the divine Will for them: "In greeting you, Sirs, I greet men inspired by God."[44] At the construction site of Port Said he encouraged the employees of the Company to make the dimensions of the town correspond to those of the world, unified by the canal: "Use large proportions for its enlargement, for this town is destined to receive the children of God arriving from all parts of the world." In a letter of January 12, 1863, addressed to Lesseps, he confirms his conviction regarding the universalist vocation of the Canal: "God has willed to reserve for you the two glories and the two merits of digging at one and the same time the maritime canal and the fresh water canal. No intelligent person can doubt that your work is a true benefit to humanity, and at the same time useful in general, the advantages of which will flow out to most of the earth's inhabitants, from one end to the other. We pray to the Most-High that He may facilitate its achievement and realize the joining of the waters."[45] The letter refers explicitly to the Koran: "God it is who hath joined the two seas: one is sweet and agreeable to taste; the other is salty and bitter. Between them He hath placed a barrier, a limit which cannot be crossed" (25:53). The isthmus (*barzakh*), here translated by "barrier," is a central notion in Sufi terminology, referring to an intermediate "space" between two worlds or two realities.

---

from the development of the border of the canal. In the end, the suggestion could not be fulfilled owing to obscure political dealings regarding which he returns to in his article in the May-June 1883 edition of *La Nouvelle Revue*.

44 F. Charles-Roux, "Abdelkader et Ferdinand de Lesseps," pp. 9-11.

45 "Le canal de Suez et Abd el-Kader," *Annales agricoles de la Dordogne*, vol. 24, 1863, pp. 220-221.

In the spiritual retreat which he entered during this same period, Abd el-Kader explored the "isthmus of isthmuses" (*barzakh al-barazikh*), described in *Mawqif* 89 as pertaining "to the subtle and imaginal world to which the spirits go after death." The encounter and cooperation between Ferdinand de Lesseps and Abd el-Kader illustrates perfectly the type of relationship that the Emir had envisaged between East and West; a technical project to which, aside from his charisma over the Muslim populations, he brought a spiritual depth.

Abd el-Kader was of course invited by Ferdinand de Lesseps to the inauguration of the Canal on November 16, 1869. The ceremony was grandiose: "This cosmopolitan crowd, gathered to acclaim the dawn of a new age of commerce and civilization, constituted a majestic display, and no one of those present has not remembered it as one of the greatest events he has ever witnessed."[46] On the official platform, surrounding the viceroy of Egypt, were gathered the crowned heads of Europe. "In the midst of the glitter of uniforms stood out the austere and energetic figure of Abd el-Kader, draped in his white burnous and, as his sole ornament, wearing on his breast the insignia of the Grand-Cross of the Legion of Honor. It was a fair and generous thought to have invited this defeated hero to the union of East and West."[47] The nuptial dimension which this witness, F. Charles-Roux, gives to the event doubtless did not escape Abd el-Kader. For him, a fecundation cannot exist if there is no encounter. At this same period, the Emir was at a turning point in his metaphysical speculations. His interpretation of the events was eschatological, and he viewed this project of unifying the two seas as the announcement of new times during which the encounter of the two entities, both geographic and metaphysical, would give birth to a new humanity. The road had been long prior to this arrival of such a celebration. It was crowned by an ecumenical ceremony which unfolded between two pavilions; in one of them were the ulemas, imams, and shaykhs of the mosque, and in the other the Western Catholic bishop, the Franciscan monks, and the Eastern patriarchs, archimandrites, and priests. Muslims and Christians, Arabs and non-Arabs, all gathered within one and the same project. Too irenic a vision? Certainly, for pessimistic minds. Europe was on the eve of the

46 Émile de la Bédollière, *De Paris à Suez, souvenirs d'un voyage en Égypte* (Paris: Librairie Georges Barba, 1870), p. 17.

47 F. Charles-Roux, "Abdelkader et Ferdinand de Lesseps," p. 49.

invasion of France by the Prussian states and the fall of Napoleon III, who had freed the "illustrious captive." But the Emir foresaw that if it was not union, at least it held the premises of a reconciliation of the great human family around one of the leading projects of modernity.

A Modernity Reconciled with Tradition

During this middle part of the nineteenth century, Europe underwent successive phases of rupture with its religious tradition, entering into a process of secularization, which in the eyes of its theoreticians defines modernity. The "death of God," which Nietzsche would not be long in prophesying, was already in germinal form, and triumphant rationality, a kind of modern demiurge, had recourse to new tools and languages to apprehend and master the real. Human progress was reduced to technical and social progress, aimed solely at ameliorating man's lot. The desire for the marvelous and the sublimation of the real were in the process of being considered as productions of the imagination. God was no longer in the minds of the builders of modernity save as an object of study, a "word dreamed up in order to explain the world,"[48] according to the saying of Alphonse de Lamartine. At last man had become "the measure of all things," like a new god, ready to fashion the world in his image. While institutional religion lost influence, the religious instinct nonetheless remained intact but transformed by the "intellectuals" of modernity, who established the cult of progress and technical mastery of the world: a project which would in due course provoke individual aberrations and collective disasters. Abd el-Kader the visionary, whose enthusiastic confidence in modernity was balanced by a lucidity without concessions, had certainly had a premonition of the existential impasse towards which Western society was heading, involving the rest of the world with it. Since 1848 he had alerted the French, and through them the Westerners, that they had lost the "way of Heaven."[49] In his eyes, European modernity had substituted discursive reasoning for the transcendent spirit and material enjoyment in the form of an alienating consumerism for the inner quest. Modern thought denied the spiritual specificity of man in the

---

48 Alphonse de Lamartine, *Harmonies poétiques et religieuses* (Paris: Ch. Gosselin-Furne et Cie-Pagnerre, 1847), p. 201.

49 Papiers Eynard, Ms. suppl. 1980-f. 32-40.

midst of Creation. Thus divested of that which constitutes his dignity, modern man closes himself to all the "useful sciences," whose aim is the knowledge of God.[50] Modern society, in its blind pretention to wish to suffice unto itself by excluding all superior authority, in its will to power and to master the destiny of the world, proceeds irremediably towards its fall for, wrote the Emir, "The moment one says: it is perfect, beware: annihilation is near,"[51] and concludes: "True perfection belongs solely to God Most High alone."[52]

Whereas fascination with technical progress fed national prides and attempts at hegemony, the lone voice of Abd el-Kader called his contemporaries to humility before the complexity of Creation. To the pharaonic pretention of modern man to wish to compete with God's omnipotence, Abd el-Kader opposed a modernity reconciled with an authentic transcendence which would restore meaning to man's existence and a center to his inner being. It is only by orienting his being towards God that man, borne by the divine Breath, could transcend himself and discover his divine face. And in the ties he established with the actors of modernity, Ferdinand de Lesseps having been one of its most eminent representatives, the Sufi Abd el-Kader had no other will than to infuse a Spirit into a soulless modernity.

50 *Lettre aux Français*, chap. 1, p. 18.

51 Ibid., conclusion.

52 This affirmation ends his epistle *Call to the Intelligent*.

CHAPTER 7

The Accomplishment

We shall show them our signs in the universe and in themselves,
until they see that it is the Truth (*al-Haqq**).
Koran 41:53

Am I not your Lord? They said:
Yea, we bear witness to it.
Koran 6:172

Time after time each day ye die.
Abd al-Qadir al-Jilani

The Emir in Damascus: A Studious Ascesis

During the first days of the month of December 1855, the arrival of the Algerian exile in Damascus did not go unnoticed: popular jubilation and official welcome worthy of a foreign ruler marked the local chronicles: "The entire Muslim population, men, women, children, went out to welcome him. Outside the doorways, for more than a mile, the way was lined on both sides with people of all ranks and classes dressed in their festive clothes."[1]

In the land of Saladin, his reputation as a legendary hero had preceded him several years earlier. His titles of *sharif* and emir, the prestige linked to his past, and his natural charisma explain the excitement he generated. His home was always full: notables of the great Damascene families, religious dignitaries, agents of foreign consulates, Europeans, Arabs, Levantines, Maghrebians. The Emir rapidly became one of the most visible personalities of the city. But this popularity, which had not diminished during the nearly eight years of retirement from public life, was a source of uneasiness for the French authorities. In Damascus a strong community of Algerian immigrants had formed, which in successive waves had fled their native land to settle on the outskirts south of the city. Their presence was sufficiently numerous to arouse the suspicions of those within the government who believed that the

1 Charles H. Churchill, *La Vie d'Abd el Kader*, pp. 305-307.

Emir was still capable of harming the interests of France. After 1830 and the conquest of Algeria by the Africa army, numerous Algerian families left for exile. A good many of them settled in Alexandria and Damascus, traditional stages on the way to Mecca. The proportion of applicants for exile and settlement in Damascus is indicated in particular by a letter of the Governor of Algeria, General de Martinprey who, in an official document dated June 13, 1860 wrote: "I have become certain by means of all the indications I have collected for several months that the Emir Abd el-Kader intends to play a part once again. I do not think that he has the idea of returning to Algeria, despite the prestige his name still has. Rather, I think, judging by the precarious state of the East, he has gauged the position which he might conquer with the force of his intelligence, energy, and ability, backed by his intrepid and devoted companions. It is the emigration that sends them to him from Algeria. They are not just anybody, but rather the most vigorous, coming from warrior tribes and provided with resources of money from the transfer of properties they used to possess. . . . Is it the intention of the Emperor that Abd el-Kader play a part in the East? If so, we must let the emigration take its course. If not, it is for us to moderate it. What interest would we have in seeing Islam restored?"[2]

If the cultural and religious crossroads that was the capital of *Sham* altogether suited its new guest, official measures forbade him from traveling outside it without authorization. The Emir discovered this to his dismay when the French consul, Max Outrey, refused to let him travel outside the Syrian province. He complained to his friends and supporters in Paris, regretting that the consul did not have "the courtesy of the French."[3] The exile would have to wait until 1863 to be able at last to go on pilgrimage to Mecca. For the time being, during 1857, after several secret negotiations, he was authorized to go to Jerusalem, *al-Quds*, the third holy place of Islam,[4] on condition however of being accompanied by Georges Bullad, the French agent who took orders directly from the Minister of Foreign Affairs, Count Walewski. Abd el-Kader remained only a few days in the Holy Land; time for him to

2 Archives des Affaires étrangères, Damascus, vol. 6, fol. 15, cited in Bruno Étienne, *Abdelkader, isthme des isthmes*, p. 274.

3 S. Aouli, R. Redjala, and P. Zoummeroff, *Abd el-Kader*, p. 453.

4 The pious visit to the Holy Land is recounted in detail in the biographical essay of his son.

visit the historical sites and to pray in the Muslim sanctuaries in the company of the local religious dignitaries. His welcome in Jerusalem, where a crowd came for the occasion, probably reawakened the fears of the French authorities. Only his past as an implacable adversary and his abiding influence could explain such suspicion, because at present, and after the signed surrender addressed to Napoleon III, the Emir had definitively renounced playing any political role. It would not be until the summer of 1860 and his action in favor of the Christians in Damascus, which caused a worldwide sensation, that the suspicion would be transformed into good will.

In Damascus, the son of the *zawiya* surely found with satisfaction an atmosphere conducive to prayer and meditation. The old city did not lack places of recollection, mosques, madrasas, mausoleums, which he visited regularly. There he encountered faithful of all the monotheist faiths and diverse nationalities, among them a large European colony. Along with consular agents, numerous English and French travelers had included in their romantic wanderings the city written, according to the French poet La Martine, "by God's finger on earth." This cultural and religious diversity probably nourished the Emir's meditation on the universal. His adaptation to this new homeland was rapid, for it was not entirely foreign to him as he had traveled there some thirty years earlier. He entered into the local life contributing "regularly more than twenty pounds each month to charitable works."[5] Among those whom he materially supported were a number of young scholars who comprised his entourage. In return, they most often took charge of teaching his children. Among other good works, Abd el-Kader financed the rehabilitation of one of the most ancient religious institutions of the city, *ad-Dar al-Hadith al-Ashrafiyya*, which he inaugurated with a public lecture. However, the man of transmission which he had never ceased to be, dedicated most of his time to study and teaching. Georges Bullad specifies this in his first report to the French Minister of Foreign Affairs, dated March 1856: "The Emir reads a great deal; he dedicates to study, which he loves passionately, all the time left to him after prayer and religious practices and the care given to the education of his children."[6] The same report in addition specifies that the exile quickly formed relationships with the literary men of the city, who

5 Charles H. Churchill, *La Vie d'Abd el-Kader*, p. 321.

6 Cited in Bruno Étienne, *Abdelkader, isthme des isthmes*, p. 466.

formed a study circle around him: "He sees few people, but gladly admits into the circle of his friends Marabouts, Shaykhs, student scholars with whom he spends entire hours in meetings that usually deal with religion or literature. The different opinions of the commentators of the Koran are reviewed, each person gives his opinion, they discuss in order to clarify, etc. These gatherings take place rather frequently, and are one of the favorite occupations of the Emir."[7]

The initial education of Abd el-Kader, his years of captivity, and his exile in Bursa enabled him to deepen his knowledge of the texts of the tradition, the exoteric as well as the esoteric. His epistle, *Call to the Intelligent*, reveals an erudition that transcends the bounds of religion. In it he freely cites Ptolemy, Galen, Socrates, Plato, Aristotle, Zarathustra, Hermes, Manes, al-Firdausi, Avicenna, Rhazes, etc. We know that during this time he requested the French consul in Tangiers to advance money to his brother Mustafa in order to buy manuscripts and recent works. Books had always occupied a place in the life of the Emir, and they had played a major role in his inner life. Those which he cites and which form the material of his teachings give an idea of his erudition and eclecticism. To the Koran and the collections of Hadith are joined the works of the masters of the Path, to whom the Emir most often refers: 'Umar ibd al-Farid, Abu Madyan, Ibn 'Arabi, Ibn al-Mashish, Abu'l Hasan ash-Shadhili, Ibn 'Ata'illa,[8] and others. To these classics of spiritual science are joined those of the scholastic theologians, among

---

7 Ibid., p. 467.

8 All these masters, through their charisma and their writings, have profoundly marked the history of *tasawwuf*. 'Umar ibn al-Farid (tenth century, Egyptian), named the "Sultan of the Lovers," is the author of *The Wine Song (al-Khamriyya)*. Sidi Abu Madyan (twelfth-thirteenth centuries, born in Andalusia, died in Tlemcen) is the author of numerous poems and aphorisms. His contemporary, the Shaykh Ibn 'Arabi, is another major figure of Andalusian Sufism. A prolific author (his spiritual summa, the *Futuhat al-Makkiyya* comprises several thousand pages) and a great pilgrim, he ended his days in Damascus. Ibn al-Mashish (twelfth-thirteenth centuries) is the author of the *Mashishiyya*, a poem-prayer of great density. He lived in retreat until his death on a mountain named the "Mountain of the Sign" (*jabal al-'alam*) in northeastern Morocco. There he encountered his sole disciple, who became his spiritual heir, Abu'l-Hasan ash-Shadhili (thirteenth century); an eminent master who was born in Morocco and died in southern Egypt, he became the eponymous founder of the important *Shadhili-yya tariqa*. Sidi Ibn 'Ata'illa became the second successor of the Shaykh ash-Shadhili. A charismatic figure, he was the author of several writings including the famous *Sayings* or *Aphorisms (Hikam)*.

whom Ibn Taymiyya and Fakhr ad-Din Razi[9] occupy a central place. Let us add finally that the Emir had certainly collected one of the best endowed libraries in Damascus.

Charles Henry Churchill, who met with him regularly at the end of the year 1859, describes his typical day: "He arises two hours before dawn and devotes himself to prayer and religious meditation until sunrise. He then goes to the mosque. After having passed half an hour in public devotion, he returns home, has a light meal, then works in his library until mid-day. The call of the muezzin invites him once again to the mosque, where his class is already gathered, awaiting his arrival. He takes a seat, opens the book chosen as the basis of discussion and reads aloud, constantly interrupted by requests for explanations which he gives by opening his many treasures of laborious study, investigations and research accumulated throughout his turbulent life. The session lasts three hours. After the afternoon prayer, Abd el-Kader returns home and spends an hour with his children, his eight sons, examining the progress they have made in their studies. Then he dines. At sunset, he is once again at the mosque, where he instructs his class for an hour and a half. His work as a professor is now over for the day. He still has two hours before him; he spends them in his library, after which he retires to rest."[10] Invited to give public and private lectures, the Emir teaches Koranic exegesis—he was a *hafiz* at the age of fourteen—as well as the science of *hadith* and in particular the *Sahih al-Bukhari*, the most important collection of *hadith*, established in the ninth century by the Imam al-Bukhari. In other locations, and to a more restricted group, he teaches *tasawwuf*. It is known that he gave a series of talks on the *Kitab al-Ibriz*, an exceptional exposition on spiritual realization by the Moroccan master of the eighth century Abd al-'Aziz Debbagh. But it is his commentaries on the monumental work of the Shaykh Ibn 'Arabi, the *Meccan Illuminations* (*Futuhat al-Makkiyya*), which give the full measure of the erudition and spiritual degree attained by the Emir; we shall return to this.

9 Ibn Taymiyya (thirteenth-fourteenth centuries), theologian and jurist from southeastern Turkey. A prolific author, he became well-known for his intransigence and his condemnation of certain writings of the Shaykh Ibn 'Arabi. Fakr ad-Din Razi (twelfththirteenth centuries), major theologian from Persia, was the author of an important commentary on the Koran, the *Mafatih al-Ghayb*.

10 Charles H. Churchill, *La Vie d'Abd el-Kader*, p. 323.

We have said that at the occasion of his first great pilgrimage
the son of Muhyi ad-Din had frequented the entourage of Shaykh
Khalid,[11] master of the Naqshbandiyya, and had probably received an
initiatic attachment to this *tariqa*. It is precisely in this Naqshbandi
milieu that he would meet his most intimate companions in the Way,
who attended regularly and assiduously the spiritual sessions which
were organized spontaneously, and later regularly, around him. To
these persons, who for the most part came from the local religious
aristocracy, were later added the Algerian exiles who arrived to the
city in 1847, in the wake of the former lieutenant of Sebaou, Ahmad
Ben-Salem. Let us also mention the Shaykh 'Abd ar-Rahman 'Illaysh
who belonged to a family of Egyptian scholars, and whose father,
Muhammad al-Kabir, a Malikite jurist, had previously supported the
cause of the Emir by the promulgation of a *fatwa*.* The encounter
between this elite of young scholars was of an exceptional intellectual
and spiritual fruitfulness and would literally unveil the hidden face
of the Emir Abd el-Kader.

If the Emir had always practiced the Way and had a profound veneration for his masters, his assimilation of the doctrine was accomplished only gradually. The themes broached in the words of the masters frequently make use of enigmatic allusions which sometimes are
disconcerting for insufficiently prepared minds. The Emir confided in
one of his writings that since his youth he liked to study the works of
the masters although not without some intellectual tensions: "During
the course of this study I happened to fall upon comments, coming
from some of the greatest among them, that made my hair stand on
end and oppressed my soul, despite my faith in their words according to the meaning they had wished to give them: for I was certain of
their perfect sense of spiritual propriety and of their eminent virtues"
(*Mawqif* 13). It was only later, and in a more definite manner during his
eastern exile, that he would go through a decisive stage in his under-

---

11 Shaykh Khalid Diya ad-Din (1776-1827), from Iraqi Kurdistan, received a traditional
religious education. He began a spiritual quest which led him as far as India. Invested
with the title of Shaykh in the Naqshbandiyya *tariqa* of the *Mujaddida* branch, he initiated a major reform movement in traditional studies in the first third of the nineteenth
century. He settled in Damascus in 1823 and created numerous teaching circles. In
1826, the young Abd el-Kader, accompanied by his father, met Shaykh Khalid, from
whom they probably received an initiatic attachment. The Shaykh passed away at the
ancient capital of the Umayyads in 1827.

standing of phenomenal and spiritual realities. Although the preceding periods of his life had been so many stages of his initiatic path and had not been devoid of spiritual events, it is in Damascus that the Emir would realize his full spiritual maturity, the last stage of which would unfold in Mecca. The ecstatic experiences (*jadhba*) and the intuitive unveilings (*kashf*) of which he was increasingly the object would nourish his writings and would constitute the heart of his spiritual *summa*, the *Mawaqif*, a work impregnated with the metaphysical doctrine of a major figure in *tasawwuf* and whose tomb was in Damascus: the Shaykh Muhyi ad-Din Ibn 'Arabi.

The Emir Abd el-Kader ben Muhyi ad-Din and the Shaykh Muhyi ad-Din Ibn 'Arabi

Abd el-Kader, son of Muhyi ad-Din: it is tempting to see a sign of providence in the similitude between the name of the fleshly father and that of the one who would become his spiritual father, an Andalusian of the thirteenth century, the Shaykh Muhyi ad-Din Ibn 'Arabi. The affinities between these two spiritual figures, separated by almost seven centuries, are varied and range from the most concrete situations to the most subtle spiritual events, which elude ordinary categories of analysis. How could it be otherwise for these two men whose earthly course, so rich, was but a field of exploration and transmission of a spiritual reality impenetrable to sense perception and to discursive reason?

A geographic affinity brings them closer, both men having been born in the west of the Muslim world. Shaykh Ibn 'Arabi was born in what the Arab geographers named *al-Andalus*, and the Emir was born in *al-Maghreb al-awsat*, the middle-west. Both saw the light of day on the threshold of profound political upheavals that would bring non-Muslim armies into *Dar al-Islam*. Until his definitive departure from Andalusia in 1200, the Andalusian was witness to a *Reconquista* that nothing could halt. The regency of Algiers in the nineteenth century experienced a succession of political and military events which disrupted its history. Both men thus lived in an atmosphere of *jihad* and in fear for the integrity of their land as well as for the perennity of their faith. If Ibn 'Arabi evolved on the margin of the political events of his time, Abd el-Kader, on the contrary, would be plunged into the heart of a battle that would occupy more than a quarter of his life. But if each took a different direction at the beginning, it was only to better meet in the eastern exile of Damascus which also corresponds to a journey in the vertical sense. The choice of the capital of the *Sham* was not motivated exclusively by political reasons. At the center of the Muslim world, the third city after Mecca and Medina to be the seat of the Sunni Caliphate, the *Sham* had been blessed by the Prophet: "Go to Syria, for it is the purest of God's countries and the elite of His creatures live there." And the eschatological tradition of Islam also grants a central place to the several thousand year old city that according to tradition will welcome the second coming of Christ.[12]

But before evoking their encounter at the heart of the Muhammadan Reality, which makes of them both inheritors of the spirit and of the work of the Prophet, let us dwell on their period of formation and the total change of their destiny.

The son of an officer placed in the service of the Almoravid and afterwards Almohad princes, the way of Muhyi ad-Din Ibn 'Arabi was marked out: he would follow a military career. The young man, moreover, had a pronounced taste for all the activities of the nobility of the sword. He was both a good hunter and a gifted horseman, with a natural predilection for arms and horsemanship. He himself confirms this predisposition towards the craft of arms: "From the time I reached the age of wearing a sword belt, I incessantly rode chargers, sought out nobles, examined swordblades, and paraded in military camps."[13] Fascinated by power and luxury, the adolescent was nonetheless endowed with a lucidity which gnawed at him and prevented him from being satisfied with the appearance of things. What the future metaphysician would term his *jahiliyya*, his period of ignorance, in reference to the age preceding the coming of the Prophet Muhammad, was brusquely interrupted at the age of nineteen. It was while seeing a member of the princely family in prostration during a collective prayer that the young Ibn 'Arabi had a revelation as sudden as it was radical. He then retired from the world and entered into retreat, an experience during which the visions he received would literally transfigure him. From that moment, he had not the shadow of a doubt regarding his vocation. To the frequenting of princes and the handling of arms, Ibn 'Arabi would

12 For further details on the legendary and eschatological dimension of the city of Damascus, see Ibn Battuta, *Voyages et périples*, in *Voyageurs arabes* (Paris: Gallimard, 1992), p. 459.

13 Cited in Claude Addas, *Ibn 'Arabi et le Voyage sans retour* (Paris: Seuil, 1996), p. 15.

henceforth prefer the existence of an ascetic and seek the company of the poor in God; a life dedicated to the quest of God (*al-Haqq*), in whom he extinguished himself in order that only "He who has never ceased being remain." He who henceforth was designated by the title of Shaykh al-Akbar, "the greatest of masters," left to posterity one of the most astonishing metaphysical works that the human mind has produced: the *Meccan Illuminations*, of which the Emir Abd el-Kader would become one of the best interpreters of his generation.

The Emir too experienced a reversal of destiny. Coming from the religious aristocracy, he would not have left it, but the political events would decide otherwise. Let us recall that it was in Mecca that Sidi Muhyi ad-Din knew through a visionary dream that his son, then nineteen years old, would become "Ruler of the West." After more than fifteen years of fighting, it was only in his fortieth year that the Emir Abd el-Kader voluntarily put an end to his political and military life. The five years of captivity that followed, as we have seen, were like a veritable purgative retreat in which the man of power was totally effaced in order to enable another reality to emerge.

In the Maghreb of the nineteenth century the doctrine of the Shaykh Ibn 'Arabi was known in broad outline. The powerful network of the *zawiyas*, the numerous exchanges with the East, notably thanks to the pilgrimages and to the wanderings of the "brothers," reactualized from generation to generation the memory of the spiritual masters and their teachings. There is no doubt, in our mind, that the young Abd el-Kader had included in his spiritual culture the name of the Shaykh Ibn 'Arabi. Just as he already knew the aphorisms and sayings of the major figures of Sufism, among them another Andalusian, Abu Madyan, and the Egyptian Ibn 'Ata'illa, whom the Emir evokes in the writings of his captivity. And it is doubtless through the traditional way of the father that the young man had been introduced to the doctrine of the Andalusian master; introduced, but not initiated in the traditional sense of the term, for the complexity of the Akbarian doctrine requires conditions which, it would seem, were not integrally present at the *zawiya* of Oued al-Hammam. This hypothesis, moreover, is qualified by the following fact. We know from the family history that the grandfather of the Emir, Sidi Mustafa, had met a notable Akbarian from India, Sayyid al-Murtadha az-Zabidi, who died in 1791. Thus the event would have taken place at the end of the eighteenth century in Egypt. Did he receive on this occasion the transmission of the *khirqa akbariyya*, the mode of initiation proper to the spiritual inheritors of the Shaykh al-Akbar? If that were the case, as the same sources affirm,[14] it would mean that the father of the Emir and the Emir himself had inherited the *baraka*, the blessed spiritual influence and the divine protection that accompany this type of initiatory attachment. It is also possible that this attachment took place in Damascus, when the young Abd el-Kader and his father traveled there in the course of the voyage that took them to Mecca. The encounter with Shaykh Khalid an-Naqshbandi, of whom the Emir speaks in the best terms, may allow one to suppose that he himself and his father received a teaching impregnated by the Akbarian doctrine, of which the Naqshbandiyya *tariqa* was one of the chains of transmission. Let us add that among the holy places of the Umayyad capital visited by the young Abd el-Kader was probably the mausoleum of Ibn 'Arabi, located in the same house in which the latter had lived. In all likelihood then, it was in 1826 that he visited for the first time the place in which he himself would be buried fifty-seven years later, both men dying at the age of seventy-five. And it is in this symbolically charged city that the two men, each endowed with a comfortable pension, chose to settle and to end their days in a studious ascesis.

But it was a book that would nourish this relation *in divinis*. The *Meccan Illuminations*, the monumental work of Ibn 'Arabi, occupies a special place in the history of universal Islamic spirituality. Over the centuries it has aroused as many enthusiastic testimonies as bitter critiques. Heretical for the literalists of Islam, inspired for the people of the Way, the *Futuhat* has rarely left indifferent those who risked approaching them. For the major work of the Shaykh al-Akbar is not of easy access, far from it. By its size, in the first place: several thousand pages of dense writing, which often sufficed to discourage lukewarm readers. Next, the subject matter broached: a subtle metaphysics which encompasses the entire sphere of the known and the unknown. One is dealing neither with a literary work nor with a philosophical essay, nor with a scholastic theological treatise, even though, from a certain standpoint of interpretation, the *Illuminations* could have that appearance. An enigmatic composition, a concise style, and an unusual manner of narrating, all serve to make this a unique work. The circumstances of its writing clarify it somewhat. No personal ambition or will is at the origin of the text: Ibn 'Arabi said that he composed it at the dic-

14 In the *Tuhfat*, p. 929.

tation of the Prophet Muhammad. It undertakes a tireless exploration of the physical and metaphysical realities of the Messenger of God.

To properly understand the centrality of the figure of Muhammad in all spiritual initiation in Islam, it is necessary to recall certain points: according to Sufi doctrine, the Prophet closed the cycle of Revelations, which makes of him the Seal of Prophecy; if he is the last in order of appearance of the prophets in history, he is however the first in the metaphysical order. A tradition in fact reveals that it is from the Muhammadan Reality (*al-Haqiqa al-Muhammadiyya*) that creatures proceed, and it is from it that the prophets who preceded him draw their light.[15] According to another tradition, God, usually designated by the Name *al-Haqq*, that is the Real or the divine Reality, was a "Hidden Treasure," and it is because He wished to be known that He created the universe.[16] If God, *Allah*, is unfathomable in His Essence, He may nonetheless be known through his attributes or Names (*asma' al-husna*), which are infinite in number and which manifest in His creation. These divine attributes often work in pairs of opposites such as the First (*al-Awwal*) and the Last (*al-Akhir*), the Outward (*az-Zahir*) and the Inward (*al-Batin*). The creation, as the support by which the Names or divine Attributes are manifested, is therefore a mirror in which God is reflected. And the Muhammadan Reality is precisely this allegorical mirror,[17] which also receives the name of Isthmus (*Barzakh*) between the uncreated and created, metaphysical and physical, divine and human levels. The omnipresence of God in His creation through the manifestation of His Attributes is termed by the Akbarians the "Oneness of Being" (*wahdat al-wujud*). As the fundamental Principle in the doctrine of the Andalusian master, it was the focus of the main criticisms by his detractors. These, comprising mainly traditionalists, saw in it nothing but a reformulation of pantheism, that is, an associationism (*shirk*) between the created world and God, which in their eyes constituted a negation of the fact of monotheism, hence liable to be condemned by the religious law. At all times, the Sufis have practiced prudence in

15 In this *hadith* the Prophet declares: "I was a Prophet when Adam was between water and clay."

16 According to the *hadith qudsi* in which God said: "I was a hidden treasure, I wished to be known, so I created the world."

17 One of the names given to it by the Emir Abd el-Kader is "God's Mirror" (*Mi'atu 'l-Haqq*), in *Mawqif* 89.

order to avoid pointless as well as risky controversies and polemics with the theologians. The work of Ibn 'Arabi is directed above all to the heart of man, to his inmost consciousness. Only he who has realized the state of 'ubudiyya, that is, who has grasped with full awareness his fundamental servitude before God, can "recognize" the Real through the multiplicity of the manifested forms, which the Shaykh al-Akbar terms the "Vast Land of God." Transfigured man contemplates the Real in every form, in every place, and at each moment: he is the Perfect Man (al-insan al-kamil) or, according to another translation, Universal Man. Following the Andalusian master, the Emir defined him as God's "Vicegerent" on Earth (Khalifat Allah), as he who has the capacity to manifest the totality of the Divine Attributes (Mawqif 178) and in whom all the manifested contraries in the phenomenal reality are harmonized. Thus he is considered as the living proof of the existence of God on earth. According to Muslim tradition, Adam, and therefore all his posterity, received the knowledge of all God's attributes or Names (Koran 2:30). Hence this knowledge constitutes the archetype of the "Vicegerency" of God on earth (Khalifat Allah). This also explains why the angels prostrated to Adam.

It is not too much to say that the Meccan Illuminations is an ocean; an ocean which itself represents but a drop of the Koran, the true "Ocean without shores" according to the Shaykh al-Akbar. And it is into this primordial ocean, from which all possibilities arise, that the Emir Abd el-Kader would in his turn be plunged. It is in the work of Ibn 'Arabi that he would draw, not his inspiration—for all authentic spiritual experience is drawn directly from its own source—but a language and a style for attesting to the inexpressible.

Often considered as being reserved for an elite even by the Sufic brotherhoods, the Meccan Illuminations has discouraged more than one neophyte on the Way. A discursive understanding is not enough to exhaust its content, for the work has a depth which only rare aspirants have been able to penetrate. The Akbarian doctrine demands a true spiritual inspiration and an intellectual genius which constitute a real challenge for generations of wayfarers: the Emir Abd el-Kader was one of these rare "spiritual heroes" to have taken up its challenge, moved by an inextinguishable thirst: in one of his poems he would write all the water on earth would not suffice to "extinguish my thirst."[18] It is by

---

18 *Poèmes métaphysiques*, translated by Charles-André Gilis (Paris: Éditions de l'Oeuvre, 1983), p. 51.

orientation towards the "Source of Mercy" (*ayn ar-Rahma*), another name of the Muhammadan Reality, that the Emir approached the work of him whom he designated as the Imam of the Knowers.

Without being able to affirm it definitively, everything leads one to believe that it was during his exile in Bursa, between 1853 and 1855, a city in which the Shaykh Ibn 'Arabi had also stayed, that the Emir Abd el-Kader for the first time had access to the manuscript of the *Illuminations* conserved in the city of Konya. But it is in the Syrian capital, with a handful of the "brothers in God," that he would refine his knowledge of the Akbarian doctrine within the framework of reading sessions of the *Futuhat*. Those attending very quickly perceived that the words of the Algerian exile were not merely the fruit of a brilliant mind accustomed to dialectic. The nuanced commentaries, the ease with notions known to be difficult, the resolution of enigmas, the multiple meanings derived from a single notion, managed to convince this group of erudites of the inspired character of his words. A small nucleus would increasingly form around the Emir and would meet regularly in one of his residences in the center of the city. The existing documents enable one to have a rather precise idea regarding the participants at these sessions. Let us mention those who are present most often: Al-Khani, Al-Baytar, At-Tantawi, At-Tayyib, 'Illaysh. This circle certainly evolved over the years, but the names mentioned are those which seem to make up the core of the most assiduous individuals. These sessions, which apparently became regular, were open only to initiates. For, regarding the subject matter of gnosis, the Emir was not unaware, following the example of his masters, that "it is not good to tell every truth" if he wished to keep himself away from "contradictors and trouble makers" (*Mawqif* 132), referring to the irresponsible attitude of certain Sufis who, due to a purely speculative approach and to an immature spiritual state, proclaim "inner truths" which inevitably bring about their condemnation. This prudence was inspired by the Prophet's saying, which imposed the rules of propriety, of which the Emir had a tried and tested knowledge and a scrupulous respect: "Speak to men according to their degree of understanding." Relating to the teaching of esoteric doctrine, it is also necessary to refer to the testimonies of the Imam 'Ali or to the companion of the Prophet Abu Hurayra, who declared: "I have guarded preciously in my memory two treasures of knowledge which I received from the Messenger of God: one I have made public, but if I were to divulge the other, you would

slit my throat." The Emir's manner of proceeding was rigorous and methodical; the seriousness of the subject demanded it. As a scrupulous
scholar and wise professor, he knew that, as regards inward realities
(*haqiqa**), the authenticity of the source documents is fundamental.
He therefore assured himself of the fidelity of the copy of the *Futuhat*
in his possession by sending two of his close companions to Konya
to study the manuscript which was kept there. This voyage of study
would have taken place in 1870. The two companions in question seem
to have been Muhammad at-Tantawi and Muhammad at-Tayyib, who
during the course of their study of the manuscript corrected some er-
roneous passages mistakenly attributed to the Shaykh al-Akbar.

Between Abd el-Kader and Ibn 'Arabi there exists a double complicity, spiritual and intellectual. Although both men composed numerous poems in the line of the classical Arab poets, it is above all
analytical writing which dominates their respective works. The methodical construction and rigor of intellectual analysis employed by
the author of the *Futuhat* certainly captivated the Emir Abd el-Kader,
whose intellectual parentage with the Andalusian master seems evident. As for the spiritual complicity, it does not lie in the form, and
eludes the usual rational points of reference. To properly understand
this singular relationship, here is what the Emir himself has to say of
it: "The Shaykh Ibn 'Arabi is our treasure from whence we draw that
which we write, drawing either from its spiritual form or from that
which he himself writes in his works."[19] According to his own words,
the Emir is aided in his investigations by the *ruhaniyya*, the "luminous"
or "invisible" presence of the Shaykh al-Akbar. At the very heart of the
nineteenth century, there begins a fruitful dialogue between these two
spiritual figures, in which the disciple interrogates the master, who answers, advises, corrects, and sometimes exhorts him concerning the
arduous notions of a doctrine that goes back to the thirteenth century.
It must be understood that the commentaries of the Emir have nothing in common with ordinary speculative analyses. And although the
Algerian was recognized by his contemporaries as a brilliant man, the
intellectual faculty in him remained subject to direct experience, that
which the Sufis usually term "taste" (*dhawq*), and which makes of him
a representative of the people of intuitive unveiling (*ahl al-kashf*). It is
precisely his lively intelligence, coupled with great spiritual acuity, that
would comprise the originality of his commentaries on the *Futuhat*.

19 *Écrits spirituels*, p. 28.

In their form, the spiritual writings of the Emir stand out by their freshness and by the daring of the themes broached. This opus, of a rare modernity, is characterized by its refusal of the rhetorical embellishments usual in most of the writings of his contemporaries. Under his direct and concise pen, a metaphysical thought, seven centuries old, is actualized in a language adapted to modernity. For, masterly though it may be, during every age every work needs to be interpreted to assure its perennity and universality. If the Emir is included in the line of the great guides of the work of the Shaykh al-Akbar, he is certainly one of the most brilliant and innovative among them by the work of revivification undertaken.[20] His privileged place is attested to by the placement of his name in a number of initiatic Akbarian chains, making him a depository of the heritage of the Andalusian master (*al-warith al-akbari*).

The Book of Halts: A Spiritual Testament

The first published book of the Emir, *Reminder to the Intelligent, Warning to the Indifferent*, mingles, as we have seen, historical, religious, and scientific considerations, and intends in the first place to be a praise of reason. According to Abd el-Kader, the discursive faculty is what most clearly distinguishes man from animals. The recipient of this manuscript, the Asiatic Society into which the Emir had just been received as a member, explains in part the concern for rationality that runs through the work. But Abd el-Kader himself always demonstrated a pronounced taste for intellectual knowledge and speculation, a taste which was affirmed during his constrained stay in France where he had familiarized himself with the rationalist culture of his former adversaries. After his geographical exile, he passed from a horizontal to a vertical approach, intensifying his exploration of what lay beyond reason by a metaphysical reading of reality. The *Kitab al-Mawaqif* or *Book of Halts*, published some twenty years after his death, attests to this. Composed of fragments of texts written at different times, this

---

20 As is confirmed by the specialists of the *khirqa akbariyya*, for whom the renewal of Akbarian studies observed in the second half of the nineteenth century is associated with the name of the Emir Abd el-Kader. Concerning this question, we refer to the in-depth work undertaken by Michel Chodkiewicz (Abd e-Kader, *Écrits spirituels*) and to the excellent synthesis of Itzchak Weismann in his work *Taste of Modernity* (Leiden: Brill, 2001).

posthumous work is in many respects close to being a spiritual autobiography and offers precious clues regarding the inner path and the
degrees of the Emir's realization.

It was the regular reunions with his "brothers in God," the bold
questions of these and the audacious responses of the Emir, which constituted the work's raw material. The idea of composing a work on the
basis of notes taken during these exchanges by Muhammad al-Khani,
Muhammad Tantawi, and Abd ar-Razzaq Baytar—all of whom would
play a major role in the transmission of *tasawwuf* in general and of
the Akbarian doctrine in particular—only surfaced progressively. The
Emir himself probably received this idea with a certain reserve, mainly
for reasons of spiritual propriety, *adab*, which was a permanent and
longtime concern of his, often expressed in the form of a petitionary
prayer: "May God accord us, by his Favor and Grace, respect for seem-
liness towards Him and towards His creatures!" (*Mawqif* 124). In many
passages of this book, the wayfarer is warned against the temptation
to "divulge the favors which God has granted him, above all as regards
the secrets of the Divine Unity" (*Mawqif* 158). Hence we may suppose,
on the basis of several Way Stations (*mawaqif*), that this book contains
only that which its author has deemed possible to communicate to his
interlocutors. By its very nature and also out of propriety, the spiritual
experience of the Emir was ineffable. His recourse to the written word
was probably driven by a wish to express gratitude, and also a way of re-
lieving his being from the states he passed through during his contemplation. It is unlikely that Abd el-Kader, who by nature was prudent,
would have accepted that certain passages, notably the introductory
poems, would one day be made accessible to non-initiates. The next
reason would be humility: the Emir often states in advance his position of inferiority compared with the masters of the Way, under whose
authority he places himself. He refused all comparison of his spiritual
states with those of his masters: ". . . far from it! Far from it! Far from
it! Their station is more glorious, their state more complete and more
perfect" (*Mawqif* 13). Despite these reservations, he did however accept
the idea of a compilation and, it would appear, supervised its development, attributing his decision to a divine inspiration: "God enjoined
me to proclaim the graces that I have received from Him through the
order of general import which he gave to the Prophet: 'And as for the
grace of thy Lord, proclaim it!' [Koran 93:11]. Indeed, any order God
addresses to the Prophet is an order for his community with the excep-

tion of that which, without a doubt, concerns him exclusively. But God has in addition given me this command in a particular manner several times by means of this noble verse: 'And as for the grace of thy Lord, proclaim it!'" (*Mawqif* 13).

The structure of the work is in the image of the spiritual states then traversed by the Emir: discontinuous and at times incoherent, or apparently so. Without titles, the themes set forth and which most often start from a verse of the Koran, are not linked, are repeated, and sometimes contradict each other. [21] However, with a close reading it is possible to follow the tangled threads of the spiritual movements; there then appears an initiatic course marked by successive stages. When the teaching proper to each step or station is assimilated by the entire being, the wayfarer is propelled towards the next stage. *Al-mawqif*, the "way station," designated, as its name indicates in Arabic, a standing pause between two stages. A pause during which the wayfarer is prepared to cross over to the next stage. This process evokes the interval between the end of one exhalation and the following inhalation. It is at this moment, having returned to himself after an ecstatic rapture, that the Emir takes stock of the teaching received in the station traversed.

Divine inspiration (*ilham*), intuitive unveiling allowing access to the suprasensible reality (*kashf*) and the subtle assistance of the departed masters (*ruhanniya*), make *Kitab al-Mawaqif* a unique book. Both in an allusive manner or explicitly, Abd el-Kader affirms that he was merely the instrument of the writing. Through the path of ecstasy, he drew directly from the source of pure Knowledge (*ma'rifa al-fitriyya*): "I have not written in accordance with my desire but in accordance with what was inspired in me" (*Mawqif* 253), he specified; or again, regarding intuitive unveiling: "All that is found on this page, and that is found in these *Mawaqif*, is of this nature" (*Mawqif* 1). In relation to certain difficult points raised by his interlocutors, he replied: "The solution to this problem is not rational, it is intuitive" (*Mawqif* 309); a "grace" which also may be understood as the result of a great vigilance and complete absorption in the remembrance of God (*dhikr Allah*),

21 In *Mawqif* 253, Abd el-Kader says that it is precisely because the commentaries he produces are inspired that contradictory commentary can arise: "I have already commented this same *hadith* in this book according to an interpretation that contradicts this one, due to the effect of an inspiration that contradicts that which occurs to me at the moment. I do not write in accordance with my desire, but in accordance with that which has inspired me."

for in this state of receptivity thoughts, he writes, are "none other than His envoys" (*Mawqif* 252). Nonetheless, the Emir establishes a distinction between thoughts that are "oriented," that is, inspired by the Real, and mere conjecture, which he terms a false discourse, since, precisely, "it proceeds from psychic suggestions with which the demon inspires his friends" (*Mawqif* 236). It is a matter of freeing oneself from discursive thought:[22] "O thou slave of thy thought, cease! I see thee unaware, on the edge of a crumbling river bank. Thou guidest thine own intelligence, thou turnest towards its light. . . . God is in the East, human intelligence in the West; between the two, what an abyss!"[23] Thus ecstasy is nothing other than a total forgetfulness of self by watching over the senses and the reason. The "brothers" who questioned Abd el-Kader did not, moreover, expect from him answers drawn from books of exoteric science, of which they already had an excellent mastery. *Kitab al-Mawaqif* has the particularity of having been built up only with responses inspired from a suprasensible dimension. The authentic experience gives the usual style a tone that does not deceive. The writing therein, however, is supported by rational and scriptural arguments: in bolstering his commentaries by precise doctrinal references, Abd el-Kader attests to the orthodoxy of his reasoning. And when he does not receive an inspiration on a point submitted to him, he limits himself to replying with a laconic "I do not know," which according to him constitutes "half of knowledge" (*Mawqif* 271).

This mode of subtle inspiration that the Emir would experience is not rare in the written sources of *tasawwuf*. It is even considered the gauge of an authentic spiritual experience. The full title of the *Kitab al-Mawaqif*, the *Book of Halts Regarding Certain Subtle Allusions Concealed in the Koran Concerning Spiritual Secrets and Knowledges*,[24] specifies the nature and spiritual orientation of its content and its distinction from the classical exegeses. The interpretation given by the Emir to verses of the Koran, serving as a kind of promontory for the

---

22 Regarding the limits of reason, having arrived at a certain stage of spiritual progression, Jalal ad-Din Rumi said: "Reason is good and desirable until she brings you to the door of the King. Having arrived at His door, set reason aside, for at that point it leads you to your perdition" (cited in L. Anvar-Chenderoff, *Rumi* [Paris: Médicis-Entrelacs, 2004], p. 200).

23 *Poèmes métaphysiques*, pp. 47-48.

24 *Écrits spirituels*, p. 187n.

ascensional movement of each Way Station, is drawn from the present Moment, eternally renewed: ". . . each time someone has had his inner sight opened and his heart illumined by God, he will draw from a verse or a *hadith* a meaning that no one before him has been led to discover" (*Mawqif* 1).

Because the spiritual path is marked with temptations and perils, the wayfarer must exercise extreme vigilance. The tradition evokes the necessity of a guide (*murshid*) who himself has followed the Way; we shall return to this later. Before finding one, the Emir had been helped by the spiritual forms of deceased masters, but also by "visitations" of the Prophet Muhammad in the subtle modality. The relationship between the Emir Abd el-Kader and he who had been his model throughout his life was not limited to merely observing the precepts inherited from the tradition. As the citation from the Koran that opens the first Way Station says: "In the Messenger of God ye have an excellent model" (Koran 33:21). For the Emir, the verse alludes both to the historical reality of the Prophet, but more fundamentally to his metaphysical reality of which he said that it is "an immense sea, beginningless and endless. All that has been able to be written on the sciences of this lower world or of the next is contained in this allusion without equal" (*Mawqif* 1).

The Muhammadan heir, following the steps of the Prophet, conforms outwardly and inwardly to the "excellent model." Outwardly, he takes on his virtues and qualities; inwardly he benefits from influx of the Prophetic inspiration: "When He [God] wished to give me a command or a prohibition, announce good news or warn me, teach me a science or respond to a question that I had posed to Him, it was His custom to ravish me from myself, without affecting my outer form, and then to project upon me that which I desired by a subtle allusion contained within a verse of the Koran; after which, He restored me to myself, armed with this verse, consoled and fulfilled. Then he would send me an inspiration concerning that which He had wished to tell me through the verse in question. The communication of this verse would take place without sound or letter, and could be situated in any direction of space. I received in this way, and by the Grace of God, roughly half the Koran, and I hope not to die before possessing thus the entire Koran" (*Mawqif* 1). This testimony reveals the closeness of the inner reality of the Emir to that of his illustrious ancestor. According to Muslim tradition, Muhammad is the preeminent vessel of the

Word of God, a Word which inhabited him to the point that his wife 'Aisha said of him that "the Koran was his nature." This *hadith* was one of the scriptural bases starting from which the Sufis developed a subtle exegesis concerning the nearness of the Divine Word and him in whom It indwells. They established an analogy, on the one hand between the Virgin Mary and Jesus and, on the other hand, between Muhammad and the Koran. Symbolically, the Virgin Mary and Muhammad, who in this respect are one and the same symbolic reality, are compared to the Mercy—etymologically also meaning the Womb, here understood as a universal reality—that gives birth to the Word of God. In other words, Jesus, the Word of God, proceeded from Mary, as the Koran proceeded from Muhammad. Now, the experience which the Emir had of "Grace" is so close that it went as far as extinction in the Prophet. The event took place at the beginning of the month of Ramadan of the year 1864. At the time, the Emir was in retreat in Medina in the mosque of the Prophet, where he gave himself up to the invocation: "Sleep overcame me. I had a vision in which the noble person of the Prophet was fused with mine to the point that we became one being: I looked at myself and I saw him; he became me. Filled with dread and joy at one and the same time, I arose, made an ablution, and entered the mosque to greet the Prophet" (*Mawqif* 13).

We have already said that if on the physical plane Muhammad is invested with the function of the Seal of Prophecy, on the metaphysical plane he is the supreme manifestation of the Muhammadan Reality, which represents the final threshold of the intelligible beyond which abides the Inexpressible, without form or name. Regarding this Reality, the Emir writes that it is "the *Materia Prima* of the Universe, the Reality of realities, the substance of all that is 'other than Allah'" (*Mawqif* 325). He devotes to this the densest pages of his spiritual testament (see especially *Mawqif* 89). While recognizing that it remains an impenetrable mystery, he offers some precisions regarding one of its aspects: "This Muhammadan Reality is thus the Isthmus separating unconditioned Being from pure nothingness. It is also the degree of the perfect Man who plays the part of isthmus between the function of Divinity and creatures, being thus the link between the manifested and unmanifested worlds" (*Mawqif* 235). The Perfect Man or Universal Man, the subject here in question, is a fundamental principle in Sufi doctrine. It is part of the "Knowers through God" (*'arifun*), those who draw their knowledge of God in God Himself. And he is distinguished from all other creatures because he "manifests in their fullness the Divine Names and Attributes" (*Mawqif* 17). Pertaining to this world and to the other, he permanently contemplates the universal manifestation of the divine attributes through all the aspects of the Creation. It is he who is referred to in this holy tradition (*hadith qudsi*), often commented upon by the people of the way: "My servant does not cease to draw near to Me through supererogatory works until I love him, and when I love him, I am the ear with which he hears, the eye with which he sees, the hand with which he grasps, and the foot with which he walks. If he asks of Me, I surely will grant it, if he seeks refuge near Me, assuredly I will give it to him." The Universal Man, writes the Emir, "contemplates God manifesting as Agent, Shaper, and Creator in all the atoms of the universe" (*Mawqif* 275). Regarding the Oneness of Being, already discussed, the author of the *Kitab* goes still further: "God is in Himself Naught and Being, the inexistent and the existent. For there is nothing that can be felt, known, written about or uttered that is not Him" (*Mawqif* 287). A daring metaphysical formulation of the testimony of the Divine Unicity (*tawhid*), the first pillar of Islam. However, the Emir is lucid regarding the "scandalous" nature of these words, which is why he declares that reason cannot apprehend such truths for, he writes addressing the reader: "Beware, O thou who readest this, of accusing us of professing incarnationism, the union of God and creature, atheism or heresy. For we bear no responsibility for thy twisted understanding and foolish attitude" (*Mawqif* 64).

Kitab al-Mawaqif gives an insight into the spiritual path of its author and the teaching that he received in the intimacy of his consciousness. Regarding prophets and saints and the teaching of which they are the depositories, the Emir wrote some lines which could be applied to himself: "God Himself takes on the charge of teaching some of His servants. . . . The science that He teaches is the only true one: for it is the immutable Science that is not shaken by any doubt nor affected by any uncertainty" (*Mawqif* 269). On the eve of his encounter in 1863 with his fleshly master, Sidi Muhammad al-Fasi ash-Shadhili, the Emir had not yet attained this certainty. His spiritual state still suffered from imperfection and instability. And it is in the Shadhiliyya *tariqa*, to which he would attach himself, that the final grafting would be accomplished.

Sidi Muhammad al-Fasi ash-Shadhili: The Final Grafting

When he arrived at Damascus, the Emir was a spiritually mature man; it is not excluded that he was already a Knower by God or Gnostic (*'arif bi-Llah*). The Knower, according to the author of the *Kitab al-Mawaqif*, is he who, even though he outwardly seems like an ordinary man, has an "interior which is divine for having taken on the Divine Qualities and having realized His Names" (*Mawqif* 17). Moreover, the Emir compares the Knower to an empty recipient or container ready to "contain" the divine; a capacity reserved for the spiritual organ of the heart, in reference to the famous *hadith qudsi*: "Neither My earth nor My Heavens can contain Me, but the heart of My believing servant containeth Me." Knowledge, which has no limits (*Mawqif* 359), nevertheless has degrees. So long as he has not reached the Station of Permanence (*maqam al-baqa'*), the Knower is in an incessant inner movement. Only one who has attained the final Station of effective realization has reached the end of the journey. God Himself takes charge of him and grants him "the great liberation and the supreme Happiness" (*Mawqif* 320). One of the conditions *sine qua non* to attain this end is recourse to a "means of access" (*Mawqif* 197), which is none other than the teaching master.

In the tradition of *tasawwuf*, the master or shaykh is defined as the preeminent servant. He knows the Way for having himself traversed the entire course, and it is by a divine mandate that the initiated aspirant becomes an initiating guide. Thus he is the companion in the Way, who knows all its subtleties and all its dangers. The genuineness of a master and his authority are based on "a true knowledge of the Way, of the deficiencies that are obstacles and the maladies which prevent attaining to gnosis, who possesses a tried and tested therapeutic science of the dispositions of the temperaments and of the remedies that are appropriate" (*Mawqif* 197). This indispensable master the Emir met only in 1863, in Mecca, in the person of Sidi Muhammad Mas'ud al-Fasi ash-Shadhili.

Let us recall that Sidi Muhyi ad-Din was the first spiritual guide of Abd el-Kader. It is in his company that in 1826, in Damascus, there had taken place another important encounter for the young aspirant, that with Shaykh Khalid an-Naqshbandi. However, despite the role that both of these could play, the two filiations had only a symbolical import on the spiritual plane. At that time Abd el-Kader was a young novice in the phase of apprenticeship and discovery more than in a maturely consented adhesion. The landing of the French Africa Army and his own political engagement moreover did not allow him to concretely take up a methodical way under the guidance of a master. An atypical person, he would also follow an uncommon spiritual way.

During his first years as a Damascene exile, the Emir was a fulfilled man. Granted a comfortable pension, he could dedicate himself to his spiritual investigation and to philanthropic works. As the head of a family with numerous children whose education he assured, he was also the mentor of several hundred Algerian expatriates who lived in the outskirts south of Damascus. The prestige linked to his name had already made him a historical figure and a legendary personage. His action in favor of the Christian community of Damascus spread his renown to the entire world. In spite of the cascade of distinctions received in tribute to his action, which would have dazzled more than one person, the Emir never deviated from his course, which his ancient French jailer, Estève Boissonnet, designated as a "fixed idea": to go to Mecca. This plan, as has already been mentioned, had its opponents in the French government: the affair of the summer of 1860 would alter the situation. Two other events which took place during that time would precipitate his departure. Lalla Zuhra, the Emir's mother, who had been one of his main supporters and who had accompanied him in captivity and then in exile, died in 1861. The same year, it was the turn of his elder brother, Muhammad Sa'id, to give up his soul. Muhyi ad-Din's successor, as head of the Qadiriyya, had settled shortly before in Damascus where he assured the continuity of the paternal legacy for his Qadiri disciples. The loss of his two "guardians" made the Emir an orphan, an aspirant in search of his master in the likeness of the Prophet: "The orphan in this case is none other than the disciple in whom the master . . . has discerned the predispositions and the aptitude to become an accomplished man. That is why God gave His Envoy the name orphan, because of all the possessors of hidden treasures, he was incontestably the most sublime, and his treasure was without doubt the most precious" (*Mawqif* 158). The inner process was henceforth initiated that would lead the "orphan" Abd el-Kader towards the one who would help him discover the "treasure" buried in his own being.[25] The Sufis use many metaphors to designate the master: "door" which gives access to the Real, "spouse" who makes fertile the "receptive vessel"

25 See Koran 18:82.

that is the disciple, or again a sort of wise man who helps the disciple give birth to himself. In *Mawqif* 19, Abd el-Kader writes: "The Master is the door that gives the disciple access to God; and every favor God wishes to give the disciple He gives through the intermediary of the Master."

It is paradoxical, to say the least, that an individual of the Emir Abd el-Kader's stature should decide to have recourse to a master. His double filiation, religious and spiritual, his election to the title of Commander of the Faithful, his stature as teacher and erudite, the subtle experiences he had, might enable one to believe that it was not indispensable for him to place himself under a spiritual authority. Such, in any case, was the opinion of a close relative who, in a letter of 1863, and in a tone that borders on reproach, questions the Emir on the nature of the tie that he had just sealed with Sidi Muhammad al-Fasi: "During your voyage [to Mecca] we were told that you met an accomplished master and attached yourself to him, which astonishes me! Your station is that of a Knower, not that of a simple disciple! If this information were to be verified, it would be among the oddest of the times."[26] Inspired by social considerations, this curious reaction could only be at odds with the purely spiritual intention of the Emir. As with his previous commitments, the Emir acted as a free man, detached from social rankings and earthly contingencies. In spiritual matters, only inner necessity was law; and at this time the Emir intensely felt the need of a master. For some time he had been beset by supernatural inspirations, theophanic flashes, and other spiritual events which disconcerted him and plunged him into a kind of confusion: thus at this stage of his way, the master, as he would later write, becomes an imperious necessity (*Mawqif* 197). According to Sufi tradition, the aspirant's travel on the way takes place according to two distinct modalities: methodical itinerary and ecstatic rapture. The itinerant proceeds step by step, progressively integrating the teaching proper to each spiritual Station, until he arrives at the "Divine Proximity" (*walaya*), an initiatic path which is considered by those who have practiced it to be demanding and trying. As for the ecstatic, he may, in a manner that is lightning-like and unpredictable, and apparently chaotic, live superior states of consciousness and benefit from spiritual sciences without having followed a marked itinerary. It is to this category that the Emir pertained on the eve of his attachment to his master. But this way of spiritual

26 *Tuhfat*, p. 714.

realization, although it is "the shortest and surest," suffers from imperfections, according to the Emir. It is probably at the onset of the year 1860 that he decided to take the gradual and demanding journey of the itinerant. Thus, free of all concerns, placed under the gaze of God, he enables one to perceive in this decision a degree of moral and spiritual exigency which he had often exhibited in the past. This disposition of mind reminds us also that despite his effective knowledge of the doctrine, the Emir never laid claim to the function of master.

Almost forty years after his first voyage to the Hijaz, the Emir once more took up the pilgrim's staff. In January 1863, he left Damascus and headed towards the "Mother of cities," *Umm al-Qura* (Koran 6:92). His geographic and spiritual peregrination would last a year and a half. Like the tens of thousands of faithful, he answered the call with the sacred formula: "Here I am at Thy call, My God, Here I am. . . !" If the *hajj* is a legal prescription which every able Muslim must heed, for the Sufi it is above all situated within him. The orientation towards the "Abode of God," the name given to the *Kaaba*, is at the same time an orientation towards the heart of the being (*Mawqif* 276): "The *hijra*[27] accomplished in view of God must above all be made in the heart" (*Mawqif* 185). A heart must be empty of all alienating passions and await receiving the visit of the Worshipped.

To get to the geographic heart of Islam, the Emir crossed what would become the isthmus of Suez—of which he was one of the main promoters—which joined the Mediterranean to the Red Sea. This crossing of a canal joining two seas strangely evokes, on the plane of inwardness, the crossing of the spiritual isthmus (*barzakh*), which every wayfarer crosses in his spiritual ascension. When he arrived at the holy city, Abd el-Kader was welcomed by the religious dignitaries and notables with 'Abd Allah Pasha, the emir of Mecca, at their head, who secured a house for him in the proximity of the sanctuary. From the moment he had gotten settled, he was assailed by unexpected and continual visits of personalities or simple faithful coming to pay him homage. Probably it was to escape them that the Emir, wishing to dedicate himself fully to prayer and meditation, sent no news to anyone after his departure for the city of Ta'if. His family became alarmed, and the

---

27 An explicit reference to the migration of the Prophet from Mecca to Medina, which marks the beginning of the Muslim calendar. [Translator's note: This *Mawqif* is a typical instance of the way the Emir, as a Sufi contemplative, above all always had in view the spiritual or symbolical meanings comprised in the religion.]

uproar over his disappearance soon became a rumor announcing his death, echoed by the regional and European newspapers. It was finally quelled when he departed from the Hijaz. A very significant anecdote, for since the Emir was quite alive at the end of the year of 1863, he probably underwent an initiatic death. It is only for those who "give up their souls," in accordance with the Prophet's injunction "Die before ye die," that transformation can take place. And the Emir Abd el-Kader had already long been prepared for it.

It is in Mecca that the pilgrim would encounter his spiritual master for the first time. We possess very little information concerning the circumstances of this meeting, just as there exist few biographical elements concerning Sidi Muhammad al-Fasi, who died in 1872 in Mecca, where he is buried. We know that he was born in Morocco, and that after having studied theology according to the Malikite rite, he attached himself to one of the most active brotherhoods of the beginning of the nineteenth century, the Darqawiyya *tariqa*, a branch of the Shadhiliyya *tariqa*. Its founder, Mulay al-'Arabi ad-Darqawi, had had many disciples who, after his death in 1823, founded their own branches in their turn. Among them figured Sidi Muhammad ibn Hamza al-Madani. It is to him that Muhammad al-Fasi attached himself. He immigrated with his master to Tripolitania where he served him for eighteen years. After the death of the Shaykh, he left Libya for the Hijaz, where he settled with some disciples. He nonetheless continued to travel to Egypt, Yemen, and India, where he created many *zawiyas*, from which his teaching, a balance between exoteric and esoteric elements, spread, and which it seems was part of the reformist current of his time.[28]

This authentic teaching, open to its age, could not but captivate the Emir Abd el-Kader. However, the relationship between the master and the disciple eludes purely objective motives. A contemporary of the Emir recounts that when the Emir finally met his master, the latter, unsurprised, told him: "I have been waiting for you for twenty years." The Emir, henceforth a simple disciple, must have surely been struck by this remark confided to him, which took him back to the year 1843, one of the most trying periods of his political and military career. Desolation had spread through the province of Oran, he had lost one after the other of his fortresses, years of work were reduced to nothing. His *smala*, his mobile capital, fell into the hands of the Duke of Aumale,

---

28 Itzchak Weismann, *Taste of Modernity*, p. 102.

he had lost his best men, among whom were his first lieutenant of the province of Miliana, Sidi Muhammad Embarek ben 'Allal—so many calamities which probably had made him dream of quitting the field of battle in order to begin a new life of verticality in the East. Only the sacred word given to his father and to his followers to defend the honor of Islam had prevented him from answering that inner call.

Master and disciple probably concluded the pact of allegiance (*bay'a*) in Mecca. During this solemn ceremony, which reproduces a major event in the life of the Prophet Muhammad,[29] (85) the disciple literally abandons himself to the master. The Sufi tradition compares this abandonment to that of a corpse in the hands of the washer. Henceforth, the disciple Abd el-Kader methodically followed the instructions of his Shaykh, who prescribed an ascetic discipline for him, the retreat and the major combat (*jihad al-akbar*), this fight against the passions and the rebellious soul of which the Emir had already had a long experience, but which gains in efficacy when it is guided: "One cannot trust in the spiritual combat undertaken in the absence of a master, save in exceptional cases, for there is no single *jihad*, conducted in a single manner: the dispositions of beings are varied, their temperaments differ greatly from one another, and what is profitable for one may be harmful to another" (*Mawqif* 197). The days are made rhythmical by the ritual prayers, completed by the *wird* and the *dhikr* proper to the Shadhiliyya *tariqa*. The culminating point of this spiritual ascension would be accomplished in a rocky cave named Hira: the very one where tradition situates the initial encounter between Muhammad and the archangel Gabriel. Situated near Mecca, on a slope of the Mountain of Light (*jabal an-Nur*), it is in this grotto, symbolizing both the tomb and the heart,[30] that the transfiguration was brought about: the son of 'Abd Allah became Muhammad Messenger of God (*rasul Allah*). The Emir Abd el-Kader, following in the steps of his illustrious model, would in his turn experience this death-resurrection.

---

29 Following an agreement signed by the Prophet with the polytheistic tribes, which gave them an advantage over the Muslims, some of the Prophet's companions expressed reservations over the decision. There ensued a renewal of the pact of allegiance to the Prophet (*bay'a*), an event referred to by the chapter "The Victory" (Koran 48:10).

30 This double symbolism refers back to the initiatic death and to the revelation. It is because he was dead to himself that Muhammad son of 'Abd Allah could receive and conserve the divine revelation in his heart: "And lo! it is a revelation of the Lord of the Worlds, which the true Spirit hath brought down upon thy heart" (Koran 26:192-193).

The several lines dedicated in the *Tuhfat* of Muhammad Sa'id to this episode in the life of his father,[31] and the indications given in the *Kitab al-Mawaqif*, allow one to believe that his traversing of the spiritual stations was as fulgurating as it was prodigious. In every way it amounted to a "flight towards God" (Koran 51:50), which propelled the itinerant Abd el-Kader into a state of amazement, to which he would give expression in a testimony of incantatory power: "What perplexity is mine! What can I do? I can do no more. Why go on? See! My entire being is at the point of dividing and dispersing. Now I melt like snow on water: it returns to its original element and dissolves therein. Each time I have said, 'This is the way out!' it has been shut before me: I cannot overcome the obstacle."[32] Abd el-Kader admits having been tempted to escape from this, but "there was no refuge, no shelter, no escape" (*Mawqif* 320). Overwhelmed by the weight of the theophanic avalanche, he implored God to enlarge the receptacle that was himself, by the saying attributed to the Prophet: "O God increase me in perplexity regarding Thee." The secrets of Lordship were revealed to him one after the other, and the Divine Attributes were unfolded; the Names of Beauty succeeded the Names of Majesty, the states of dilation and appeasement (*bast*) succeeded the states of contraction and anguish (*qabd*). Regarding these unveilings, which subjugated him as much by the dazzling brilliance of the veils of light as by the terrifying depth of the veils of darkness, he wrote: "All these successive unveilings were in fact so many trials. Will the wayfarer let himself be stopped by them or not? Some stop at the first unveiling, or at the second, and so on, until the last of these trials" (*Mawqif* 18). In this exploration of his "inner kingdom" (*malakut*),[33] the trial is in proportion to the object of the quest. Sinking into an abyss without end, at the threshold of despair, the aspirant is confronted with a dark night "without stars and

---

31 *Tuhfat*, pp. 695-699.

32 *Poèmes métaphysiques*, p. 39.

33 Sufi terminology terms the manifested world *al-Mulk*, and the suprasensible world veiled from the ordinary senses *al-Malakut*. In *Mawqif* 222, Abd el-Kader writes: "The outwardness of a thing is its *mulk*, its interior is its *malakut*," in reference to the attributes and Names of God: the Inward or Hidden and the Outward or Apparent. These are two dimensions in which the divine theophanies are unfolded and to which this Koranic verse alludes: "We shall show them Our portents on the horizons and within themselves until it will be manifest unto them that it is the Truth" (41:53).

without the light of the moon."[34] The harrowing testimony of the Emir reproduces the suffering undergone: "One day I entered into retreat . . . my soul was broken, I lost hope, and my heart fainted. All that I knew seemed false to me, all company seemed like solitude, every good thing, something painful. . . . The day was night for me, and the night accursed."[35] After having endured what amounted to the torments of agony, the itinerant arrived at the effective awareness of his ontological indigence. *Kitab al-Mawaqif*, and even more eloquently, the collection of poems that introduces it, give an idea of the experience of annihilation which Abd el-Kader lived then: "In this state of intoxication, of effacement, of non-being, I arrived, in truth, where there is no longer either place or beyond."[36] The solid rock, which had resisted all the joltings of a turbulent existence, would literally be shattered to pieces under the violence of the states traversed: "I faint. The mountain of our being collapses.[37] Let come, then, what will come."[38]

Having arrived at the end of his quest, Abd el-Kader the aspirant realized within himself the fundamental principle of the Oneness of God (*tawhid*). *La ilaha illa 'Llah*, "there is no god but God" or, according to an initiatic acceptation, "there is no reality but Reality," which constitutes the first pillar of Islam, and is also the first word breathed into the ear of a new-born and the last recitation to the dead. Here it becomes an attestation that emanates from the heart of the being, "it is not a simple word. . . . He [God] leads you to your extinction and to lose consciousness, to leave your mind and your senses. You are present in all its phases at the Resurrection of the dead; the shroud, the washing of the mortician, the tomb, are prepared for you. It is there that you acquire certitude; you realize Unity; you know the source and the estuary. Thus is extinguished that which was already close to extinction, thus remains He upon whom all is ceaselessly founded."[39]

34 *Tuhfat*, p. 695.

35 Translation of d'Henri Teissier, in *Église en Islam* (Paris: Le Centurion, 1984), p. 24.

36 *Poèmes métaphysiques*, p. 29.

37 An explicit reference to the Koranic passage (7:143) referring to Moses struck down and the disintegration of the mountain upon which he stood.

38 *Poèmes métaphysiques*, p. 29.

39 Ibid.

Certitude[40] based on vision and no longer on belief, is here compared to death, which also leads to the stripping away of all that is other than God. Emptied, like the cube of the *Kaaba*,[41] the heart of the itinerant is henceforth ready to welcome Him whom "neither the Earth nor the Heavens" can contain. What remains, then, of this soul emptied of itself? For this, the Emir refers to his own name, which signifies, let us recall, "servant of the Powerful": "They call him 'servant of the Powerful'; yet only one Powerful one abides."[42] In other words: the servant (*'abd*) is extinguished in the Powerful (*al-Qadir*), the creature in the Creator. The author continues in more sibylline terms: "I am not this being whom you know. Seek actively who is He who speaks to you." In another poem, the answer springs forth in a last breath in which the aspirant, extinguished from himself in an overflow of the Divine Reality which he bears within himself, writes: "I am Uncreated,[43] I am creature; I am Lord, I am servant—I am the Throne and the matting one treads; I am fire; I am air and earth—I am the 'how much' and the 'how'; I am presence and absence—I am essence and attribute; I am nearness and farness—All being is my being; I am the One Alone; I am the One and Only."[44] The use of the first person reveals the annihilation of the witness[45] in the object of contemplation: "He has returned

40 A verse of the Koran (15:99) calls upon the believer to worship until God grants him certitude.

41 The word *Ka'ba* precisely means "cube" in Arabic. The emptiness of the heart corresponds, on the plane of ritual, to the position of prostration: a "prostration of the heart" from which the servant "never arises" according to a saying reported by the Shaykh at-Tustari. See Abd el-Kader, *Écrits spirituals*, note 112, p. 209; see also *Mawqif* 149.

42 *Poèmes métaphysiques*, p. 29.

43 The Arabic text is *Ana Haqq* (without the article *al*), which means literally "I am Real," but what follows, "I am a creature," allows one to think that which preceded could be translated as "I am the Creator" or "I am God," this last solution being the one retained by Michel Chodkiewicz in his translation. For our part, we prefer "I am Uncreated," which seems to us more in conformity to the spirit and the letter of the Emir Abd el-Kader's text. I thank Denis Gril and Éric Geoffroy for their clarifying arguments.

44 *Écrits spirituels*, p. 177.

45 As in Greek, the words "martyr" and "witness," in Arabic *shahid* and *shahid*, have one and the same origin or root, sh-h-d. Symbolically, this etymological unity recalls that only he who has sacrificed his individual soul, his limited I, can become the "wit-

to God and he sees Him by Him" (*Mawqif* 271). In another passage of *Kitab al-Mawaqif*, the Emir comes back to this experience of the inexpressible in equally eloquent terms: "God ravished me from my [illusory] I and has drawn me close to my [real] I and the disappearance of the earth has entailed that of heaven. The whole and the part are fused. The voyage has reached its end and that which is other than He has ceased to exist" (*Mawqif 7*).

Abd el-Kader is not unaware of the scandal that such attestations can arouse, and that is why he ends this *Mawqif* with a reference to Al-Hallaj,[46] which rings out a warning against all mistaken interpretations that would involve a saying which, he writes, "was uttered for me without my expressing it myself. This saying is understood and accepted by those who are worthy of it; those who do not know its meaning and who reject it are those who are overcome by ignorance."[47]

In this process of transfiguration, the Emir Abd el-Kader says that only he who has totally abandoned himself (*taslim*) can hope to arrive at the end of this "voyage with no return," as the Shaykh al-Akbar designates it. And it is through the subtle energy (*himma*) of his fleshly master, Sidi Muhammad al-Fasi, that the disciple Abd el-Kader was able to attain to the supreme realization. In a long poem, the Emir pays tribute to him who permitted the junction: "O Mas'ud. The time of joy, of blessings, and of deliverance hath come. . . . Muhammad al-Fasi hath the noble traits from Muhammad the Chosen One: He is his legitimate heir; full moon amongst the holiest stars."[48] From this realization the Emir obtained the certitude, following an ecstatic ravishment, that it was a pure grace, reflecting the edifying humility of the Emir as much as the mystery of his election: "When I recovered my senses, I praised God anew, for this verse informed me that all the favors granted me were neither the result of my science nor of my works, nor of a spiritual state, nor due to any merit whatever, but solely by an effect of the

---

ness" of the universal, unconditioned Soul, into which the soul "content in His good pleasure" is reabsorbed (Koran 89:27-30). Let us also recall that *ash-Shahid*, the supreme Witness, is one of the divine attributes fixed by tradition.

46 Mansur al-Hallaj (ninth century), a Sufi from Iraq, who was condemned to death for having exclaimed, in a state of ravishment, "I am the Real" (*Ana 'l-Haqq*).

47 *Écrits spirituels*, p. 45.

48 There exist several versions of this poem. The one retained here is found in the *Tuhfat* of Muhammad Sa'id, pp. 695-699.

[Divine] Grace and Favor" (*Mawqif* 83). At the end of his letters, and more especially it seems in those of the Damascene period, the Emir most often signed "Abd el-Kader, son of Muhyi ad-Din," without any mention of a title of nobility: a simple name followed by that of his father. Sometimes he used an expression signifying the state attained: "Abd el-Kader the wholly poor before the All-Rich."

This total metamorphosis necessarily marks the one who has undergone it. When the Emir Abd el-Kader returned to his family, he was not altogether the same: those near him could see appreciable changes in his face and in his attitude. His gaze was softer and his eloquence more delicate than before. "Fountains of wisdom flowed from his tongue,"[49] wrote his eldest son. As testified by the Emir himself: "This transformation should be understood as being purely inward. As for the outer man, he was not modified one iota. He continued to behave in the manner that conformed to the sacred Law and is praiseworthy according to custom and to natural law, practicing the activities proper to his situation and his rank among his peers" (*Mawqif* 172). This testimony recalls that the way which leads to perfection paradoxically ends with full conformity to the Law: a conformity which, according to Ibn 'Ashir, a famous Sufi, leads to "the greatest charismas."[50]

The great mystics of Islam are unanimous in saying that the return of the new man to society is difficult. For the Emir Abd el-Kader, it seemed to unfold between sobriety and serenity. After the final rituals of the *hajj*, in June 1864, he set out for home, and his first stop was to visit the construction sites of the isthmus of Suez with Ferdinand de Lesseps.

In July 1865, the Emir Abd el-Kader was in Paris, where he stayed in a hotel near the Étoile, on Lord Byron Street. His schedule, managed by the French consul of Damascus who accompanied him, was busy. He attended a solemn meeting at the headquarters of the Suez Canal Company (*Compagnie Universelle du Canal Maritime de Suez*), after which he was received officially by Napoleon III, who presented him with the Grand Cross of the Legion of Honor. Then he visited the Imperial Stables, the Louvre, the Sorbonne, and so on. This voyage to Paris was interrupted by a short trip, strictly private, to England, reported by the *Morning Post*: "During the four days that the Emir Abd

---

49 *Tuhfat*, p. 695.

50 Ibn 'Ashir, cited in A. Cheddadi, *Ibn Khaldun, l'homme et le théoricien de la civilisation* (Paris: Gallimard, 2006), p. 81.

el-Kader spent in London, he visited Westminster Abbey, the palace of Parliament, the British Museum, the National Gallery, and all the other sights of our capital."[51] The visit of almost two months in the French capital was also the occasion for the Emir to see old acquaintances again, among whom those who previously worked for his freedom. Charles Eynard made a special trip to Paris to see again him with whom he shared "a common trust in God." There was a warm reunion between the two men. In a letter dated July 1865 addressed to his wife, the Genevan sketched the portrait of the Emir, whom he had not seen for thirteen years: "His face hadn't changed much, his beard is very black, . . . he has become a little less grave and more expansive, and it is his goodness which is most apparent, above all in his gaze and his smile."[52] The Parisian photographic studios, through its great names, A. Disdéri, E. Carjat, L.-J. Delton, requested sessions with the Emir, who accepts to pose for them. The Emir offered the portraits in the form of visiting cards to those who asked for them. He often affixed the same dedication reminding one that he was no longer entirely the same man: "Although this picture gives you my appearance, it could not, however, give you our loftiest image, for behind my features lies a veiled personality, whose spiritual energy raises its aspiration beyond the heavens."[53]

The man who wandered in public buildings attending solemn gatherings, meeting with distinguished personalities, invited to worldly receptions, was inwardly absorbed in the contemplation of Divine Reality. Abd el-Kader, after having attained the supreme degree of illumination, did not flee from the world. Having barely emerged from his spiritual retreat, he returned to the heart of the preoccupations of his contemporaries, sharing with them their doubts and hopes while dedicating himself to religious and spiritual practice. In all this he is among those of whom the Koran says that "neither commerce nor profits distract them from the remembrance of God" (24:37). A columnist for a French journal perspicaciously used the title "complete man" to desig-

---

51 Marie d'Aire, *Abd-el-Kader*, pp. 220-221.

52 Papiers Eynard, Ms. suppl. 1910-f. 120-123.

53 The dedication appears in the 1884 book by Léon Roches (*Trente-deux ans à travers l'islam*) and was reprinted in Paul Azan (*L'Emir Abd el Kader*). The photograph, dated to 1865, taken by the brothers 'Abd-Allah of Istanbul, was recovered in the collection of P. Zoummeroff, now at the CAOM [Centre des Archives d'Outre-Mer].

nate the Emir Abd el-Kader: "For not only is he a man of action, but also a man of study and meditation. Does not thought nourished by study prepare one for action? From this happy alliance between speculative study and the active life is in fact born true philosophy which, according to the ancients, is none other than practical wisdom. *Virtutis omnis laus in actione consistit.* Thinking and action, therein lies the complete man."[54] The man referred to would define this completeness in a different way in a letter written a year before his death: "The generality of men today are occupied solely with the things of this world; the complete man is one who is preoccupied with his acts and writings of this world as well as with the hopes of the next," a position clearly evoked by a *hadith* of the Prophet: "Work in this world as if you were to remain in it eternally, and for the other as if you were to die tomorrow."

The grafting of fruit trees is a delicate art requiring expert hands; the Emir himself probably had had experience with it on his plantations surrounding Damascus or in the fertile region of Hawran. On the spiritual plane, he had had recourse to the expert hands of his master, who proceeded to graft the individual soul onto the universal Soul. After this grafting, the relationship between the two men evolved to become simply "a relationship of company, fraternity, and cooperation" (*Mawqif* 185). In 1868, four years prior to his death, the Shaykh al-Fasi, after a trip to Egypt, went to Damascus where he visited his most eminent disciple. On the occasion of this event, most of the "brothers in God" of the Emir, who frequented his circles of study, attached themselves to this Shaykh. There were *fuqara'* of the Shadhili, Naqshbandi, Qadiri, Rahmani-Khalwati and probably of other *turuq* there. This event proves, as we have already pointed out, that the Emir did not have the function of an initiating master and that he never claimed to. The doctrine of *tasawwuf* states that even when the disciple surpasses his master, he maintains the condition of disciple.[55] No mastership, therefore no disciples, yet a need to share and spread knowledge, and to announce "the good news," in reference to the verse, "And as for thy Lord's blessing, declare it" (Koran 93:11).

---

54 A. Wicquot, "Le Livre d'Abd-el-Kader," *Mémoire de la revue d'Arras*, vol. 34, 1861, p. 120.

55 Concerning this subject see the clarifying commentary of a contemporary master, in Jean-Louis Michon, *Le Shaykh M. al-Hashimi et son commentaire de l'Échiquier des gnostiques* (Milan: Archè, 1998), pp. 153-154.

CHAPTER 8

The Man of Unity

To God belong the East and the West.
Whereso'er ye turn, there is the Face of God.
Koran 2:115

Verily, this community of thine is a single community.
Koran 21:92

The Ecumenist

"O mankind! We created you from a male and a female, and made you into peoples and tribes, that ye may know each other" (Koran 49:13). In this verse of the Koran, the diversity of worship and culture, far from being an evil, is on the contrary considered a mercy inviting one to fully accept the other in respect of that which differentiates him. For if God had so willed, says another verse, "He would have made you one people. But He hath willed to try you by that which He hath given you" (Koran 5:48 and 12:118). This divine gift is the multiplicity of human communities whose origin is one through Adam, the Father of mankind. The "sons of Adam" are therefore ontologically "brothers," one fraternity which must be actualized in history. This path from the multiple to the One resonates with that which gradually leads the Sufi towards the inner realization of God's Unity (*tawhid*). The Emir Abd el-Kader will follow it to the end, passing from dialogue with just the Christians, to an Adamic brotherhood, above and beyond confessional and philosophical particularities.

Islam presents itself as a revealed message addressed to all humanity, recapitulating and synthesizing previous revelations. Just as the Koran sums up all the revealed books preceding it, the Prophet Muhammad, Seal of the prophets, brings to completion the previous prophetic missions, as is emphasized in the following Koranic verse (2:136): "Say (O Muslims): We believe in Allah and that which is revealed unto us and that which was revealed unto Abraham, and Ishmael, and Isaac, and Jacob, and the tribes, and that which Moses and Jesus received, and that which the prophets received from their Lord. We make no distinction between any of them, and unto Him we have surrendered." Thus the biblical stories are familiar to the Muslims; the prophets of Israel, as well as "those who are Jews, and Christians, and Sabaeans—whoever believeth in Allah and the Last Day and doeth right" (Koran 2:62) are surrounded with deep respect. Regarding the attitude that must be observed towards the "People of the Book" (*ahl al-Kitab*), the Koran is very clear: "And argue not with the People of the Scripture unless it be in a way that is better, save with such of them as do wrong; and say: We believe in that which hath been revealed unto us and revealed unto you; our God and your God is One, and unto Him we surrender" (29:46). Abd el-Kader's ecumenism is inspired by this exhortation to a dialogue of good will, while calling for respect for monotheism, as he expresses it in his *Reminder to the Intelligent, Warning to the Indifferent*: "Concerning the fundamentals and principles of religion, the different prophets, from Adam to Muhammad do not contradict one another in the least. All of them call on creation to proclaim the Oneness of God, to magnify Him, to believe firmly that all things in the world are His work, and that He, the Most High, is the sole cause of all existence,"[1] a text that takes up the *hadith* reported by Abu Hurayra: "Prophets are brethren from one father, but from different mothers, and their religion is one." Thus, every form of anathema is excluded: "Religon is one. And it is so by the agreement of the prophets. For they differ in their opinion only regarding certain details in rules. Indeed, they resemble men who have the same father, each of them having a different mother. To accuse all of them of lying or accusing one of lying but believing another, amounts to the same thing: it is to thoughtlessly transgress the essential rule of religious duty."[2] The goal of dialogue is to reveal the principles common to all religious traditions, not to oppose them nor to serve proselytism.

Aside from some Jewish communities which settled there generations ago, the province of Oran at the beginning of the nineteenth century sheltered a homogeneous Muslim community, essentially of the Malikite rite. For the young Abd el-Kader, the experience of others was limited to encounters with students coming from different tribes and sometimes different countries, but who shared the same beliefs. As for knowledge he would have possessed of the People of the Book and of Christianity in particular, he essentially owed it to books. The clas-

1 *Lettre aux Français*, p. 114.

2 Ibid., p. 120.

sical Arab authors integrated in their reflections on Christianity only the Eastern Christian traditions. In the small essay, *Miqradh al-Hadd*, composed during his captivity, Abd el-Kader often refers to the Melkite, Nestorian, and Jacobite traditions. Even if his journey to the Levant had enabled him to discover Arab Christians of the Eastern rite, his true encounter with Christian reality took place during the war of conquest by the French and the landing of their troops in Algiers. The son of the *zawiya*, according to the world view that had been transmitted to him, believed that at issue was the invasion of Muslim territory by Crusaders. The Christian enemy was conflated with the "infidel" who had to be fought in the name of Islam. But to the extent he had contact with French soldiers, mainly prisoners and deserters from the Africa Army, Abd el-Kader would come to have a less stereotypical idea of these "Crusaders of modern times": the religious slackening which he then noted caused him to lose a number of illusions regarding the vitality of the faith of his adversaries. Indeed, most French soldiers had been cut off from their Christian roots: the generation born from the French Revolution were noteworthy for their religious indifference, even their anti-clerical attitude.[3] The fact that the Emir confided his reactions to many people shows that he felt genuinely disappointed, and that it was also the starting point for understanding the loss of the religious sense and the spiritual destitution of his Western contemporaries.

While respecting the religious integrity and the freedom of worship of the French prisoners, Abd el-Kader also manifested a genuine curiosity regarding Christian rites, concerning which he questioned the soldiers and the French emissaries with whom he came into contact, and he "did not fear discussing with Christians concerning religious matters, which he did with acuteness and politeness."[4] Moreover, it seems that the Emir possessed a Torah and that he had tried without success to procure a volume of the Gospels in Arabic. His attitude on the whole was a natural one for a literary man, just as the art of

---

3 According to certain chronicles of the time, it was a remark of the Emir on the absence of religious practices among the French that subsequently led to the decision to found the Trappist abbey at Staoueli, in Algeria! This fact has not yet been verified, but if it were confirmed, it would demonstrate the influence of the Emir even outside his cultural environment.

4 E. Pellissier de Reynaud, *Annales algériennes* (Paris: Anselin et Gaultier-Laguionie, 1836), vol. 2, p. 358.

dialectic and theological debate that he practiced with his coreligion-ists came naturally to him and would henceforth widen to include the "People of the Book." While these dialogues with some military men remained sporadic and improvised, they would take on greater ampli-tude after 1841, on the occasion of an exchange of prisoners during the course of which the Emir met, for the first time it seemed to him, a true representative of the Catholic Church.

In the spring of 1841, when Father Suchet, accompanied by an in-terpreter, entered the camp of the Emir, he already knew of the Arab chief's reputation for tolerance. His *Lettres édifiantes et curieuses sur l'Algérie* ("Edifying and Interesting Letters on Algeria"), appeared the year following the encounter, allowing one to suppose that the author fell under the spell of "that powerful Chief of the Holy War" compara-ble to a "holy bishop of France"![5] Once the negotiation concerning the prisoners was completed, Abd el-Kader took advantage of the guest's knowledge to satisfy his religious curiosity. The dialogue that followed is sufficiently edifying for us to reproduce a large extract:

"After a moment of silence, he told me, indicating the Christ that he saw on my chest: 'Is that the image of Sayyiduna 'Isa [Our Lord Je-sus]? Yes, I told him, it is the image of Jesus Christ, our God. — What is Jesus Christ? — He is the Word of God, who has made himself man to save all men; for our God is the Father and the God of all men, Mus-lims as well as Christians. — But you have only one God like the Mus-lims? — We have but one God in three Persons.' Thereupon I gave him some explanations on the mystery of the Holy Trinity. 'But by whom was this world created? — By the Word of God. — This Word of God is His word? — Yes, It is His word incarnate out of love for men. — Did Jesus Christ die? — Yes, he truly died. — But no, he replied sharply, Jesus Christ did not die.[6] Then he asked, 'Will Jesus Christ return to earth? — Yes, he will return at the end of the world to judge all men and to give his Paradise to the good and throw the evil into hell. — Where is Paradise? — Where God is; that is, it is everywhere that God manifests Himself, such as He is, and without veils, to His elect.'"[7] The themes broached were those of the classical Islamic-Christian contro-

---

5 Abbé Suchet, *Lettres édifiantes et curieuses sur l'Algérie*, pp. 405-406.

6 The Koran affirms that Jesus did not die but that "it appeared so unto them" (4:157-159).

7 Abbé Suchet, *Lettres édifiantes et curieuses sur l'Algérie*, pp. 405-406.

versy, yet there prevailed a great freedom of tone between these men who did not fear arousing sensitivities. The exchange had to be interrupted by the confessed incompetence of the interpreter, which caused Father Suchet to say with a tone of regret: "Thus ended this interesting and very important meeting; and I am convinced that Abd el-Kader himself shared my disappointment."[8]

This singular encounter on Islamic soil doubtless constitutes a foundational date of the first religious dialogue of the modern era between two representatives of the Muslim and Christian religions. Abd el-Kader would continue it in the trying context of captivity, evolving little by little towards a declared ecumenism. The Emir and the Vicar of Algeria were to meet again on two other occasions. In December of 1847, some days after his surrender, the Emir presented his turban to the Vicar as a pledge of friendship and as requested by him; and again in September of 1849, at Amboise, were the prelate had gone with a singular gift for his friend, "a palm branch plucked by him at the tomb of his fathers at Kachrou."[9]

Upon his arrival in France, the Emir was somewhat disillusioned regarding the relationship that the French maintained with their religion. As the source of individual morality and collective ethic, religion, for the Muslim Abd el-Kader, finds its meaning in the existence and maintenance of a relationship with the Creator: every rupture of this tie is a sign of decadence. During his captivity he often returned to this question with his interlocutors. In Toulon he broached it with Colonel Daumas: "You acknowledge God, His Books, His prophets; except you have left the path they traced out for your fathers."[10] This assessment perturbed him all the more in that he did not grasp its cause. And neither the power nor the prosperity of the French nation tempered his judgment: "You have civilization, commerce, the arts, but not the path to Heaven,"[11] he told one of his visitors. In other words: you do not have the essential. The Emir regretted not having met more Christians capable of having a profound exchange regarding the one thing needful in his eyes. And we shall see later that when such exchanges took place, his interlocutors were not without ulterior motives of evangelism.

8 Ibid., pp. 406-407.

9 Khelfa Benaissa, "La Zawiya d'Amboise," p. 77.

10 Paul Azan, *L'Émir Abd el Kader*, pp. 246-247.

11 Papiers Eynard, Ms. suppl. 1980-f. 32-40.

In Abd el-Kader the need for exchange and dialogue with others was of an intellectual as well as spiritual order. As a man of learning, he took advantage of all the possibilities of learning more, as much about his own tradition as about that of others. On the spiritual plane, dialogue nourished the inwardness of his being and helped progress towards the truth, a truth multiple in its expressions, each tradition receiving a share, like children from the same father born of different mothers. If the skillful dialectician he was took pleasure, during the course of these theological discussions, in trying to overcome his Christian partners, he nonetheless did not seek to convert them. His position as a captive and his past actions respecting the faith of his prisoners confirm it. He possessed a feeling for the other and a tolerance not shared by all his Christian interlocutors. Political and military men and ecclesiastics awaited the conversion of the Arab chief, convinced that it would entail the submission of the entire country: the policy of conquest often went hand in hand with evangelism. Most Christian believers who went to the Commander made no secret of such a hope. Father Suchet, since 1841, alluded to it in his *Lettres édifiantes*. In 1845, Father Creuzat tried to join the Emir Abd el-Kader, who had taken refuge in Morocco, to convey to his heart "Christian ideas, demonstrating the sublimity of our religion."[12] This project, born of a "divine inspiration," had the blessing of the bishop of Algiers. It is precisely this bishop who should be referred to when seeking the main cause of such missionary activism. Monsignor Dupuch fully shared in the Pauline vision of the apostolic mission which starts from the principle that the salvation of humanity passes through the conversion of the non-Christian to the evangelical message; a denial of the fact of otherness. The apostolic zeal of the bishop was well known in Algiers, and had several times aroused the wrath of Marshal Bugeaud. In a letter to Pope Gregory XVI, Monsignor Dupuch recalls his intention of "announcing the Gospel of God to the infidels" and complains of having been "continually thwarted [by the Governor-General]."[13] But after the exchanges of prisoners in 1841, the prelate did not conceal his admiration for the Muslim chief. It changed into esteem after their

12 Jacques Caillé, "Le curé de Mascara et l'émir Abd el-Kader", *Revue africaine*, 88, 1944, pp. 230-231. Jean-Baptiste Creuzat was the priest of the church dedicated to Saint Peter, established in the mosque of Bou Maza in Mascara.

13 Ibid., p. 237.

first encounter at the castle of Henry IV in Pau, in September 1848. Yet despite his affection for the illustrious captive, and his action in favor of his liberation, the former bishop of Algiers does not seem to have abandoned the idea of converting him.[14]

This ambition becomes pathetic when it is known that the Emir, who considered himself the victim of a perjury, especially feared being forced to abjure his faith:[15] if France had been capable of betraying its given word, nothing could prevent it from trying to attack his religious integrity. Despite this gnawing anxiety, he continued to welcome all visitors who asked to see him and to respond to all the questions that were asked him, even the most impertinent. Out of regard for them, he accepted holy images which Christians offered him; as far as possible he smoothed over differences in points of view, going so far as to suspend cultural customs, such as serving wine to one of his guests.[16] As Alexandre Bellemare recounts, this good will was sometimes badly interpreted, and had "as a result making one highly placed member of the French clergy believe that he had led Abd el-Kader to embrace the Christian religion."[17] But this was to misunderstand the person. His solid religious and intellectual formation, his faith forged in the crucible of a difficult existence, had made of the Emir a man of conviction, deeply rooted in his tradition. The close friend that showed through in intimacy remained inflexible on certain theological matters. His Christian interlocutors were not long in realizing that he was not a man easily convinced; one of them would even say that he was "armored by the Koran."[18] To those who insisted on the divinity of Jesus, Abd el-Kader recalled the place occupied by prophets, and the noblest

14 An intention that appears in several places in his works, as in this extract in which, speaking of himself, Monsignor Dupuch writes that "he scarcely ever despairs of seeing him [the Emir] draw closer to Christianity" (*Abd el-Kader au château d'Amboise*, p. 18).

15 The most convincing testimony regarding this fear is found in the notes of Daumas taken in part from the library of Alexandre Bellemare but also in the Emir's poems during the Emir's captivity.

16 "Abd el-Kader has invited the prelate to share his breakfast. He insisted that he change nothing of his habits, and had him served a bottle of white wine" (CAOM, Report from Boissonet from September 1 through 10, 1848, cited in Khelfa Benaissa, "La Zawiya d'Amboise", vol. 1, pp. 105-106.

17 Alexandre Bellemare, *Abd-el-Kader*, pp. 452-453.

18 Papiers Eynard, Ms. suppl. 1980-f. 78-80.

among them, "our Lord Jesus Christ is very venerated by us, but we do not acknowledge him as the Son of God; he is a Prophet like the others."[19] To another who blurted: "Your God is not mine," the Emir retorted: "Our Gods are not as different as you say; we are children of two different mothers, but of the same father."[20] The Count de Falloux, the future minister of Public Education, visiting Pau in the fall of 1848, admitted failing in his attempt at converting the captive, and did not hide his admiration in the face of his refusal to become "a defector from his Religion, like a man who would pay for his ransom with an apostasy." The Genevan Charles Eynard ended by acknowledging that regarding this conversion "God alone can do something."[21] Having respect for beings and things, the Emir surely received with indulgence these repeated attempts at evangelizing and perhaps even took them as a mark of esteem. He concluded that the religious zeal, at times inconvenient on the part of some of his "hosts," merely reinforced his own faith, leading him also to view it differently. The Emir knew how to ridicule these excesses. When a priest from Mâcon asked to be received so as to convert him, he replied with a faint smile: "This must be a good man, for he has good intentions. Write and tell him to come, it is I who will convert him."[22] In the same way, he was often the object of misplaced prayers calling for his entry into "the religion of truth." Regarding this, Father Louis Rabion, the abbot of Amboise, who had received the surname of Sidi Babaz and had become an intimate of the small community of captives, had received from the Emir Abd el-Kader a magnificent chandelier for his parish church. At the moment of placing this imposing gift in its place in the choir of his church, the abbot made a short prayer: "May this ornament remain always before God, and with our prayers contribute one day to obtaining from His Divine Goodness the lights of the truth for this eminent spirit so worthy of knowing it."[23] A prayer to which the Emir would certainly have

19 Paul Azan, L'Émir Abd el Kader, p. 246.

20 A.F.P. Falloux, Mémoires d'un royaliste, vol. 1, pp. 363-374.

21 Papiers Eynard, Ms. suppl. 1980-f. 114-115.

22 Alexandre Bellemare, Abd el-Kader, p. 453. In the biography dedicated to him by his eldest son, Abd el-Kader does not employ the word "convert," he says: "It is I who will put him on the straight path. . .".

23 Le Journal d'Indre-et-Loire of December 14, 1852.

said "Amen," he who knew that "God guideth to His Light whom He will" (Koran 24:35).

The spontaneous dialogue that developed with the Christians who visited him soon led the Emir to study the Old Testament and the Gospels. It is the Protestant Charles Eynard and his Catholic friend Albert de Rességuier who procured for him eight volumes of the "the Word of God," some of which were intended for his companions in captivity, and a volume of the Gospels. No sooner had he received them than he plunged into "St. Matthew, paying no heed to the persons present around him and with an admirable seriousness and simplicity."[24] He did not hesitate to call upon Monsignor Dupuch as a guide in his study: he wrote to him: "I have undertaken to read the book of your law, the Bible; and during your stay with me allow me to ask you for certain explanations concerning it."[25] According to the prelate, who reported the following saying of the Emir, his readings led him to a settled conclusion: "The more I study the Jewish religion, the more it seems to me to be harsh and at times terrible, whereas the religion of Jesus Christ more and more seems to me to be sweet, indulgent, the very goodness of God."[26]

It is precisely the figure of Christ who would dominate the exchanges with his Christian hosts. His miraculous birth, his role at the end of times, his message founded upon universal love, and his being qualified as the "Word of God," place the son of Mary at the heart of the spiritual tradition of Islam, but it is also a classical theme of controversy between Christian and Muslim theologians over the course of centuries. It is with Charles Eynard that the dialogue was most sincere and free. His good knowledge of the Word of God, his religious fervor tainted with mysticism, his nationality, which for the Emir guaranteed a certain political neutrality, brought the two men closer together. During one of their meetings, Abd el-Kader, direct and precise as usual, asked him: "I know that among Christians there are different beliefs, some regarding Jesus Christ as the son of God equal to His Father as a son is equal to the Father in nature, others as the son of God, but inferior to his Father, others as a great prophet. What is your opinion?"[27]

---

24 Papiers Eynard, Ms. suppl. 1910-f. 30-31.

25 Cited in Mgr. Dupuch, *Abd el-Kader au château d'Amboise*, p. 18

26 Ibid., p. 32.

27 Papiers Eynard, Ms. suppl. 1984-f. 32-35.

Charles Eynard's answer attests to the spiritual intimacy that existed between them: "I believe that Jesus Christ is the son of God and God like his Father, but in his humanity inferior to his Father. In this sense I would not call his mother the mother of God." The response, sincere and daring, satisfied Abd el-Kader "for," wrote the Protestant, "he reproached Catholicism for having denatured God by this title of the Virgin."[28] Having a nuanced knowledge of Christianity, he discussed other questions with his friend, among them the apocalyptic period and the Second Coming of Christ, perhaps because of the upheavals occurring in the world during this year of 1848. The erudition of the Emir struck Charles Eynard as it would strike Count de Falloux, who was convinced that only the Pope could overcome the arguments of this "brave representative of Islam." To the Count's great surprise, the Emir calmly received this proposal, as daring as it was novel, of meeting with the head of the Catholic Church: "I respect the Pope and I know of the existence of his capital. I consider him as a friend of sincere believers, whoever they may be. I have asked that the vessel which would take me to Mecca allow me to remain for a time in Rome. If the Pope would like to organize a conference there between his priests and mine, I would be happy to take part in it. Ask the Frenchmen who have accompanied me since I came to your country whether these desires are familiar to them."[29] After his liberation, other French personalities suggested to the Emir that he meet with the Pope; this was the case of Émile Ollivier and of Dom Régis, a Trappist monk of Notre-Dame de Staoueli.

Abd el-Kader had done much to avoid the spirit of "annoying controversy"[30] and at the outset would warn his interlocutors on the incompatibility of such an attitude with true brotherhood between "lofty spirits." The annals have preserved only one infraction of this rule of etiquette, on the occasion of the publication of the *Soirées de Carthage* ("Evenings in Carthage"), which its author, Father Bourgade, had sent to the Emir. Presented in the form of an imagined dialogue between two Muslims, this polemical work ends with the conclusion that Islam is "treacherous, a breaker of oaths," and that the "true Mus-

28 Ibid.

29 A.F.P. Falloux, *Mémoires d'un royaliste*, vol. 1, pp. 363-374.

30 Ibid.

lim is the Christian."[31] The Emir wrote a short theological essay to reply to these "false insinuations," the title of which alone is an irrevocable condemnation: *Sharp Scissors to Cut-off the Tongues of Liars Who Criticize Islam.*

Abd el-Kader was led by an idea of brotherhood which viewed the other, whether familiar or stranger, a fellow creature, another "me." During the war, he had treated the French prisoners like his own soldiers. In Damascus, he had risked his life to save Christians out of humanity. In the letters written in captivity, he addresses family and strangers in the same manner: the same formulas of civility, the same religious references, the same prayers, with the persistent will of treating one and all on the same footing of equality. Muslims and non-Muslims, all believers, above and beyond all dogmatic differences, are "brothers," including those whose function placed them in the position of adversaries. To Colonel Daumas, the agent of the Ministry which unjustly kept him in captivity, the Emir wrote: "Between my brothers and you I make no difference; it is as if we all came from the womb of the same mother, I swear to you by the head of the Prophet."[32] The fraternity evoked is no simple formula of courtesy, but profound conviction, as attested by the final oath.

The manner in which he addresses Charles Eynard, the "well-beloved in God,"[33] is particularly eloquent. The Protestant friend is the "well-beloved who has loved us in view of the Face of God Most High,"[34] in another letter,[35] the "Knower by God" (*'arif bi-Llah*)! If the formula is usually reserved, as we have seen, for a certain category of Sufi aspirants who have been "extinguished" (*fana'*) from themselves in view of self-realization in God, the Emir here seems to acknowledge the possibility for a Christian, in this case a Protestant, of spiritual re-

---

31 Abbé Bourgade, *Soirée de Carthage* (Paris: Firmin Didot Frères, 1847). Father Bourgade published a sequel with the title *La Clef du Coran faisant suite aux Soirées de Carthage* (Paris: J. Lecoffre et Cie, 1852). He was the president of the Association Saint-Louis which undertook a "peaceful crusade with the aim of spreading Christian civilization among the Muslims through works written or translated in their language."

32 M. Perras and E. Boislandry Dubern, "Abd-el-Kader en exil," pp. 356-357.

33 Papiers Eynard, Ms. suppl. 1910-f. 9.

34 Papiers Eynard, Ms. suppl. 1910-f. 10-11.

35 Papiers Eynard, Ms. suppl. 1910-f. 18.

alization at the heart of his own religion. In fact, Charles Eynard had confided to the Emir Abd el-Kader that when he was twenty years old he had had a spiritual experience which had transformed him. To a religious, he asked to pray for him and his family because "your heart is attached only to God." In a letter dated October 17, 1852, to Sister Saint-Pierre, the General Superior of the *Présentation de la Vierge*, at La Bretèche, near Tours: "You and your nuns live to do good; you are generous and magnanimous, for you have left the world and its enjoyments in order to attach yourself to God alone and to care for human beings." And in a letter of December 10, 1852, to Sister Providence, the Superior at Amboise: "To you who are our friend, and towards whom we feel great sadness at leaving you, know that such a loving and compassionate heart as yours we will never meet with again. May God reward you because of us!"[36] He sent a petition to Monsignor Dupuch addressed to the representatives of the Church: "By His inspiration, your tender compassion, and the powerful intercession of the bishops, may you never fail a suffering heart."[37] More than out of simple tolerance, Abd el-Kader recognized the right of religious difference to the Christian, and implicitly, the possibility of salvation through his own tradition. A religious outlook that already announced the Sufi turned towards the universal.

The brotherliness of Abd el-Kader, his innate sense of welcoming the stranger to his home—*bayt*, a term whose metaphorical meaning takes one to the heart—had the effect, like a mirror, of transforming the view the French had of him. In turn, they came to view him as an *alter ego*, a fellow-man who was different. The cultural and religious differences were glossed over to allow only the man in his simple humanity to shine through, and upon whom each person could project a religious and spiritual ideal, as this fervent Protestant visiting Pau, who saw in him, "the simplicity and cordiality of a brother in Christ."[38] One of the charitable nuns of Amboise wrote in turn: "Allowing for certain exceptions of principle, there is no Christian virtue which Abd el-

---

36 "Lettres inédites," pp. 186, 191.

37 During his forced stay in France, the Emir Abd el-Kader would meet numerous members of the Church of France, including Monsignor Donnet from Bordeaux, Monsignor Morlot from Tours, and Monsignor Bonald from Lyon.

38 Papiers Eynard, Ms. suppl. 1980-f. 23-26.

Kader does not practice in the highest degree."[39] And Charles Eynard, as sarcastic towards his co-religionists as he is laudatory towards the Emir, had this radical judgment: he is "infinitely more pious and more edifying than three-quarters of the Christians one meets with."[40] Abd el-Kader had managed to break prejudices, but he had also fascinated the Christians to the point of becoming a religious model!

After his liberation in the fall of 1852, the Emir was offered a complete visit of the "monuments which make Paris the capital of the world."[41] When he was asked what he wished to see most, he replied spontaneously: a church! And he was taken to the Madeleine. Before the altar he remained, wrote an eyewitness, "in a pious immobility, and prayed for several moments with an indescribable recollection." Although not unique, such an attitude is sufficiently rare to be pointed out. Abd el-Kader had not been the only Muslim among his contemporaries to visit a Christian religious building. The Qa'id of Tlemcen had preceded him, in 1846, to the Madeleine, but unlike the Emir, he had expressed judgments concerning the idolatrous character of the statuary which he discovered in the interior of the Church, and concluded that "only the Muslims are faithful to God"[42] Subsequently, the Emir visited other churches in Paris but also in Lyon, where Cardinal de Bonald awaited him in order to visit the Primatial Church of the Gauls (Cathedral of St. John the Baptist). The visit to Notre-Dame de Paris was also a subject of choice for the chroniclers of the time. Charles H. Churchill wrote: "Passing through Notre Dame, he halted there in order to examine all the artistic marvels and relics that it contains with an interest which, on the part of a Muslim, surprised those present. Its sculptures, paintings, the court mantle worn by Napoleon I for his coronation, and the fragment of the true cross donated by Beaudoin to Louis IX, all this successively held his interest."[43]

---

39 "Mémoire et images d'Abd el-Kader," p. 99.

40 Papiers Eynard, Ms. suppl. 1980.

41 E. de Civry, *Napoléon III et Abd-el-Kader*, p. 355.

42 "Visite de Mohamed el-Dhqal, caïd de Tlemcen, à Paris," *Revue algérienne et coloniale*, 1847, vol. 3.

43 *La Vie d'Abd el Kader*, p. 298. His voyage toward his place of exile had led him to make a stop in Sicily, in Messina, on Christmas Day 1852, at a Benedictine monastery. The Emir Abd el-Kader received "a hospitality worthy of the Middle Ages . . . where

By now, Monsignor Dupuch certainly had reason to stress that the judgment of the Emir on the religiosity of the French had evolved during his constrained stay in France. "He had heard our bells night and day call to prayer those whom previously he believed to not even be worshippers of God."[44] Similarly, during the five years duration of the captivity of the Arab chief, the Amboisians were able to hear from the top of the tower of the "Garçonnet" the call to prayer of the muezzin. This remarkable similarity between the bells and the *adhan*,* was for Abd el-Kader the manifestation of a possible coexistence between the "People of the Book." With Count de Falloux, who in less than two months after their meeting was named as head of the Ministry of Public Education, he had envisaged the possibility that in Algeria the children of all confessions might undertake their schooling in one and the same establishment.[45] Such a project was not at all utopian and despite the warlike context between France and Islam, he was convinced that there was no other alternative than that of dialogue and peaceful coexistence, even while being aware of the obstacles that were against it and noting with regret that the minds on both sides were not yet prepared for it.

After his liberation in the fall of 1852, it was in exile, firstly in Turkey and then in Syria after 1853, that the Emir Abd el-Kader would continue his meditation on ecumenism, a theme that would be the core of an epistle matured in captivity and completed in the city of Bursa.[46] The title he gave his epistle is evocative: "Brief Notes Intended

they [the Emir and those who accompanied him] attended the midnight Mass piously celebrated by the good religious. The descendent of the Prophet edified them all by his recollection and by the silence which he observed, in accordance with the long silence before and after the ceremony" (Marie d'Aire, *Abd el-Kader*, p. 197).

44 Mgr Dupuch, *Abd el-Kader au château d'Amboise*, p. 32.

45 In October of 1848, at Pau, he declared to the Count of Falloux: "If freedom of worship were guaranteed in Africa, your children and ours could be raised together."

46 Considered as the first capital of the Ottomans, Bursa was a cosmopolitan city where Turks, Armenians, Jews, and Greeks rubbed elbows. It seemed that the Emir Abd el-Kader had great difficulty in adapting to his new environment. After a series of earthquakes that occurred between the end of February and the beginning of March in 1855, and the devastation of a large part of the city, the Algerian exile, passing through Paris the summer of the same year, requested authorization to settle in Damascus. It is not impossible that in this event, which coincided with the Crimean War, he had seen a sign of the end of the Ottoman Empire.

for Those Who Understand in Order to Direct the Attention to Essential Problems." The work saw the light of day in a particularly tense international context: the Crimean War (1854-1855) which opposed the Russian empire and a coalition composed of the Ottomans, France, and England. Reflecting the rivalries of the great powers of the age centered on the dismemberment of the Ottoman Empire, it certainly influenced the tone of his work.

In the end, the Crimean War would preserve the territorial integrity of the Ottoman Empire. During a journey to Paris in 1855, Abd el-Kader attended the *Te Deum* celebrated in Paris on the occasion of the taking of the Malakoff tower by the French and the English on September 8 1855, an event that marked the end of the Crimean War and the victory of the allied troops. On the occasion of this journey, the manuscript of his epistle was sent to Mr. Reinaud, member of the National Institute of France and president of the Asiatic Society: this gesture marked the entry of the Emir Abd el-Kader into the prestigious institution. Addressed to the French, the epistle was not published and translated into the language of Molière until 1858 by Gustave Dugat with the title *Reminder to the Intelligent, Warning to the Indifferent*.[47] Whereas discourses in France were dominated by stigmatization, the author, as a direct consequence of the war of conquest in Algeria, breathes into his essay a spirit of tolerance, emphasized by the translator in his preface: "The impression made by reading the work of Abd el-Kader, is that the moral and religious ideas of peoples are not as opposed as is commonly imagined; they do not appear as divergent except through the prism of ignorance and prejudice. What is it that most often has been lacking in them to arrive at conciliation, if not that they needed to know one another, hear one another, and establish between them the interchange of the intelligence?"[48] And it is precisely a role as conciliator that the Emir Abd el-Kader seems to endorse. In the lines that follow, which certainly constitute the heart of his message, it is the whole authority of a master and of a visionary which speaks: "If the Muslims and the Christians had wished to pay attention to me, I would have made them cease their quarrels; inwardly and outwardly they would have become brothers. But they did not pay attention to my words: God's Wisdom decided that they would not be reunited in

47 *Lettre aux Français.*

48 Ibid.

one and the same faith. He will not make them cease their divergences until the Messiah comes. But not by speech will he reunite them, even though he raise the dead and heal the blind and the leprous. Only by the sword and battle to the death will he reunite them. Were someone to come to me who wished to know the way to the truth, provided that he understood my language perfectly, I would without difficulty lead him to the way of the truth, not by driving him to adopt my ideas, but simply by making the truth appear before his eyes, so that he could not but recognize it."[49] The incantatory tone and the eschatological reference point both to the urgency and the immensity of the task to be accomplished. The challenge did not frighten Abd el-Kader, who intended to make it known by presenting himself as a possible intermediary between Christianity and Islam and, on a symbolical plane, between West and East.

An Abrahamic Figure

Although he is designated by the Koran as a "Muslim," namely, one who is "submitted to the will of God," Abraham is known in Islam as a common reference to the religions of the Book. As a "guide for men" (Koran 2:124) he is the father of a community that rises above religious differences and, beyond that, above the human community altogether. He is also designated as the preeminent model of a monotheist (*hanif*). "Abraham was not a Jew, nor yet a Christian; but he was a *hanif* who had surrendered (*musliman*) (to *Allah*), and he was not a polytheist" (Koran 3:67; 16:120). Prior to his mission as Messenger of God, Muhammad had been considered as *hanif*, a pure monotheist. In this, he was Abraham's heir as well as his descendent. This is why numerous traditions recall the closeness between the two figures, particularly in their conception of the human community. As the Prophet understood it, especially in the Medina Constitution (*sahifa*) it included Muslims but also the "People of the Book," and the polytheists. Thus the Islamic tradition teaches that this Abrahamic specificity is transmitted to Abraham's descendants, and Abd el-Kader, after having received a visionary dream, acquired the certitude that he was one of his inheritors: "By this vision, I knew that I would obtain a part of his spiritual heritage, and that creatures would love me" (*Mawqif* 83). But obtain-

49 Ibid., chap. 2.

ing the same favor as Abraham and becoming a common reference to the three monotheist religions necessarily entails passing through the realization of unity as such. It is in Damascus, whose cosmopolitanism goes back to Antiquity, in many respects sheltering a microcosm of humanity, that the Emir would acquire the full knowledge of the fundamental unity of mankind.

Like Abraham's tent, open to the four cardinal points and welcoming indistinctly all passing guests, the Algerian exile had made of his home a place of hospitality; it rapidly took on the aspect of a *zawiya*. People went there to settle differences, receive alms, and so on. An Austrian visitor to the Emir, in 1856, offers this testimony: "Two barefoot old men, wearing white turbans and brown-striped light robes, hurried into the room and began loudly to recount the details of a quarrel between them. The Emir raised his right hand, and seemed to order them to cease with his index finger raised. They both immediately fell silent and humbly approached to clasp the hem of his garment. He had them each speak in turn, which they did with great passion, the subject of their dispute being the possession of a horse. The Emir uttered several firm words, and they again clasped his hem, and then withdrew."[50] In Churchill there is this description: "Abd el-Kader is punctual in his charities. Every Friday, the street leading to his residence can be seen filled with poor people, gathered for the customary distribution of bread. The poor who die penniless, not only in his neighborhood but in all of Damascus, are buried at his cost. It is enough that a case of distress be brought to his attention for him to alleviate it immediately. He regularly dedicates more than twenty pounds each month to charitable works."[51] The work of conciliation, a major virtue in Islam, does not lead to results unless undertaken by an individual who has realized it inwardly: in other words, it is because he was engaged in a process of unification of his own being that the Emir could contribute to the unity and reconciliation of his fellow men. As the Commander of the Faithful, he had already distinguished himself by fighting against the spirit of discord prevailing among the Algerian tribes, and by his will to unite them around a common principle. It was the same quality that enabled him to rule by surrounding himself

50 R.P. Beaton, *The Jews in the East*, pp. 282-290.

51 *La Vie d'Abd el Kader*, p. 321.

with lieutenants of very different personalities. In Damascus, his status as a *sharif*, his prestigious past, his experiences as a statesman, his erudition, in short, his personal qualities, attracted representatives of most of the intellectual, political, and religious currents. Increasingly, he found himself at the center of a multitude of realities that were often opposed in their principles and for which he became their point of junction. In France, the former enemy was praised by all the humanist currents in the country, by philosophical circles or fraternal societies.[52] All of them emphasized the closeness of their ideas with his and paid tribute to him. Increasingly engaged in conciliation, the Emir refused no possibility of dialogue and accepted entering into a relationship with the Henry IV Lodge of the Masonic French Grand Orient. Despite the prejudices that he had in the past against Freemasons, which at the time he considered to be "people without beliefs, without laws, ready to disturb the order of society,"[53] he agreed to affiliate himself with the Lodge. When one realizes that Freemasonry and secret societies in general were the object of some ten Encyclicals from the Vatican, one can better appreciate how unique this decision was on the part of such an eminent representative of Islam![54]

After the riots of the summer of 1860, an acute tension reigned between the Syrian religious communities, and also between the European chanceries in the very midst of the Ottoman administration. The explosive situation drove the Algerian exile to a process of dialogue everywhere and in search of associates who shared his ideal of peace and fraternity. It is in this light that the adhesion of the Emir to Freemasonry should be understood. At the time of the initial contact, in the fall of 1860, he had only a vague knowledge of the organization. His affiliation in principle was made solely on the basis of a brief but

---

52 One example among others is the case of Louis Tourreil, the founder of the *doctrine fusionienne*, presented as a pantheistic "universal religion" numbering many adepts in France.

53 S. Aouli, R. Redjala, and P. Zoummeroff, *Abd el-Kader*, p. 510.

54 The Emir was not the only Muslim to be interested in a Masonic lodge. Later, one of his closest companions, the Shaykh 'Illaysh, an Egyptian theologian and eminent scholar of Ibn 'Arabi, would begin reflections on the possible analogies between the Masonic symbols and Islam, as would also be done by a great disciple of Shaykh 'Illaysh, René Guénon. Regarding this subject, see Michel Valsan, *L'Islam et la Fonction de René Guénon* (Paris: Éditions del l'Œuvre, 1984). On Freemasonry and Abd el-Kader, see Bruno Étienne, *Abd el-Kader et la Franc-maçonnerie* (Paris: Dervy, 2008).

brilliant letter whose content he could not but agree with: "The moral principle of Freemasonry is the existence of God and the immortality of the soul, and the basis of its actions is the love of humanity, the practice of tolerance, and universal fraternity."[55] This coincidence is also true as regards the initiatic rites and symbols used by Freemasonry, giving it the aspect of a traditional spiritual brotherhood, which could not but appeal to the Emir.[56] Among these symbols there is the reference to a "Great Architect of the Universe." In his correspondence with the Masonic "brothers" the Emir used the name of the "Great Architect" in Arabic: *al-Sani' al-'alim al-'adhim.*[57] In his eyes, the Names of God were infinite and this Name had the advantage of taking up a constant theme in the Koran. The relationship was continued regularly for five years. After the return from his pilgrimage to Mecca, in the spring of 1864, Abd el-Kader was initiated into the Lodge of the Pyramids in Alexandria, in the name of the Henry IV Lodge of which he would remain an active member. The same year, in a letter of August addressed to those whom henceforth he designated as "brothers," he affirmed his adhesion to the ideal of fraternity: "I have understood that the foundation of this noble society is to do what is useful to the creatures of the Most High, to repel that which is harmful, and to proceed on a path full of humanity and fraternity."[58] By accepting the Masonic initiation, officially confirmed the following year in the French capital,[59] the Emir

---

55 S. Aouli, R. Redjala, and P. Zoummeroff, *Abd el-Kader*, p. 493. See also the letter of Abd el-Kader to the Henry IV Lodge, dated January 27, 1861 (Ibid., p. 582).

56 The initiatic questionnaire submitted to the Emir must surely have reminded him of those used in the Qadiriyya *tariqa*. See the description of a questionnaire and the procedures of a ritual of reception for a Qadiri novice in Louis Rinn, *Marabouts et Khouan*, pp. 190-196.

57 See the original letter of Abd el-Kader addressed to the Henry IV Lodge, dated January 27, 1861, in S. Aouli, R. Redjala, and P. Zoummeroff, *Abd el-Kader*, p. 581.

58 S. Aouli, R. Redjala, and P. Zoummeroff, *Abd el-Kader*, p. 569.

59 Abd el-Kader was officially initiated into the Henry IV Lodge during his voyage to France in the summer of 1865. An initial meeting organized for his initiation, which the Emir did not attend, while forgetting to warn them, was postponed to a later date. The delay gave rise to a certain tension and loosened tongues somewhat! Some of the "brother" masons openly expressed their discontent: regarding the Emir, one of them declared that "awareness of etiquette is still somewhat lacking in him," while another declared that his "mystic physiognomy ... inspired little sympathy" before concluding that the French masons had nothing "to learn from him" (in S. Aouli, R. Redjala, and

did not desert his own convictions for others, he did no more than affirm his idea of a human fraternity which excludes none of its components and which draws its inspiration and its principles from God—a fundamental point for him. But after his voyage in 1865 to the French capital, his attachments to Freemasonry would be strained, and finally broken. The reference to God and to religion, enunciated in the first article of the founding text of the Masonic organization at the beginning of the eighteenth century, was called into question, thus relativizing the existence of God and the immortality of the soul.[60] Under the pressure of the republican and laic spirit, the French branch of Freemasonry evolved towards secularization. Concretely, this was manifested by the fact of no longer invoking the "Grand Architect of the Universe" at the beginning of Masonic works. At that point the Emir had no reason to remain affiliated to an order which had nothing initiatic about it except symbols, thereby removing in his eyes that which precisely had given it its life and its legitimacy. Moreover, his relationship with the Freemasons had convinced him that they no longer were interested in exchanges with Islam and its spirituality which could enrich them, but rather that they were seeking Muslim representatives capable of extending their influence and propagating Masonic ideas in the East.

This experience, as with all his past encounters, would give the Emir Abd el-Kader occasion to further unveil his universalist thought, and it is in the initiatic questionnaire which the Henry IV Lodge submitted to him[61] that it would be expressed most eloquently. In particular, the Emir would make use of the circle as a symbol of all humanity to set forth his demonstration. Each point constituting the circle represents an individual soul, all these souls being linked by the center, which for the Emir corresponds to the Universal Soul, a reference to

P. Zoummeroff, *Abd el-Kader*, p. 510).

60 In 1877, during the course of a general assembly of the French Grand Orient, the obligation to believe in God and the immortality of the soul was definitely eliminated in the name of freedom of conscience. This led to the rupture with the GLU of England. The Grand Orient of France would become one of the main constituents of the large laic element in society.

61 The answers of the Emir Abd el-Kader to the questionnaire of the Henry IV Lodge were reproduced in their entirety in the original version accompanied by their translation, in the work of S. Aouli, R. Redjala, and P. Zoummeroff, *Abd el-Kader*, pp. 571-580.

the Koran 7:189: "He it is who created you from a single soul."[62] He concluded his symbolical demonstration by recalling that man must "consider the soul of his fellow men and his own as coming from the same origin, and that there is no difference between them save for clothing and appearances."[63] Humanity is fundamentally one for Abd el-Kader, and in this he follows the tradition of the Prophet that "all Creation is the 'family' of God" (al-khalq 'iyal Allah). By "clothing and appearances" must be understood not only differences in physiognomy, character, sensibility, class, but also religion, culture, language, and philosophy. The unity of this multiplicity is founded on their single origin, whose imprint each person bears within himself; and that is precisely why, wrote the Emir, man can "love himself in another."[64] Love, therefore, stems from the awareness that humanity is one, and the Emir even grades faith in accordance with the degree of love it engenders: "What greater happiness can surpass the love of man for humanity? If there is no love in us, would we pertain to true religion? Certainly not. Love is its sole foundation. Now, God is the God of the Whole; hence we must love this Whole."[65] Abd el-Kader then proceeds to comment upon a poem of Ibn 'Arabi, whose doctrine evokes in analogous terms an indissoluble faith in universal love: "I profess Love, wheresoe'er its caravans may lead—and Love is my law and my faith." This Christ-like emphasis is met with in the spiritual writings of Abd el-Kader and still more in those written after his pilgrimage to Mecca, from which he returned transfigured. Extinguished from himself and from the world, he contemplated in each being and in each aspect of creation the manifestation of the Merciful (ar-Rahman). The love of Abd el-Kader for the Creator henceforth extended to all His creation without any exclusion. This spirit of universal compassion inspired these words written to his friend Charles Eynard: "Small as I am, I possess a great zeal and tolerance to a high degree, which makes me have consideration for all

62 The word "circle" in Arabic, da'ira, has the same root as "house" dar, or "group of habitations," da'ira [the French transliteration is deïra] du'ar, etc. Let us also note that the smala of the Emir, composed of many thousands of tents sheltering tens of thousands of inhabitants, was organized in a circle at the center of which was the tent of the Commander of the Faithful.

63 S. Aouli, R. Redjala, and P. Zoummeroff, Abd el-Kader, pp. 574-580.

64 Ibid., p. 575.

65 Ibid., p. 582.

men, of whatever belief and whatever religion. I even go so far as to protect animals, and I do not seek to do evil to anyone, but on the contrary desire to do good to them."[66] These lines, written in the month of March 1862, are those of a fully accomplished man. He who has sought his entire life to be unified in himself, is led by the consciousness of God's Oneness (*tawhid*). In the *Poèmes métaphysiques* which he composed during this period, the Emir often returned to the desire for metaphysical union: "Where, then, is He who will reunite me with myself: that I may be His forever?"[67] He is the witness of unity within multiplicity and where ordinary mortals see contradiction, he sees only harmony. The transfigured vision he has of the world places him at its center, equally distant from every being and every thing, where he can welcome the other, the different, the stranger, as the manifestation of the Divine Reality (*al-Haqq*). Divine Reality, being Absolute, cannot be confined to any religion, doctrine, or belief. Each community which claims to do so worships God only according to the conditioned and therefore limited knowledge that it has of God. God cannot be worshipped "in a form exclusive of all others" (*Mawqif* 246) for "God embraces the beliefs of all His creatures," wrote the Emir, "just as His Mercy embraces them" (*Mawqif* 254). The tonality of these writings does not conceal the "eye of certitude" (*'ayn al-yaqin*) that he brings to bear henceforth on the matter: "Our God, that of the Christians, the Jews, Sabeans, and all the separated sects, is One, as He has taught us. But he has manifested Himself to us by a different theophany from that by which He has manifested himself to the Christians, or the Jews, or the other sects. . . . Despite this diversity, He who manifests Himself is One" (*Mawqif* 246). And this creed, which grants to each authentic tradition its legitimate share in the Truth, suffered no exception, for it even included those who professed no religion: "There is not a single being in the world, even among those called 'naturalists,' 'materialists,' or otherwise, who is truly atheist. Infidelity (*kufr*) does not exist in the universe except in a relative way" (*Mawqif* 246).

The Emir did not expose this vision, prodigious and scandalous in more ways than one, to all and sundry, but only to a restricted group of his students capable of understanding his statements. Despite this precaution, he gives numerous warnings in the *Kitab*, such as here,

66 Marie d'Aire, *Abd-el-Kader*, p. 215.

67 *Poèmes métaphysiques*, p. 52.

referring to *Mawqif* 246 cited previously: "All this is part of the secrets that it is appropriate to keep from whomever does not follow our path. Beware! He who divulges them must be counted among those who tempt God's servants; and no blame can be attached to the doctors of the Law if they accuse him of being an infidel or a heretic whose repentance cannot be accepted." Thus he was deeply aware of the possible accusation of heresy on the part of the traditionalist milieus. The orthodoxy which he exposes clearly in his writing and exemplifies in his actions, results from a concern for a *praxis* based on a balance between the normative Law (*shari'a*) and the inner reality of the Law (*haqiqa*) excluding all religious syncretism or cultural relativism. It is on the basis of a tested spiritual experience, and starting from the heart of Islam, that the Muslim Abd el-Kader arrived at the conclusion that all men, without exception, are in search of God, including those who deny His existence. At this time of his life, the thought of the Emir unfolds along the boundary line of a clear and unambiguous adhesion to Islam as an instituted religion, and an affirmation of that which the Koran terms the immutable Religion (*din al-qayyim*), the primordial worship which, according to tradition, was professed by Adam.[68] Such a position, however, raises a question: how can two conceptions of the universal coexist? For Abd el-Kader the response does not proceed from a reflection, but from a superior inspiration. It is in his *Poèmes métaphysiques*, born in the wake of his ecstatic raptures and of intuitive unveilings, that his unified vision is expressed with even more passion and daring. Ravished from himself, the Emir, whose individual "I" is then extinguished in the universal "I," bears witness to absolute Oneness: "I am Love, the Lover, the Beloved all together . . . whether in folly or amazement I cease not being Myself. In Me are all the anticipations

---

68 Koran 6:161; 9:33; 30:30; 98:5. The immutable Religion, also called the primordial Religion, is the archetype of the worship given to the One God prior to the appearance of the historical religions, and was the religion of Adam. Its distinction from the religion of Abraham (*al-Hanifiyya*), which represents pure monotheism, is not clearly established in Islam. Verse 161 of the Sura "Cattle" seems even to conflate the two notions: "Say: Lo! As for me, my Lord hath guided me unto a straight path, a right religion, the community of Abraham, the upright, who was no idolater." The immutable Religion such as it appears in Sufi doctrine has a more universal character and includes men outside the monotheist family. In this it rejoins the Greek notion of the *sophia perennis*, which was at the heart of René Guénon's reflections on the "Primordial Tradition."

and hopes of men: for him who wants it to be 'Koran,' for him who wants it to be 'Discriminating Book,' for him who wants it to be 'Torah,' for some other to be 'Gospel,' the flute of the Prophet-King, Psalm or Revelation. For him who wants it to be 'mosque' where he prays to his Lord, for him who wants it to be 'synagogue,' for him who wants 'bell' and 'crucifix.' For him who wants it to be the Kaaba where the Stone is piously kissed, for him who wants images, for him who wants idols, for him who wants seclusion where he may dally with his beloved."[69] In these words, born from an overflow of ecstasy, definitively free of all conditionings, Abd el-Kader lets the quintessence of the universal which he bears within himself burst forth. Having arrived at the highest degree of the Testimony of Faith (*Shahada**) and of the Divine Oneness, He attests to the universal manifestation of God: "To God belong the East and the West. Wheresoe'er ye turn, there is the Face of God" (Koran 2:115).

The Harmony of Contraries

"True poetry, complete poetry is in the harmony of contraries," wrote the young Victor Hugo in 1827.[70] This manifesto of romantic literature could be applied to the inspired poems of the Sufi Abd el-Kader and to the man himself, to such an extent are his texts an emanation of his inner being. According to the tradition of Islam, man, constituted by the four elements of creation, is a microcosm of the universe. Composed of clay (Koran 7:12; 17:61; 38:71) and the Divine Breath in the image of Adam the father of mankind (Koran 15:29; 38:72), he unites the opposites within himself. The author of *Cromwell* wrote of man that he is "the point of intersection, the common link between the two chains of being which comprise the creation, the series of material beings, and the series of incorporeal beings, the first starting from rocks to arrive at man, the second starting from man to end in God." This definition of the human condition seems to meet its exact incarnation in the personality, at once complex and simple, of the Emir. Indeed, a duality emerges from most of the portraits that have been sketched of him: "A fierce *hajji* with calm eyes, the pensive Emir, ferocious and gentle" in *Les Châtiments* by the pen of Victor Hugo; "strength veiled by

---

69 *Poèmes métaphysiques*, p. 53.

70 Victor Hugo, *Cromwell, drame* (Paris: Ambroise Dupont et Cie, 1828).

grace"[71] by that of Eugène de Civry; a "fair ideal of moral and physical grandeur"[72] in the biography of Churchill, who saw in him the result of a perfect combination of feminine and masculine qualities. These European voices, among others, allow a deeper reality to be discerned. For before being aesthetic, this superior harmony between the spiritual and the temporal, grace and rigor, action and meditation, modernity and tradition, in the case of the Sufi Abd el-Kader refers above all to an inner reality. In the image of his inwardness, the whole existence of the Emir, from the dawning of his taste of the Absolute to the final stage of its accomplishment, was penetrated by opposing currents which he had maintained on the same course. An odyssey in which the wayfarer, passing through all the states and discovering all the facets of his being, returns to himself after having acquired self-knowledge. In this voyage of an identity always in movement, never fixed, the world is like a mirror in which the wayfarer is revealed to himself. The relationship between spirit and matter, inward and outward, the metahistorical and the historical, is a projection of the Absolute in the relative, or in other words of the manifestation of the Creator in His creation. And at the heart of this creation is man, the preeminent support of the manifestation of the Divine Reality in which the divine Attributes of Beauty and Majesty compete. Each Attribute exists only in virtue of its opposite Attribute, and their interaction generates the movement of life. In *Mawqif* 230 Abd el-Kader specifies: "The Names of God enter into competition, they confront one another and repel one another, and this is so even within the intimate interior of a person." And in *Mawqif* 225 he writes: "Balance engenders nothing." Only the Name *Allah*[73] has no opposite, for it is in this totalizing Name that "the contraries and opposites combine" (*Mawqif* 30). The Universal Man (*al-insan al-kamil*), whose archetype is the Prophet Muhammad, is he who has inherited the vicegerency of God in the manifested world,[74] conferring upon him the capacity to reflect in their fullness the Divine Attributes, and thus

---

71 Eugène de Civry, *Napoléon III et Abd-el-Kader*, p. 178.

72 Charles H. Churchill, *La Vie d'Abd el Kader*, p. 287.

73 *Allah* is the Name of the Essence, *ism adh-dhat*, which is absolutely transcendent and which contains the totality of the Divine Names.

74 Adam was taught all the Names of God. This knowledge is the archetype of the "Vicegerency" of God on earth (*Khalifat Allah*). This also explains why, according to Koranic tradition, the angels prostrated before him.

of integrating in himself all opposites. If Abd el-Kader was able to pass through an existence made of contradictions, he owes it to his fidelity to the Prophet Muhammad in his historical and metaphysical reality. It made of him a Muhammadan inheritor (*al-warith al-Muhammadi*) who, having arrived at the end of his spiritual progression after reintegrating his primordial nature (*fitra*), contemplates the unfolding of the possibilities starting from the center of his own being, just as pure white light is refracted into an infinite number of colors. If the aspects are multiple, each of them bears the imprint of the common origin; an imprint which can be compared to a "point," receptacle of all possibilities, according to Sufi symbolism.[75] And it is also in this initial and final point that the whole life, spiritual and historical, of Abd el-Kader al-Hasani can be summarized.

---

75 The symbolism of the "point of origin," to be found especially in the doctrine of the Shaykh al-Akbar, is based on the *hadith* according to which "All that is in the Koran is in the *Fatiha* [the first Sura of the Koran]; all that is in the *Fatiha* is in the *Basmala* [the introductory formula: "In the Name of God, the Clement, the Merciful"]; all that is in the *Basmala* is in the *Ba'* [the second letter of the Arabic alphabet, which has the form of an upturned crescent, underneath which is a point] and all that is in the *Ba'* is in the point."

CONCLUSION

The Legacy of Abd el-Kader

Whosoever killeth a human being for other than manslaughter
or corruption in the earth, it shall be as if he had killed all mankind,
and whoso saveth the life of one, it shall be as if he had
saved the life of all mankind.
Koran 5:32

He who knows himself and the others will also know this:
East and West cannot be separated.
Goethe, *East-West Divan*

To retain only the image of the hero and the saint that historians and
storytellers have bequeathed us each in their own way, is to forget the
human dimension of Abd el-Kader. "Dehumanizing" him as it were
from above, risks making him inaccessible and ultimately foreign to
his condition as a man. Behind the person of legend there is the figure
of a being endowed with strength as well as fragility, sharing the lot of
joys and sorrows common to all. His existence, from the most ordinary
facts to the most remarkable exploits, shows that the Emir had a deep
awareness of the impermanence of beings and things; he had lived
with the conviction that nothing is ever definitively acquired and that
life is an effort at every moment. Fatally, his tumultuous journey was
not exempt from false steps or from errors of judgment. For, as Jacques
Berque very rightly wrote, "great souls are particularly designated for
grief."[1] Abd el-Kader escaped no trial in his public as well as private
life. Is it necessary to recall that he experienced treason, violence, illness, the death of near ones, and in particular several of his children?
Despite being made of stern stuff, there comes through his letters and
his poems a feverishness and anguish which drove him to the point of
despondency, and he was no stranger to the feeling of melancholy. He
did not remain impassible under the blows of destiny, or insensible
to physical and moral suffering. It was precisely this permeability to
suffering, inherent in the human condition, that brought him close to
the common man. Abd el-Kader was a hero only to the extent that he

---

1 Jacques Berque, *L'interieur du Maghreb*, p. 516.

was able to sublimate the trials he underwent. In the biography which he dedicates to him, Mohamed Chérif Sahli recalls that the virtuous qualities of the Emir were not one of those gifts which Providence grants to a rare elect, but the "fruit of an incessant work on himself, of a will that applied itself to fashion the being, to correct it."[2] It is this capacity to always push further back the limits of human nature that make Abd el-Kader a model of accomplishment. "Princes in the guise of slaves":[3] thus does the Shaykh Ibn 'Arabi designate the "spiritual knights" (*fata*). Emir Abd el-Kader without a doubt pertained to this category of beings whose spiritual "virility" (*muru'a*) enabled them to attain to inward plenitude. A small work which appeared at the beginning of the twentieth century, *Âmes viriles* ("Virile Souls"),[4] placed the Emir among the "illustrious persons of all times and countries." It is precisely by the chivalric dimension of the person that the testimony of his life is sealed within time and that his memory remains so alive today; a memory which, however, gives rise to numerous conflicting interpretations. How could it be otherwise given the complexity of his existence and the multiple facets of his personality which, if they are sometimes complementary seem often to contradict one another? A truly free man, the Emir had the peculiarity of being just where one least expected him to be. Moreover, in his will to adapt to the truth, he had an astonishing capacity to challenge himself. Those who claim to pertain to his spiritual, intellectual, political, or simply human heritage have unfortunately had a tendency to neglect his transformations and eclecticism, reducing his personality to only one of its aspects and drawing only a partial portrait of him. The import of his word and of his message are thus reduced or even denatured: a *de facto* negation of his own universality. Abd el-Kader had been everything at once: an edifying symbol of the Algerian national consciousness, a daring inspirer of religious reform (*islah*) which, wrote Mohamed Chérif Sahli, "enlightened opinion in the present Muslim world claims to represent,"[5] a precursor of the Arab cultural renaissance (*nahda*) occupying, according to Henri Pérès, "a good rank among the Arab literary figures of the

---

2 Mohamed Chérif Sahli, Abd el-Kader, chevalier de la foi, p. 54.

3 Claude Addas, *Ibn 'Arabi et le Voyage sans retoir*, p. 40.

4 Collectif, *Âmes viriles* (Paris: Albin Michel, n.d.).

5 Mohamed Chérif Sahli, Abd el-Kader, chevalier de la foi, p. 44.

nineteenth century,"[6] a eulogist of tolerance claimed as one of their own by European humanists, or again, according to Michel Chodkie-wicz, the pivot of the movement of the "transmission of the spiritual heritage of Ibn 'Arabi."[7] W.S. Blunt even puts forth the idea that he could have been the new Caliph of Islam, an enlightened guide of the whole Muslim community.[8] But these acknowledgments are posthu-mous. Like all men ahead of their time, the Emir was misunderstood by his contemporaries as regards the essential of the message which he incarnated and tried to transmit. He himself was conscious of this and already in 1855, in his *Recall to the Intelligent*, he regretted not be-ing heard. It has to be admitted that the "Abdelkaderian" inspiration has not drawn the Muslim world into its wake. To the Islam turned towards the universal and open to its time, Islamic orthodoxy has pre-ferred an Islam that singularly lacks daring and generosity. The fears of the Emir Abd el-Kader have been realized: Muslim society has ended by becoming sclerotic and modernity with a European face has turned out to be soulless.

The most eloquent heritage bequeathed to us by the son of Sidi Muhyi ad-Din is beyond doubt the example of his life. A life marked with a seal of the Divine because he was able to cultivate his human-ity in all circumstances, showing that aspiration to God renders man infinitely perfectible. For God, Abd el-Kader seems to whisper to us, reveals Himself only to the being who has accomplished his humanity. The veil is then transformed into a mirror, and the two faces, divine and human, are both reflected in the most perfect harmony. The Koran teaches nothing else when it exhorts man to perfect himself by taking as his model the Prophet Muhammad, the paragon of humanity whom Lamartine thanked for having been able to "make God present to man and man present to God."[9] In another one of his inspired poems, the

---

6 Henri Pérès, *La Littérature arabe et l'Islam par les textes, les xixe et xxe siècles*, 4th ed. (Algiers: Impr. la Typo-Litho et J. Carbonel, 1949), p. 34.

7 Introduction to Abd el-Kader, *Écrits spirituels*, p. 37.

8 W.S. Blunt, *Secret History of the English Occupation of Egypt* (1922), p. 88, cited in Jacques Berque, *L'interieur du Maghreb*, p. 519n.

9 Alphonse de Lamartine, *Histoire de la Turquie* (Paris: V. Lecou et Pagnerre, 1855), vol. 1. p. 277. In his capacity as a member of the provisional government, Alphonse de Lamartine had been the originator of the Emir's transfer from Fort Lamalgue at Tou-lon to the Henry IV castle at Pau.

most lyrical of the French politicians wrote that all is vanity, "excepting the service to God and to men for God!"[10] This thought can summarize the whole life of Abd el-Kader.

In 1839, when he was only thirty years old, the young Commander of the Faithful, taking God as witness, declared to his compatriots: "My highest desire is to be agreeable to God and leave behind a lasting and useful work to men."[11] At the beginning of the year 1883, a little less than four months before being called to God, he was solicited by Ferdinand de Lesseps for an ambitious project of piercing a canal in the Sahara with the evocative name "inner sea." The piercing of this isthmus at Gabès would have conducted sea water by canal toward the ancient dry lakes of the Sahara. Abd el-Kader replied favorably to the request and concluded his letter with these lines, which seem like a last will and testament: "Men are thus the family of God, and the Lord loves especially those who compete to do good to His family. Mankind is greatly beloved of God, its Creator, and all creatures, from the highest to the humblest, are consecrated to the good and to the service of the great whole that is called the human family."[12] A vision that shows the world its own inadequacy, and which some have considered as utopian, forgetting too quickly that Abd el-Kader the visionary did not always act in view of an immediate result.

Like the reactions of incredulity in the face of his project of a sovereign state in Algeria, for which he prepared the ground from the fall of 1832 and which did not see the light of day until one hundred and thirty years later, will his faith in a reconciled humanity not turn out to become a reality? There is no doubt that Abd el-Kader announces a new era.

10 Alphonse de Lamartine, *Souvenirs, impressions, pensées et paysages pendant un voyage en Orient, 1832-1833* (Paris: Librairie de Charles Gosselin, Librairie de Furne, 1835), p. 234.

11 Inscription placed in 1839 at the entrance of the city of Taza after having been rehabilitated and populated. The plaque is found in Paris at the Musée de l'Armée.

12 Ferdinand de Lesseps, "Abd-el-Kader," p. 735.

CHRONOLOGY

1807-1808

Birth of Abd el-Kader Nasr ad-Din, son of Muhyi ad-Din and Lalla Zuhra, in the Guetna of Oued al-Hammam, in Ghriss.

May to July. On orders of Napoleon I, the commander of the Génie Boutin is sent on a mission to draw up a map of Algiers and its surroundings in view of an expedition to the Ottoman regency.

1825-1827

The young Abd el-Kader accompanies his father to make the *hajj*. They cross Tunisia, Egypt, Greater Syria, Iraq, and finally Arabia.

1827

Upon returning from the pilgrimage, Abd el-Kader marries his cousin Khaira bint Abu Talib.

April 30. Tensions between France and the Regency of Algiers after Dey Husayn strikes the French consul Deval with his fly-swatter.

1830

June 14. The Africa Army lands in the Bay of Sidi Ferruch.

July 5. In accordance with a signed agreement between General Bourmont and Dey Husayn, French troops enter Algeria.

July 10. Departure in exile of Dey Husayn.

July 27-29. Revolution in Paris.

July 31. Charles X abdicates.

August 9. Louis-Philippe d'Orléans becomes the French king.

1831

January 4. General Damrémont lands in Oran. Bey Hasan is exiled in turn.

1832

April 27. *Jihad* is proclaimed by Muhyi ad-Din, Abd el-Kader's father, an influential member of the tribe of Hashim, the *muqaddam* of the Qadiriyya brotherhood. Abd el-Kader takes part in skirmishes against the French troops.

End of November. A great assembly takes place in Ersibia, in the environs of Mascara. The dignitaries of the three great tribes of Hashim, Beni Amer, and Gharaba, propose that Muhyi ad-Din take command of the resistance. He declines the offer but proposes his son in his place.

November 22. Solemn investiture of the new emir.

1833
April 23. Arrival of General Desmichels in Oran.

July. Abd el-Kader takes control of the city of Tlemcen. General Desmichels occupies Mostaghanem and Mazagran. Death of the Emir's father.

1834
February 26. Signing of the Desmichels Treaty, which recognizes the sovereignty of the "Commander of the Faithful."

July 9. General Drouet d'Erlon becomes the first governor-general of Algeria, a post instituted by royal decree.

1835
January. General Trézel replaces General Desmichels in Oran. He will pursue a harsher policy than his predecessor.

June 26-28. Victory of Abd el-Kader's troops on the banks of the Macta. Generals Trézel and Drouet d'Erlon are recalled to France. The Emir establishes his new capital in Tagdempt.

December 6 and 8. Capture of Mascara and Tlemcen. First diplomatic contacts of Abd el-Kader with England and the United States of America.

1836
April-May. For almost three and a half months, the Emir lays siege to the troops of General d'Arlanges.

July 6. General Bugeaud wins a victory over the troops of the Emir at the Sikkak. Defeat of the French army before Constantine.

1837
May 30 and June 1. Signing of the Treaty of Tafna. Bugeaud and Abd el-Kader meet for the first and last time.

July. The Emir takes possession of Tlemcen.

October 13. The French army occupies Constantine.

1838

January. Abd el-Kader attempts to establish himself in the Kabylie.

March 3. Milud Ben Arrach becomes the special representative of the Emir before King Louis-Philippe in Paris.

June to December. Siege of Ain Madhi—seat of the Tijaniyya brotherhood—by Abd el-Kader's troops.

August 25. Monsignor Dupuch becomes the first bishop of Algiers.

December 1. General Valée is the new governor-general of Algeria.

1839

October 26. Governor Valée and the Duke of Orléans ostentatiously cross the Biban, territories under the administration of the Emir, which he considers to be a *casus belli*.

November 18. Letter of Abd el-Kader announcing the resumption of combat.

November 20. The troops of the Emir sweep through the Mitija. Colonists surge into Algeria.

May 12. Battle of the pass of Tenia.

May to June. Occupation of Media and Miliana by the French troops.

June 15. Battle of Mouzaia.

1841

February 22. General Bugeaud succeeds Marshal Valée to the post of governor-general in Algiers. Onset of the scorched earth policy.

May to June. Fall and destruction of the main cities of the Emir: Boghar, Taza, Tagdempt (May 25), Mascara (May 30).

October 16. On orders of General Bugeaud, Lieutenant-colonel Youssouf destroys the Guetna of Muhyi ad-Din.

October 22. The city of Saida is set on fire by the men of the Emir at the approach of General Bugeaud's troops.

1842

January 24. Tlemcen is occupied by General Bugeaud.

April 29. Defeat of the Emir at Bab Taza by General Bedeau.

November and December. Attempts of General Bugeaud to capture Abd el-Kader in the Ouarsenis.

July 13. Accidental death of the Duke of Orléans, heir to the throne.

1843

Fierce battles in the Ouarsenis between the Emir and General Bugeaud, who almost loses his life.

May 16. The Duke of Aumale takes Abd el-Kader's *smala* at Oued Taguin, while he is absent.

July 31. General Bugeaud is made marshal. The Emir and his troops retreat to Morocco.

1844

April and May. French expeditions in Kabylie.

August 6 and 15. Prince de Joinville bombards the Moroccan cities of Tangiers and Mogador.

August 14. Serious defeat of the Moroccan troops at Oued Sly.

September 10. France imposes a peace treaty on the Moroccan monarchy, which obliges it to abandon its support of Abd el-Kader.

1845

March 18. Agreement of Lalla Maghnia which fixes the borders between Algeria and Morocco.

March to May. Insurrection of the Bou Maza in the Dahra and valley of Cheliff.

June 19. Colonel Pélissier orders the smoking out of the caves of Dahra where between five hundred and a thousand members of the Ouled Riyah tribe have taken refuge. This crime scandalizes Algeria and France.

1846

April 24. Execution of the French prisoners of Sidi Brahim, presumably on orders of the Emir's lieutenant, Mustafa Ben Thami.

Spring. Pursued by French troops, Abd el-Kader takes refuge on the Moroccan border.

1847

February 27. Lieutenant Ben Salem surrenders to Marshal Bugeaud. He is exiled with his followers in Damascus.

April 13. Bou Maza surrenders to Colonel de Saint-Arnaud.

June 5. Bugeaud is removed from his post as governor-general.

October 5. The Duke of Aumale is named governor-general.

December. Taking refuge with his last troops in Morocco, Abd el-Kader, who faces attacks from Moroccan troops as well as from those of the French columns, decides to surrender to General Lamoricière.

December 23. After having negotiated the conditions of his surrender, in particular his exile to St. Jean d'Acre or Alexandria, the Emir goes to Jam' Ghazaouet, where he surrenders his sword and horse to the Duke of Aumale.

December 25. Abd el-Kader and some hundred of his followers leave for Jam' Ghazaouet aboard the frigate *Asmodée*.

1848

January. Arriving in Toulon, the Emir and his companions are placed under arrest at Fort Lamalgue. Colonel Daumas is sent on mission to him.

January 17 and February 5. Discussion in the two Chambers regarding the fate of Abd el-Kader.

February 22-24. Days of insurrection in Paris, concluding with the abdication of King Louis-Philippe.

February 25. The Republic is proclaimed.

March 13. Émile Ollivier, commissioner-general of the government, arrives on mission to Fort Lamalgue.

April 23. Abd el-Kader, transferred to Pau castle, is received on April 28 by Captain Estève Boissonet.

End of June. Riots in Paris, harshly repressed by General Cavaignac, Minister of War.

September 9. Algeria is organized into three departments integrated into France (Algeria, Constantine, and Oran). This statute is inserted into the Constitution of the Republic in its Article 109.

November 2-8. The captives are transferred to Amboise castle.

November 10. Louis Napoleon Bonaparte becomes the first president of the Second Republic. With 5.4 million votes, he greatly outstripped General Cavaignac (1.4 million) and Alphonse de Lamartine (8,000).

1849

January 13. The prince-president convenes Marshal Bugeaud and General Changarnier to discuss the Emir's situation. The Minister of War is opposed to his liberation.

Spring. Publication of Monsignor Dupuch's book, *Abd el-Kader au*

château d'Amboise ("Abd el-Kader at Amboise Castle"), dedicated
to the prince-president Louis Napoleon.

June 10. Death of Marshal Bugeaud.

July 1. Rome is taken by the French army.

July. Revolt in Algeria, in Zaatcha, an oasis of the Ziban.

August 2. Death near Alexandria of Muhammad Ali, the viceroy of
Egypt.

1850

August 26. Death of Louis-Philippe in exile.

1851

October 27. General Saint-Arnaud is named Minister of War.

December 2. Coup d'état of Louis Napoleon Bonaparte. The Assembly
is dissolved, universal suffrage is reestablished.

1852

October 9. The prince-president is in Bordeaux where he proclaims:
"The Empire is peace."

October 16. Returning from Bordeaux, the prince-president stops at
Amboise where he informs the Emir of his liberation.

End of October, beginning of November. Abd el-Kader makes several
visits to Paris and meets numerous personalities.

November 21. By plebiscite, the French approve the reestablishment of
the Empire (7.8 million votes for and 250,000 against).

December 2. The Emir attends the Proclamation of the Empire at the
Tuileries Palace.

December 21. Abd el-Kader and his followers arrive in Marseille, where
they embark on the *Labrador* for Constantinople.

December 23-25. Stopover in Sicily and a visit to Etna.

1853

January 7. Arrival in Turkey. Abd el-Kader is received by the young Ottoman Sultan Abd al-Majid.

January 17. Settles in Bursa.

1854

France, Great Britain, and the Ottoman Empire declare war on Russia
(Crimean War).

1855

February 28 to March 2. Earthquakes in Bursa. Abd el-Kader asks to be settled in another city.

May 15. Opening of the Universal Exposition in Paris.

September 6. The Emir and his followers are officially welcomed in Damascus.

September 8. Abd el-Kader visits the Universal Exposition. He presents the president of the Asiatic Society the manuscript of his *Reminder to the Intelligent, Warning to the Indifferent* (*Letter to the French*). He meets Napoleon III, after which he obtains authorization to leave in order to settle in Damascus.

1856

March 30. Signing of the Treaty of Paris which ends the Crimean War.

1857

Abd el-Kader finances the edition of the *Futuhat al-Makkiyya* ("The Meccan Illuminations") of Shaykh Ibn 'Arabi. He goes on pilgrimage to the Holy Land (Jerusalem, Bethlehem, Hebron).

1858

Publication of *Reminder to the Intelligent, Warning to the Indifferent*, translated by Gustave Dugat and edited in Paris by Duprat.

1859

June 24. Victory of the French and Sardinian coalition against the Austro-Hungarian Empire at Solferino.

August 25. Imam Shamil, hero of the Chechen resistance, surrenders to the Russian troops.

1860

July 9. Onset of disturbances between communities which culminate with massacres of Christians in Syria and in Lebanon. The Emir and his companions intervene and save from death several thousand Christians in Damascus. Abd el-Kader receives letters of gratitude and decorations from the entire world.

August 7. Decree awarding Abd el-Kader the Grand Cross of the Legion of Honor.

September 17. Brief visit of Napoleon III in Algeria.

1863

January. The Emir departs for the Hijaz, for a journey that will last a year and a half. He follows the ceremonies of the *hajj* and receives a teaching from Shaykh Muhammad al-Fasi ash-Shadhili. He makes a retreat near the mosque of the Prophet and in the cave of Hira where, according to Muslim tradition, Muhammad received the Revelation.

Alexandre Bellemare publishes *Abd el-Kader, sa vie politique et militaire* ("Abd el-Kader: His Political and Military Life") with Hachette.

Napoleon III brings up the idea of an "Arab kingdom" in Algeria.

1864

The Emir returns from the pilgrimage through Egypt. He visits the construction site of the Suez Canal and goes to Alexandria where he is received by the Masonic Lodge of the Pyramids.

1865

May 3. Napoleon III is in Algiers.

June 20. Publication of the "Lettre sur la politique de la France en Algérie" ("Letter Concerning the Policy of France in Algeria") addressed to Marshal MacMahon by the Emperor.

July 5. En route to Paris, the Emir stops over in Constantinople where he is received by Sultan 'Abd al-Aziz. In particular, he asks for clemency towards the rioters of the summer of 1860.

July 14. *Senatus-consulte* on the granting of French citizenship to Muslims and Jews in Algeria. The first week of August. Abd el-Kader makes a four-day visit to England.

1867

April 1. Opening of the Universal Exposition in Paris. Napoleon III officially invites the Emir to visit. This will be his last visit to France.

1869

November 16. According to the official press releases, Abd el-Kader attends the inauguration of the Suez Canal.

Meeting with Imam Shamil, who had obtained the authorization from the Czar of Russia to go on pilgrimage to the holy places.

1870

May 8. Plebiscite in favor of the Empire (7.35 million votes).

July 19. Onset of the war against Prussia.

September 2. Defeat at Sedan. Napoleon III abdicates and is taken prisoner.

September 4. The Third Republic is proclaimed.

1871

March. In Kabylie, the onset of the uprising against the colonial army of Bach-Agha al-Mokrani, joined by Shaykh al-Haddad of the Rahmaniyya brotherhood. Muhyi ad-Din, the son of Abd el-Kader is among the insurgents.

May 10. The Treaty of Frankfurt ends the war. France cedes Alsace and Lorraine.

Death of Shamil in Medina.

1873

January 9. Death of Napoleon III in England.

1883

Abd el-Kader dies during the night of the 25th-26th of May in his home in Damascus. He is buried near the tomb of Shaykh Ibn 'Arabi.

GLOSSARY

Adab
The code of spiritual courtesy, governing the inner attitude as well as the outward comportment.

Adhan
Call to prayer.

Amir al-mu'minin
Commander of the faithful. The word "emir" (*amir*) also has the meaning of "prince." The French term "amiral" (Eng. "admiral"), comes from *amir al-bahr*, "prince of the sea."

Baraka
Divine spiritual influx; has the meaning of blessing and protection.

Bey
Turkish word designating a dignitary of the Ottoman Empire. During the regency of Algiers it designated the governors of the provinces (*beylik*) placed under the authority of the Dey of Algiers.

Dar al-Islam
"Land of Islam." The regions where Islam is dominant and where Muslim law is applied.

Deïra
Etymologically, it means "circle." A small human collectivity grouped by family and tribe. It can be more or less important. The *smala* (*zmala*), the mobile capital of Abd el-Kader, was an assemblage of *deïra*.

Dey
Turkish word designating the Ottoman administrator of the regency of Algiers. He had under his authority the beys of the provinces.

Dhikr
The *dhikr*, a term which means "remembrance," "call," "evocation," or

again, "invocation," is a form of prayer composed of litanies which can vary from one brotherhood to another. The *dhakir*, when invoking the *dhikr* customarily uses a rosary (*sabha* or *tasbih*).

Fana'
A Sufi technical term which comprises the idea of (spiritual) extinction or annihilation.

Faqir (*pl.* Fuqara')
Al-faqir ila Llah: "the poor one towards God," according to the Koranic expression: "O ye men, you are the poor (*fuqara'*) towards God, and God is the Rich, the Glorious" (35:16). In certain Sufi brotherhoods, the term designates the disciple.

Fiqh
Law, Islamic jurisprudence. *Al-faqih* (pl. *fuqaha'*) designates the doctor of the Law, the jurist, he who possesses the science of the religious law (*shari'a*).

Fitra
Original, primordial nature, the innate nature of the human being.

Fatwa
A religious opinion concerning Islamic law, issued normally by a jurist. In Sunni Islam any *fatwa* is non-binding.

Hadith
Collection of the Traditions of the Prophet (*sunna*). Stemming from a chain of transmission, the *hadiths* are classed according to their degree of authenticity. Together with the Koran, the body of the *hadiths* constitutes one of the two sources of jurisprudence from which the *shari'a* draws. *Hadith qudsi* designates a tradition in which God addresses men through the Prophet.

Hafiz
Title given to one who learns the sixty parts (*hizb*) of the Koran by heart. Traditionally, the full apprenticeship of the Koran is accomplished starting in childhood in the Koranic schools (*zawiya* or *madrasa*).

Hajj (*fem.* Hajja)
Designates both the great pilgrimage to Mecca and the one who accomplishes it.

Haqiqah
Inner, esoteric reality of all that is created, of all law, of all religion. It is the "strait path" towards God, as opposed to the "wide path" which constitutes the exoteric law (*shari'a*). *Al-haqiqa al-muhammadiyya* is the Muhammadan Reality, the metaphysical reality of the Prophet.

Haqq (al-)
One of the Names or Attributes of God, which refers to the Real or to the Divine Reality. The Divinity as distinguished from the creature (*khalq*).

Hijaz
Region of the Arabian peninsula where the two main holy cities of Islam, Mecca and Medina, are located.

Ijtihad
The effort of interpreting the Law, whether exoteric or esoteric. More generally: judgment, personal appreciation, authorized interpretation.

Jihad
Etymologically, the word *jihad* means "effort," "fight," "struggle," and by extension, "combat." In no case is "holy war" its primary meaning.

Khalifa
From which the word "caliph" is derived. Its meaning is that of "lieutenant," representative, on the planes of politics and spirituality. In Sufism, he is the representative or successor of a Shaykh.

Khalwa (*pl.* Khalwat)
Isolation, spiritual retreat.

Mawqif (*pl.* Mawaqif)
Literally, "stops"; designates a "halt" between two spiritual stations.

Marabout (Murabitun)

Originally a man at once pious and a warrior who lived in a *ribat* (a fort). Later designating a saintly man by his actions and noble by his origins.

Muqaddam (*pl.* Maqaddimun)

Person in charge or the representative of a *zawiya* in a region or a country. He is designated by the disciples and confirmed by the Shaykh of a brotherhood.

Mubaya'a

Ceremony of allegiance in the course of which an individual is solemnly recognized as worthy of a mission. The original reference of *mubaya'a* is linked to certain companions of the Prophet (Koran, Sura "The Victory").

Qadi (*pl.* Quda)

In the Islamic world, a *qadi* traditionally has jurisdiction over all legal matters involving Muslims. The judgment of a *qadi* must be based on *ijma'*, the prevailing consensus of the *ulema* or Islamic scholars. As distinct from the *muftis* and *fuqaha'*, who were concerned more with the elucidation of the principles of jurisprudence and the laws, the *qadi* was the key person to ensure the establishment of justice on the basis of the laws and rules. In many cases, he was responsible for all the administrative, judicial, and fiscal control over a territory or a town, including the keeping of the civil records. Often, he would retain a small army or force to ensure that his rulings were enforced. In most cases, the *qadi* would pass on the title and position to his son, descendent, or a very close relative. Over the centuries, this profession became a title within the families, and the power remained within one family in a region.

Shahada

Testimony of faith of Islam, which consists in acknowledging the Oneness of God and the mission of His Messenger Muhammad (*La ilaha illa Llah wa Muhammad rasul Allah*); the first pillar of Islam and the foundation of the Muslim faith.

Shari'a
The exoteric Law, the "wide path" intended for all believers.

Sham
Greater Syria, another name for the city of Damascus.

Sharif (*pl.* Shurafa')
Title borne by the members of the religious nobility, because related to the family of the Prophet through his daughter Fatima and his two grandchildren Hasan and Husayn.

Shaykh
Old man, sage; takes on the meaning of the spiritual master in a Sufi brotherhood.

Smala. See Deïra

Sufism (Tasawwuf)
School or esoteric current of Islam. Sufism (*tasawwuf*) is a composite of Islamic sciences. As a way of spiritual initiation, it represents the mysticism of Islam and is based on an inward interpretation of the religion.

Sunna
Authentic tradition of the Prophet of Islam. Deeds and words (*hadith*) of the Prophet reported by his companions and compiled into a corpus.

Tahqiq
Spiritual realization. For the adept of *tasawwuf*, it is the goal of the Way (*tariqa*) through extinction in God (*fana' fi Llah*).

Tariqa (*pl.* Turuq)
Literally, the Way. The term can signify either the spiritual method or way as such, or the particular initiatic path or brotherhood within which the disciples follow a religious teaching and are attached to a spiritual master (*shaykh*).

Ulema (Ulama')
Doctor of the Law (*shari'a*).

Wird
Formula of prayers, litanies prescribed to the Sufi disciple.

Zawiya
Place of prayer and study, the *zawiya* is also the seat of a Sufi brother-hood. Etymologically, the term designates a corner, which symbolizes the meeting of the temporal and spiritual dimensions.

For a glossary of all key foreign words used in books published by World Wisdom, including metaphysical terms in English, consult: www.DictionaryofSpiritualTerms.org.
This on-line Dictionary of Spiritual Terms provides extensive definitions, examples, and related terms in other languages.

ACKNOWLEDGMENTS

My heartfelt thanks go to Éditions du Seuil for having marked the bi-centennial of the birth of the Emir Abd el-Kader with the publication of a new biography.

All my gratitude goes to Shaykh Khalid Bentounès for his advice and for having generously offered the use of his prodigious library. My thanks naturally also to Éric Geoffroy for having accompanied this project from its beginning. To Michel Chodkiewicz for his promptness and diligence in his replies to my questions.

Finally, there are all those, too numerous to mention, who have given their less visible but altogether useful support: they are warmly thanked.

SUGGESTIONS FOR FURTHER READING

Burckhardt, Titus. *Moorish Culture in Spain*. Louisville, KY: Fons Vitae, 1999.

———. *Fez: City of Islam*. Cambridge, UK: Islamic Texts Society, 1992.

Eaton, Charles le Gai. *Islam and the Destiny of Man*. Cambridge, UK: Islamic Texts Society, 1994.

Gammer, Moshe. *Muslim Resistance to the Tsar: Shamil and the Conquest of Chechnia and Daghestan*. Abingdon: Frank Cass, 1994.

Guénon, René. *The Reign of Quantity and the Signs of the Times*. Hillsdale, NY: Sophia Perennis, 2004.

Kiser, John W. *Commander of the Faithful: The Life and Times of Emir Abd el-Kader*. Rhinebeck, NY: Monkfish Book Publishing, 2008.

Lings, Martin. *Muhammad: His Life Based on the Earliest Sources*. Cambridge, UK: Islamic Texts Society, 1991.

———. *A Sufi Saint of the Twentieth Century: Shaikh Ahmad al-Alawi, His Spiritual Heritage and Legacy*. Cambridge, UK: Islamic Texts Society, 1993.

Macnab, Angus. *Spain Under the Crescent Moon*. Louisville, KY: Fons Vitae, 1999.

Schuon, Frithjof. *Understanding Islam*. Bloomington, IN: World Wisdom, 2011.

Shah-Kazemi, Reza. "From the Spirituality of *Jihad* to the Ideology of Jihadism." In *Islam, Fundamentalism, and the Betrayal of Tradition: Revised and Expanded*, edited by Joseph Lumbard. Bloomington, IN: World Wisdom, 2009.

BIOGRAPHICAL NOTES

AHMED BOUYERDENE was born in Algeria in 1967, but emigrated with his family to France when he was five; he has both Algerian and French nationality. He is an independent researcher in history and a specialist on the Emir Abd el-Kader. Bouyerdene completed his PhD on the life of Abd el-Kader at the University of Strasbourg, France, and has since published two books and several articles on the Emir in his native French, including *Abd el-Kader, l'harmonie des contraires* (le Seuil, 2008, 2012) and *Abd el-Kader par ses contemporains* (Ibis Press, 2008). Bouyerdene has attended dozens of conferences around the world to present papers on the intellectual and spiritual qualities of the Emir. This is his first work to be translated into English. Bouyerdene lives in the Savoy region of France.

ÉRIC GEOFFROY is an Islamicist and Arabist at the University of Strasbourg, France. He specializes in Sufism and sainthood within Islam, as well as in issues of spirituality in the modern world, including globalization and ecology. Geoffroy has contributed numerous articles to the *Encyclopaedia of Islam* (by Brill Academic Publishers) and translations and books under his own name such as *Ibn 'Atā'Allāh—La sagesse des maîtres soufis* and *Initiation au Soufisme*, which was published as *Introduction to Sufism: The Inner Path of Islam* (World Wisdom, 2010).

GUSTAVO POLIT is a professional translator fluent in English, French, and Spanish. He studied Arabic at Indiana University where he received both his B.A. in Religious Studies and M.A. in Near Eastern Languages and Literature. He has rendered several traditionalist works from French into English, including *The Transfiguration of Man* (World Wisdom, 1995) and *The Eye of the Heart* (World Wisdom, 1997) by Frithjof Schuon, and *Sacred Royalty: From the Pharaoh to the Most Christian King* (Matheson Trust, 2011) by Jean Hani. Polit lives in Mexico.

INDEX

Islam, Fundamentalism, and the Betrayal of Tradition:
Essays by Western Muslim Scholars,
edited by Joseph E.B. Lumbard, 2004, 2009

Journeys East: 20th Century Western Encounters with Eastern Religious
Traditions, by Harry Oldmeadow, 2004

Light From the East: Eastern Wisdom for the Modern West,
edited by Harry Oldmeadow, 2007

Living in Amida's Universal Vow: Essays in Shin Buddhism,
edited by Alfred Bloom, 2004

Maintaining the Sacred Center: The Bosnian City of Stolac,
by Rusmir Mahmutćehajić, 2011

The Mystery of Individuality:
Grandeur and Delusion of the Human Condition,
by Mark Perry, 2012

Of the Land and the Spirit:
The Essential Lord Northbourne on Ecology and Religion,
edited by Christopher James and Joseph A. Fitzgerald, 2008

On the Origin of Beauty:
Ecophilosophy in the Light of Traditional Wisdom,
by John Griffin, 2011

Outline of Sufism: The Essentials of Islamic Spirituality,
by William Stoddart, 2012

Paths to the Heart: Sufism and the Christian East,
edited by James S. Cutsinger, 2002

Remembering in a World of Forgetting:
Thoughts on Tradition and Postmodernism, by William Stoddart, 2008

Returning to the Essential: Selected Writings of Jean Biès,
translated by Deborah Weiss-Dutilh, 2004

Science and the Myth of Progress, edited by Mehrdad M. Zarandi, 2003

Seeing God Everywhere: Essays on Nature and the Sacred,
edited by Barry McDonald, 2003

Paths to Transcendence: According to
Shankara, Ibn Arabi, and Meister Eckhart,
by Reza Shah-Kazemi, 2006

The Sacred Foundations of Justice in Islam:
The Teachings of ʿAli ibn Abi Talib,
edited by M. Ali Lakhani, 2006

A Spirit of Tolerance: The Inspiring Life of Tierno Bokar,
by Amadou Hampaté Bâ, 2008

The Sufi Doctrine of Rumi: Illustrated Edition
by William C. Chittick, 2005

Sufism: Love and Wisdom,
edited by Jean-Louis Michon and Roger Gaetani, 2006

Sufism: Veil and Quintessence,
by Frithjof Schuon, 2007

Understanding Islam,
by Frithjof Schuon, 2011

Universal Dimensions of Islam: Studies in Comparative Religion,
edited by Patrick Laude, 2010

The Universal Spirit of Islam: From the Koran and Hadith,
edited by Judith and Michael Oren Fitzgerald, 2006

Unveiling the Garden of Love:
Mystical Symbolism in Layla Majnun and Gita Govinda,
by Lalita Sinha, 2008

What Does Islam Mean in Today's World:
Religion, Politics, Spirituality,
by William Stoddart, 2012

Wisdom's Journey:
Living the Spirit of Islam in the Modern World,
by John Herlihy, 2009